MARXISM
in
LATIN
AMERICA

MARXISM
in
LATIN
AMERICA

Edited with an Introduction by

Luis E. Aguilar

Georgetown University

REVISED EDITION

TEMPLE UNIVERSITY PRESS
Philadelphia

Temple University Press, Philadelphia 19122
© 1978 by Temple University. All rights reserved
Published 1978
Printed in the United States of America

International Standard Book Number: cloth, 0-87722-106-5;
paper, 0-87722-108-1
Library of Congress Catalog Card Number: 77-81331

This book is dedicated to
VERA *and* VERITAS

For the revised edition I wish to express my gratitude to my son Luis E. Aguilar, Jr. for editing assistance, and to Lynn Bracken for her research.

FOREWORD

Marxism in Latin America is too complex a subject to be examined fully within the confines of an anthology. To the difficulties inherent in the making of any selection of articles—the sacrifice of interesting material, the inevitable partiality of the presentation—must be added, in this case, the tremendous dispersion of the materials and the consequent difficulty in obtaining them. As in many other areas of Latin American culture, Marxist productions are scattered through a multitude of articles and pamphlets, often ephemeral, and sometimes impossible to locate. Until a very short time ago, for example, it was an arduous job to find the basic works of José Carlos Mariátegui or Luis Emilio Recabarren, even in Peru or Chile.

In this anthology, in order to present important portions of the diverse facets of Marxism in Latin America—from the first socialist sprouts to contemporary Communist self-criticism—I have sought to go beyond the usual limits of those authors who are most widely known. I have also included a number of Trotskyite and ex-Communist authors. Although as broad a picture as possible has been offered, for reasons of space examples of only the most typical cases and the most important parties have been included.

I make no claim to having even remotely exhausted the subject; I hope merely to have helped arouse interest in an extremely important topic that is still practically unexplored territory.

In some cases, the reader may find a selection that is repetitious or whose conception is confused. This is not the fault of the translators, all of whom have handled extremely difficult material exceptionally well; the cause lies, rather, with the original documents, which are usually written with intense fervor and little attention to style.

Among the many people who have contributed to the production of this book I would like to express my thanks, in particular, to the following: my friend, Víctor Alba, whose suggestions and contributions of material were invaluable; many of my friends in Latin America, who went out of their ways to search remote libraries for rare material, among them Harry Hannabergh in Bogota and Arturo Martín de Nicolás in Santiago; the Institute of Language and Linguistics of Georgetown University, headed by Dr. Robert Lado, whose assistance made possible the translation of several documents; Marcia Maleske, graduate student at Georgetown University, who succeeded in obtaining several hard-to-find volumes; and Cheryl Keyser, graduate student at Georgetown University, who read the manuscript and offered many suggestions.

CONTENTS

II The Emergence of the Communist Parties and the "Hard Line" Period, 1920–1935

III The Popular Front and World War II, 1935–1945

IV   Cold War and New Crisis, 1946–1959

V   The Cuban Revolution and Its Aftermath, 1959–1968

VI From the Peruvian Military Revolution to Cuban Intervention in Angola, 1968–1977

MARXISM
in
LATIN
AMERICA

INTRODUCTION

Marx and Engels paid very little direct attention to Latin America. Their knowledge of that part of the Western hemisphere was, apparently, slight and second-hand, and was limited by the few sources of information available to them. Engels' dependence on the writings of the North American ethnographer Lewis H. Morgan, for example, explains why his reference to the American Indians in his *The Origin of the Family, Private Property and the State* are limited, almost entirely, to the Iroquois, and do not take into account the members of the great Central and South American civilizations. If Marx devoted slightly more attention to Mexico than did Engels, he did so because of the European intervention of 1862 and chiefly as a means of attacking Napoleon III.[1] Marx's comments on Bolivar and those that both he and Engels made on the war between the United States and Mexico (1846–1848) (document 1) denote a certain European, one might almost say Germanic, disdain for those peoples excluded from the main historic currents by the famous Hegelian *Urdummheit*. Not even the fact that his son-in-law, Paul Lafargue, was born in Cuba seems to have aroused in Marx any great curiosity about the new American nations.[2]

[1] See Domingo P. de Toledo y J., *México en la obra de Marx y Engels* (Mexico City: Fondo de Cultura Económica, 1939).
[2] Lafargue, in turn, showed an almost total lack of concern for the problems of his native land. While he was in Spain doing organizational work (1871–1872), Cuba was waging her

Marxist ideas, in their turn, reached Latin America late and sporadically. In the intellectual field, before 1890, alert thinkers, among them Tobías Barreto (1839–1889) in Brazil, did occasionally note the presence of Marxist ideas among European philosophical currents, but such mention did not necessarily imply any appreciable ideological influence.[3] In the field of workers' struggles, the first social theories of significance to arrive—and these theories were not of the Marxist variety—were introduced after 1870 by the streams of European immigrants—refugees from the French Commune, the Italian Risorgimento, and the republican struggles in Spain—who brought not only a new social consciousness and an impetus toward rebellion and self-organization, but also a strong anarchist influence. Initially, then, anarchism was the doctrine that penetrated the nascent Latin American workers' movement, remaining influential until about the second decade of the twentieth century. It is,

---

first war of independence against Spain. Nevertheless, the event is not mentioned in his correspondence with Engels. See Frederick Engels, Paul and Laura Lafargue, *Correspondence, Vol. I: 1869–86* (Moscow: Foreign Languages Publishing House, 1959). As for Marx and Engels, they apparently did not write anything about colonialism in Latin America, even though Latin America at the time of Marx and Engels still had several colonial regions; *On Colonialism* (Moscow: Foreign Languages Publishing House, 1961), a compilation of articles by Marx and Engels, does not contain any selections on the subject.

[3] The Russian writer Zhakob Bazarain deemed it possible to indicate a parallel between Barreto's position and that of democratic Russian revolutionaries, such as Herzen ("Tobías Barreto, illustre pensador brasileiro," *Novos Rumos* [Rio de Janeiro, June 19, 1959]). For a refutation of this parallelism see Vamireh Chacón, *História das idéias socialistas no Brasil* (Rio de Janeiro: Editorial Civilização Brasileira, 1965), pp. 267–272.

therefore, extremely unlikely that the Marxist First International had any noticeable impact on Latin American labor groups.[4] The first groups to adhere to the International, including the group formed in Buenos Aires in 1872, were made up of foreigners, the vast majority of whom were partisans of the anarchist tendencies of Bakunin.[5] At about this time, a group of "erudite and idealistic" people also tried to found a Workers' Bank in Rio de Janeiro on the bases recommended by Proudhon.[6]

Marx, whose influence was obscured by his controversy with Bakunin even when he was not being openly opposed by the anarchist groups, long remained an impressive though vague and unfamiliar figure in Latin America.[7] The writings of José Martí

[4] The slightness of that influence can be gauged, for example, in Sebastián Marotta, El movimiento sindical argentino (Buenos Aires: Ediciones Lacio, 1961), I, 25–28; Francisco R. Pintos, Historia del movimiento obrero del Uruguay (Montevideo, 1960), pp. 34–52; Hernán Ramírez Necochea, "Tuvo influencia la Primera Internacional en Chile?" Principios (Santiago, September–October 1964), pp. 34–52; Rodney Arismendi et al., En el centenario de la internacional (Montevideo: Ediciones Pueblos Unidos, 1964), pp. 76–77. (There is a work by the Russian historian V. I. Ermolaiev on that influence, mentioned in Juan A. Ortega y Medina, Historiografía soviética Iberoamericanista [Mexico City: Universidad Nacional Autónoma, 1961], p. 76, that I have been unable to obtain.) An idea of Ermolaiev's arguments is given in Benito Marianetti, Argentina, realidad y perspectivas (Buenos Aires: Editorial Platina, 1964), pp. 281–282.

[5] Carlos M. Rama, Mouvements ouvriers et socialistes: L'Amérique latine (Paris: Les Editions Ouvriers, 1959), p. 110. "Fundamentally, these groups reflected the divisions aroused in Europe . . . in 1876, a Bakuninist worker propaganda center is founded almost exclusively for the purpose of combating the Marxists," wrote Marotta, op. cit., p. 26.

[6] Everardo Días, Historia das lutas Sociais no Brasil (São Paulo: Editora Edaglit, 1962), p. 65.

[7] Lafargue complained of this same unawareness of Marx in

(document 2), Santiago Iglesias (document 4), and Diego Vicente Tejera (document 3) clearly show that for Latin Americans Marx was a remote figure whom they did not associate with the other great European social thinkers. Thus Martí, for example, while rejecting Marx's call to violence, refers to Bakunin as "tender and radiant." Iglesias shows the prestige of the obscure, messianic Marx among the Puerto Rican workers; and Tejera, founder of the ephemeral Cuban Socialist Party (1899), develops some socialist ideas whose utopianism seems to reflect a very superficial contact with Marxist sources.[8]

Of all these early contacts with Marxist thought, the most serious developed in Argentina with Juan B. Justo. Justo not only studied Marx in German but also undertook the task of translating him into Spanish, so as to make him accessible to the Spanish American socialist milieux. The Argentine group established around Justo—Américo Ghioldi, Nicolás Repetto, Alfredo Palacios, and others—represented the passage through the formative stage of the first period. They brought with them a cogent desire to participate in Argentine politics and to study the background (document 5) and social conditions of the country. Although now much weakened, the trajectory of the Socialist Party of Argentina extends to the present day.

Spain. In his letter to Engels, of October 2, 1871, he tells him: "I have met several people here . . . who were convinced that it was Bakunin who introduced communism into the International. . . . It is not only the workers who have this ridiculous idea, but also the leaders of the bourgeois Republican Party." Engels and Lafargue, *op. cit.*, p. 27.

[8] See José Rivero Muñiz, *El primer partido socialista cubano* (Cuba: Universidad Central de las Villas, 1962), pp. 29–37.

In the intellectual field, the contribution of this group was also significant. Its prestige went beyond the confines of Buenos Aires and sowed social unrest in Uruguay, Chile, Bolivia, and elsewhere on the continent. Thus, for example, in Uruguay the socialist group of Emilio Frugoni kept in close touch with the Argentines, and in Bolivia the *Argentine Sociology* of José Ingenieros, who figured fleetingly in the socialist orbit,[9] aroused in the universities the first speculative interest in historical materialism.[1]

Influenced by the example of the German Socialist Party, and somewhat by the ideas of Eduard Bernstein, the Argentine socialist group (like Frugoni's group in Uruguay, document 6) tried very early to advance beyond purely Marxist doctrine and, with a certain degree of originality, proposed less radical solutions to national problems. The evolution was anything but smooth: Struggling against the anarchists in labor circles and with the emerging force of the Radical Party on the political plane, the Socialist Party of Argentina suffered an almost interminable series of schisms and splintering actions. In 1899, the so-called Collective Socialists left the Party; in 1903, the Syndicalists separated from it; and in 1915, Palacios broke away and founded the Argentine Socialist Party. After 1917, the impact of the Russian Revolution touched off a new crisis. Justo argued in vain against what he

---

[9] Ingenieros (1877–1925) was the son of an Italian revolutionary who had been a founder of the International and director of the first socialist newspaper in Italy and had emigrated to Argentina. See Aníbal Ponce, *José Ingenieros, su vida y su obra* (Buenos Aires: Editores Iglesias y Matera, 1948).

[1] Guillermo Francovich, *El pensamiento boliviano en el siglo XX* (Mexico City: Fondo de Cultura Económica, 1956), p. 103.

called "authoritarian fanaticism": "It is, in fact, in the Socialist Party that authoritarian fanaticism has burgeoned recently under the influence of the Russian Revolution, which proclaims the dictatorship of the proletariat." [2] A minority then broke away from the Socialist Party to follow the Russian line.

Over and above the anarchists and the socialists, official Marxism—Marxism-Leninism, if you will— was making its appearance in Latin America under the aegis of the new Communist parties.

Orthodox Marxism: First Phase
(1920–1928)

To understand this period completely, it must be remembered that the appearance of the anarchist, socialist, and, later, Communist groups was only one of the many symptoms announcing a new era of political and social transformation in Latin America. The more or less apparent order and stability with which the most important areas of Latin America entered the twentieth century—the Porfiriato in Mexico, the parliamentary republic in Chile, the Régimen in Argentina, the civil presidents in Brazil, and others —was very soon to be ended by newly emerging forces. It is in the light of these changes that the origin and development of the Communist parties which appeared during the twenties must be studied.

A sketch of some of these factors would include: the continuous immigration from Europe, importing

---

[2] Luis Pan, *Justo y Marx* (Buenos Aires: Ediciones Monserrat, 1964), p. 36. For a harsh criticism of the Argentine Socialist Party from the point of view of the New Left, see Jorge E. Spilimbergo, *Juan B. Justo o el socialismo cipayo* (Buenos Aires: Editorial Coyoacán, 1964).

social ideas and social unrest; the organization of the first workers' groups with their expression in strikes and demands; the increasing influx of rural population into the cities; the emergence of a strong middle-class nucleus, full of political claims; and the economic crises that were occasioned by World War I. Thus, in rapid crescendo, the following took place: there appeared on the continent the first genuinely popular parties and political figures to transcend the minority dichotomy of liberals and conservatives (the Radical Party in Argentina, José Batlle y Ordóñez in Uruguay, Francisco I. Madero in Mexico, and Arturo Alessandri in Chile); the Mexican Revolution broke out, causing the banner of agrarian reform to be raised; the student centers were shaken by the echoes of the 1918 University Reform of Córdoba (Argentina), which thrust the students into the national political struggles; and the echo of the distant but impressive drumrolls of the Russian proletariat, summoning the workers to revolution, resounded.

The new atmosphere was, in addition, fraught with seething nationalism and Latin solidarity. North American Manifest Destiny ceased to be merely a program and became a reality that washed over the Caribbean and flooded southward. Latin American diplomacy strove to raise the feeble dike of the Drago Doctrine, but anti-Yankee invective and angry protest ran through deeper channels than the diplomatic ones. Rubén Darío's sobering question had resounded throughout the continent: "Shall we many million men speak English?" In the twenties, anti-imperialism was, for at least the minority of alert Latin Americans, not only a popular cause but almost a duty of conscience and salvation.

The environmental conditions were, then, extremely propitious for the appearance of radical political groups. Among them, the Communists had the advantage of arriving already provided with an ideological arsenal, which most of the nascent leftist parties lacked. This very doctrinal advantage, however, when it took the form of inflexible directive, on occasion proved to be more of an anchor than a spur. As a result, the expansion of the Communist parties during this stage was not in keeping with the propitiousness of the circumstances.

The Foundation of the Communist Parties

After the Russian Revolution of 1917, the first and most important Communist parties of Latin America appeared in rapid succession. In January 1918, a dissident group of the Argentine Socialist Party founded the International Socialist Party, which later, in 1920, adopted the name Communist Party. In 1919, the Mexican Communist Party was created, at least nominally.[3] In 1921, the Chilean Socialist Workers' Party was transformed, under the direction of Luis Emilio Recabarren, into the Communist Party. That same year, the Brazilian Communist Party was founded and the Uruguayan Socialist Party became Communist.[4] In 1925, the Cuban Communist Party was organized in Havana.

[3] The "official" Communist Party (there were other socialist-communist groups) was established by a native of India, Manabendra Nath Roy. Roy left Mexico in 1920 (as delegate to the meeting of the Comintern) and never returned to the country.

[4] In Uruguay, unlike Argentina, the majority of the socialists (1,007 to 110) voted in favor of changing the name of the

Almost immediately, following the pattern established in Europe by Willi Muezenberg, "peripheral" organizations were created, their purpose being to channel the activities of those who were not Communists but who sympathized with the Party's ideals.[5] Thus there appeared, in nearly all the Latin American countries where there were Communist parties, a myriad of organizations—Anti-Imperialist Leagues, Left Wing Students, Confederations of Women of America, Organizations of Professionals, etc.—which were more or less linked to the central leadership of the Party and served as sounding boards for its activities and its propaganda.

The multiplicity of names and organizations may, however, produce a mistaken impression. Throughout this entire period, the Latin American Communist parties were actually only minority groups—riven by differences in the interpretation of programs and in the bold struggle to infiltrate intellectual circles and workers' organizations in countries where the majority of workers had no class consciousness or basic education and where the labor movements were either fragmented or virtually nonexistent. In 1928, the Argentine Communist Party, according to Comintern figures, had only 2,000 members; the Brazilian, 1,200; and the Mexican, which "had doubled its members in 1927," had 1,000, 50 of whom were rural workers.[6]

---

party and accepted the Twenty-One Conditions laid down in Moscow in 1920 for admission of parties to the Communist International.

[5] For a study of these organizations, see Bernard S. Morris, "Communist International Front Organizations, Their Nature and Functions," *World Politics,* IX, No. 1 (October 1956), 76–85.

[6] *The Communist International Between the Fifth and the Sixth World Congresses, 1924–28* (London: Communist Party

Hence, the relevance of the founders and first Communist theoreticians on the continent. In Chile, Recabarren succeeded in heightening the prestige of socialist ideas by defending them openly from his position as a member of the Chamber of Deputies (document 7). In Cuba, Julio Antonio Mella (1900–1929) and Rubén Martínez Villena (1899–1933), the former a student leader and the latter a vibrant poet, enhanced the fervor of anti-imperialism and adorned the Party with a halo of martyrs.[7] With *Educación y lucha de clases* the Argentine Aníbal Ponce, a disciple of Ingenieros, contributed to raising the theoretical tone of Marxist analysis. However, Ponce's studies on Argentine history (document 9) show, at times, less profundity. Of all these figures, the one with the greatest intellectual vigor was the Peruvian José Carlos Mariátegui, whose *Siete ensayos de interpretación de la realidad peruana* (1927) remains the most serious attempt to understand a Latin American national problem from a Marxist standpoint. Mariátegui, furthermore, was ever alert to international events and frequently advanced profound judgments on them (document 8).[8]

of Great Britain, July 1928), pp. 368, 397, 400. Without exact data, the membership figures of the Communist parties, at least in their first period, must be taken as approximate. According to Leoncio Rodrigues, *Conflicto industrial e sindicalismo no Brasil* (São Paulo: Difusão Européia do Livro, 1966), p. 137, the Brazilian Communist Party in 1928 had no more than 500 members, and in 1930 only 1,000.

[7] According to one version, Mella was assassinated by agents of the Cuban dictator Gerardo Machado while in exile in Mexico. Martínez Villena died in Cuba of tuberculosis, involved up to the very end in struggles against the same dictator.

[8] The Marxist position of Mariátegui has been, and still is, a source of controversy. Such authors as Robert Alexander,

But to keep the Marxist line correct, at a time when Moscow itself was in turn first condemning leftist and then rightist deviations, was a complicated task. Nearly all these men had periods of bitter friction with the Party. In 1924, the attacks on Recabarren inside the Party were of such a nature as to compel him to engage in public controversy to defend "the present and future of the Communist Party, threatened by the vanity and petulance of novice affiliates who are ignorant of the true objective of our party," [9] and in December of that year, Recabarren committed suicide. In 1933, in the resolutions of the national conference of the Chilean Communist Party, it was still stated: "The ideology of Recabarren is the heritage that the Party must quickly overcome. . . ." [1] Insofar

Víctor Alba, San Cristóbal-Sebastián, and others have pointed to unorthodox aspects of his thought. See Alexander, *Communism in Latin America* (New Brunswick: Rutgers University Press, 1957), pp. 222–223; Alba, *Historia del movimiento obrero en la América Latina* (Mexico City: Libreros Mexicanos Unidos, 1964), pp. 192–193; San Cristóbal-Sebastián, *Economía, educación y marxismo en Mariátegui* (Lima: Ediciones Stadium, 1960). The German Communist historian Manfred Kossok, for his part, while simultaneously defending Mariátegui's Marxist soundness, also recognized his flirtations with certain concepts of Nietzsche, Bergson, and Sorel, as well as the mistaken interpretation that Communist writers such as the Russian V. M. Mirosheski have made in thinking they have found in Mariátegui's agrarian vision a Peruvian version of the Russian *narodnicestvo* (populism). See Manfred Kossok, "José Carlos Mariátegui y el desarrollo del pensamiento marxista en el Perú," *Documentos políticos,* Nos. 36–37 (Bogota, January–February 1964), pp. 61–83.

[9] Luis Emilio Recabarren, *Obras escogidas* (Santiago: Editorial Recabarren, 1965), p. 15.

[1] Cited by Julio César Jobet in *Recabarren: los orígenes del movimiento obrero y del socialismo chilenos* (Santiago: Prensa Latinoamericana, 1965), p. 70. Currently, the Chilean Communists attribute these attacks on Recabarren to the Trotskyite groups of the epoch: see José González, "Rápidamente a la

as Mella is concerned, it is a common belief among many Cubans that he had been expelled from the Party weeks before his death, and it was not the agents of Machado who killed him.[2] As for Mariátegui, the first Congress of Latin American Communist Parties, meeting in Buenos Aires June 1–12, 1929, rejected as "confusionist" his project of creating a Peruvian Socialist Party[3] and disregarded his agrario-Indian ideas. And as for the work of Aníbal Ponce, it has been almost entirely viewed askance by Latin American Marxist authors.[4]

This friction, as well as the differences that were frequently manifested in crises and expulsions from the Party, was due basically to the increasing tendency or need to adopt the line of action of the parties to the decisions of the Comintern. Beginning in 1928, when the Third International radically defined the directions to be followed, the most disciplined leadership continued to consolidate its control over the Party by steamrolling every kind of internal conflict. Victorio Codovilla in Argentina, Blas Roca in Cuba, and Luís Carlos Prestes in Brazil represent this type of leader, less given to theoretical disputations and more inclined toward the concrete problems of organization and action. Perhaps the characteristic

---

acción!" *Principios,* No. 105 (Santiago, January–February 1965), pp. 109–110.

[2] Alexander, *op. cit.,* p. 271. The thesis that Mella was in conflict with the Party has been publicly confirmed by his daughter.

[3] *El movimiento revolucionario latinoamericano: reseña de la primera conferencia latinoamericano de partidos comunistas* (Buenos Aires: Editorial La Correspondencia Sudamericana, 1929), p. 149.

[4] For a sketch of Ponce and his work, see Juan Antonio Salceda, *Aníbal Ponce* (Buenos Aires: Editorial Lautaro, 1953).

that is most salient in all of them is their desire to interpret loyally the directives of the Comintern (Third International). These directives are, then, decisive for an understanding of the period.

The Comintern and the Latin American Communist Parties

Geographically and culturally distant from Russia, and thus without direct access to information, the socialist groups of Latin America, at the time of the establishment of the Third International, could have no clear idea of what was taking place inside Russia or of the plans and programs of the Communist leaders.

We are now familiar, however, with the transformation that took place in Moscow between the First Congress of the International (March 1919), which gave it official life, and the Second (held in Moscow in July and August 1920), which issued the famous Twenty-One Conditions for the admission of Communist parties to the International. The change was crucial and aids in understanding many of the problems that beset the Communist parties of Latin America.

The First Congress—at which no Latin American Communist party was represented—was convoked in extreme haste, because of immediate international exigencies and under the general conviction of the Bolshevik leaders that the European revolution was on the point of breaking out. The basic task was, therefore, one of mobilization and propaganda. The Second Congress—at which the only Latin American country to be represented was Mexico (with three delegates)[5]—took place under more sober prospects; not only had the anticipated general European revolution failed to take place, but the only Communist regime to win power outside Russia, that headed by Bela Kun in Hungary (March–August 1919), had been overthrown. The change of attitude was reflected in the organization of the International. The Congress emphasized the need for better discipline and a firm central leadership, and the Twenty-One Conditions for admission to the International were the most manifest expression of this new policy.[6]

After the formulation of the Twenty-One Conditions, which gave rise to countless controversies and expulsions in the socialist parties of the world, this tendency toward a rigid central leadership grew more acute in the congresses of the Comintern (in 1921, 1922, and 1924). In the Fifth Congress (1924), when the Comintern recognized and analyzed the "partial stabilization of capitalism," special emphasis was laid on the "Bolshevization" of the Communist parties, which meant the reorganization of these parties in accordance with the political and organizational lines of the Russian Communist Party.

It was not until its Sixth Congress (1928), however,

[5] James W. Hulse, *The Forming of the Communist International* (Stanford: Stanford University Press, 1964), p. 194.
[6] Thesis No. 15 of the Fourth Congress of the Comintern (1922) stressed: "The fourth congress categorically demands of all sections and all members the strictest discipline in carrying out the tactical line. . . . Adherence to the twenty-one conditions involves the carrying out of all tactical decisions of the world congresses. . . . Only the sharply defined revolutionary tactics of the Comintern ensure the earliest possible victory of the international proletarian revolution. . . ." Jane Degras, *The Communist International, 1919–1943* (London: Oxford University Press, 1956), Vol. I, p. 428.

that the Comintern laid down a determined orientation in the tactics to be followed by all the Communist parties during the "Third Period," which, according to the Russian experts, was then beginning in the capitalist world.

At the Sixth Congress, Latin America was represented by Argentina, Brazil, Chile, Colombia, Cuba, Ecuador, Mexico, and Uruguay, with a total of 25 votes.[7] When this Congress was held, Trotsky had already been expelled from the Party and "leftist deviation" condemned. Still to come was the liquidation of the rightist deviation which was to be represented by the very man who was presiding over the Congress, Bukharin.[8] The Congress's conclusions therefore meant essentially a violent offensive against the rightist and left-centrist groups (particularly the socialists), as well as a return to the radicalism of the left. Such an orientation prevailed until 1935.

For the purposes of a study of Latin America, it is of interest to single out these points in the strategy outlined by the Sixth Congress of the Comintern:

1) The conviction that the masses of the colonial and semi-colonial countries had taken to the field

[7] The votes were distributed as follows: Argentina, 7; Mexico, 5; Chile, 3; Brazil, Colombia, Cuba, Ecuador, and Uruguay, 2 each. See Kermit E. McKenzie, *Comintern and World Revolution, 1928–1943* (New York: Columbia University Press, 1964), p. 306.

[8] Perhaps with a presentiment of the disaster, Bukharin, at the close of his speech said: "Discipline in our party is the highest rule. But I want to quote an unpublished letter which Lenin sent to me and Zinoviev. Lenin writes: 'if you chase all intelligent people who are not very pliable, and only keep obedient idiots, then you will certainly ruin the party.'" Quoted by F. Borkenau, *World Communism* (New York: W. W. Norton, 1939), p. 337.

in the international struggle. The heightening of the struggle against Yankee imperialism in Latin America was cited as an example. No attempt was made to define clearly the terms "colonial" and "semi-colonial." In the final program the term "semi-colonial" was extended to include the so-called "dependent countries," of which Argentina and Brazil were cited as typical.[9]

2) The condemnation of the upper bourgeoisie of the colonial and semi-colonial countries as allies of imperialism and of the small progressive bourgeoisie, usually called "national-reformist," as "opportunist" and always ready to capitulate to imperialism. The socialists ("social-fascists") were considered to be the best allies of fascism.

3) The repeated warnings against Trotskyist or Trotskyite influence, which demanded repeated purges of the leadership cadres of the parties.

The interpretation of these and other essential points produced a series of external and internal crises in the Latin American Communist parties that characterized virtually the entire period.

According to a number of authors, the principal stumbling-block in the path of the Latin American Communists was in trying to apply the conclusion derived from such theoretical premises—that the industrial proletariat necessarily had to be the leader in the revolutionary struggle—in countries that were

---

[9] The term "dependent countries" was adopted, according to McKenzie, *op. cit.*, p. 81, following the suggestion of the Ecuadorian Ricardo Paredes to include "those areas which had been penetrated economically by imperialism but which still retained a higher degree of political independence than the colonies and semi-colonies."

made up of an overwhelming majority of rural masses.[1] The point is a valid one, but not absolutely so. If we disregard the enormous difficulties that are inherent in the organization of the rural inhabitants of Central and South America, it is certain that the Comintern, the national congresses of the Communist parties, the International Congress of Latin American Communist Parties (1929), and all such groups attached special importance, at least in their programmatic concepts, to the organization of rural inhabitants and their relation to the proletariat (document 10).

Conversely, many Marxist sources have accepted as "tactical" difficulties of the period the problems that affected the development of the Latin American Communist parties: (1) exaggeration in the attack on non-Communist groups, particularly the socialists;[2] (2) underestimation of the strength and role of the national bourgeoisie as an element of transformation in the semi-colonial and dependent countries; and (3) a mistaken evaluation of nationalist sentiment.[3] Maybe

[1] See, for example, G. D. H. Cole, *A History of Socialist Thought: Communism and Social Democracy, 1914–1931* (London: Macmillan, 1958), IV, Part II, 761.

[2] Among the Marxist authors, see R. Palme Dutt, *The International* (London: Lawrence & Wishart, 1964), pp. 207–214.

[3] Points 2 and 3 were recognized and corrected, at least in part, in the Seventh Congress of the Comintern (1935). For a study on the changing role of the national bourgeoisie in the Soviet outlook see Walter Z. Laqueur, "The National Bourgeoisie," *Contemporary History in the Soviet Mirror*, John Keep, ed. (New York: Frederick Praeger, 1964), pp. 155–169. For an example of the attitude of the contemporary Russian historians on the same topic, see A. Shul'govski, "Imperialism and the Ideology of National Reformism," *The Third World in Soviet Perspective*, Thomas P. Thornton, ed. (Princeton: Princeton University Press, 1964), pp. 305–331. A Latin American Marxist interpretation is offered by Rodney Arismendi, "Acerca del papel de la burguesía nacional en la lucha anti-

to this could be added, continuing the thinking of Walter Z. Laqueur, the scant valuation of the intellectual and non-class roots of anti-imperialist sentiment in these countries.[4]

Application of the Hard Line in Latin America (1928–1935)

Application of the tactical line developed by the Comintern meant an immediate radicalization of the Latin American Communist parties. This radicalization explains, at least in part, the series of purges and expulsions that characterize the period, as well as the political isolation of these parties and their aggressive attitude toward national events.

Before 1928 the tactics of the Communist groups had been comparatively flexible, focused chiefly on infiltration of the labor movements and intellectual circles in their respective countries. In 1927, in the announcement issued in Moscow for the Congress of the Latin American Confederation of Labor Unions that was to meet in Montevideo in 1929, Lozovski, leader of the International of Red Labor Unions, warned the Latin American comrades against overestimating their own strength and plunging into the revolutionary struggle before they were ready. "There is not yet in the interior of your movement sufficient motivational strength to be able to transform all of Latin America overnight." [5]

---

imperialista," *Problemas de una revolución continental* (Montevideo: Ediciones Pueblos Unidos, 1962), pp. 475–498.

[4] Laqueur, *op. cit.*, p. 166.

[5] "A las organizaciones obreras de la América Latina y al proletariado en general," *El Trabajador latinoamericano* (Montevideo), I, No. 1, 6–8. For further details on Lozovski's inter-

After the 1928 meeting of the Comintern, such caution was disregarded. As a result, at the Conference of Communist Parties in Buenos Aires (1929) the attitudes and the programs were radicalized. It was postulated that the bourgeois-democratic revolution in Latin America was aimed at "the creation of a worker-peasant government on the basis of soviets of workers, peasants, and soldiers" and at the disruption of "the domination of feudalism, imperialism, the Church, imperialistic companies, and others." The Peasant Leagues of Mexico were criticized for having fought counterrevolutionary insurrections "as troops faithful to the government of Portes Gil" and for not having formed "soviets in the region they dominated." [6] It was affirmed that "in all the Latin American countries, the petty bourgeoisie and the nascent industrial bourgeoisie are directly linked to the imperialistic interests." [7] And mention was made of the possibility of creating "Indian republics" in those countries with large Indian populations.[8] Without any further evaluation of the historical-national situation that actually confronted them, the different Latin American Communist parties permitted this aggressiveness very quickly to permeate their activities.

Thus, the Communist Party of Argentina, in 1929 and 1930, simultaneously attacked the socialists and the Radical government of Hipólito Irigoyen, condemning them as allies of imperialism and "quasifascists." And while they were thus contributing to

vention, see Rodrigo García Treviño, *La ingerencia rusa en México* (Mexico City: Editorial América, 1959), pp. 79–83.
 [6] *El movimiento revolucionario latinoamericano, op. cit.*, pp. 89–90.
 [7] *Ibid.*, p. 93.
 [8] *Ibid.*, p. 298.

the destruction of the reputation of the old president's democratic regime, on September 6, 1930, a military coup of truly fascist nature suddenly closed off the Argentine political horizon.[9]

In Mexico in 1929, the Communist Party interpreted the rebellion of Generals Jesús M. Aguirre and José G. Escobar as a sign of the total disintegration of the Mexican political order, aggravated by the economic crisis that was then shaking the Western world; they therefore decided on open opposition to the government of Portes Gil. Many expulsions occurred as a result of that decision (Diego Rivera, David Siqueiros, and, later, Ursulo Galván, Secretary General of the National Peasants' League), which ultimately brought about the failure of the insurrectionist tactics, a harsh official repression of the Party, and the loss of almost everything that had been won in the twenties.[1]

The Communist Party of Chile, which as early as

[9] Two years later the leader of the Party, Victorio Codovilla, was to explain: "Our viewpoint, for which I am one of the chief persons responsible, was that in spite of the threats of the opposition, the coup d'état would not take place, since Irigoyenism, within which pro-fascist elements were developing, was in a position to strengthen the state apparatus in a dictatorial manner. . . . Hence we concentrated all our activity against Irigoyenism without understanding the political nature of the coup d'état that was being prepared." Quoted by Rodolfo Puigróss in *Historia crítica de los partidos políticos argentinos* (Buenos Aires: Editorial Argumentos, 1956), p. 303. The reader may also wish to consult one of the few "official" histories of a Latin American Communist party, *Esbozo de historia del partido comunista de la Argentina*, prepared by the Commission of the Central Committee of the Communist Party (Buenos Aires: Editorial Anteo, 1947). A harsh critic of the Communist Party of Argentina, from a Marxist standpoint, is Jorge Abelardo Ramos, whose *El partido comunista en la política argentina: su historia y su crítica* (Buenos Aires: Editorial Coyoacán, 1962) may also be of interest.

[1] Karl M. Schmitt, *Communism in Mexico* (Austin: University of Texas Press, 1965), pp. 14–15. In May 1929, the

1923 had nearly 2,000 members,[2] showed what was probably the greatest flexibility and progress during that period. The Communists, at a very early date, had achieved increasing influence and control over the Federación Obrera de Chile (FOCH), which in 1922 became affiliated with the Internacional Sindical Roja.[3] In the Chilean presidential election of 1925, the Party had supported the candidacy of an army doctor who was linked to a young officer group; the program he advocated was reformist democratic but not leftist radical. At the same time, the Party secured the election of two senators and seven deputies.[4] Despite this, the radicalization of the policy which now followed very quickly provoked a double crisis: externally, the Party broke away from the collective struggle against the dictatorship of Carlos Ibáñez, following the line of "claiming that the Party alone and the isolated working class could produce the revolutionary change";[5] internally, the Party split into two factions, that of Manuel Hidalgo, who gravitated toward Trotskyism and rejected the necessity of attacking all the leftist organizations, and that of Elías

United States Communist leader Earl Browder said: "the present new period of the Mexican Revolution is characterized by the emergence of workers and peasants as an independent force, carrying through the revolution *no longer with but against the petty bourgeoisie*, which has surrendered to the bourgeoisie and imperialism" [italics E. B.]. See "A New State of the Mexican Revolution," *The Communist*, VIII, No. 5 (May 1929), 228.

[2] Hernán Ramírez Necochea, *Orígen y formación del partido comunista de Chile* (Santiago: Editorial Austral, 1965), p. 37. Until 1928 the Communist Party of Chile was accepted only as a "sympathizer" by the International.

[3] Robert Alexander, *Labor Relations in Argentina, Brazil, and Chile* (New York: McGraw-Hill, 1962), pp. 254–255.

[4] Ramírez Necochea, *op. cit.,* pp. 149–151.

[5] *Ibid.,* p. 272.

Laferte, who remained faithful to the strategy of "united front from below," as outlined by the Comintern. In accordance with this strategy, when the military-civil coup of June 4, 1932, proclaimed the Socialist Republic of Chile, the Communist officials condemned the movement as a demagogic effort of the bourgeoisie.[6]

That same year the small Communist Party of El Salvador (founded in 1925), which had apparently infiltrated the army to some extent, attempted a coup against the dictator Hernández Martínez. The confused revolt, disseminated in peasant outbreaks, provoked an unusual display of United States, Canadian, and British naval forces,[7] and was drowned in blood by the dictator. According to Marxist criticism, one of the principal causes of the failure was the "leftist deviation" and "putschist[!]" approach of this movement;[8] a bit later, the Communists were accusing Augusto César Sandino, the guerrilla chief who was opposing the United States forces in Nicaragua,[9] of having gone over to the "counter-revolution" (document 12).

One of the best examples of the effects of the Com-

[6] Alexander, *Communism in Latin America, op. cit.,* pp. 186–187.

[7] The British government, "in view of the serious situation," sent a warship; the Canadian government, a destroyer; the United States, two destroyers. *Foreign Relations of the United States, 1932* (Washington: U.S. Government Printing Office, 1948), V, 615.

[8] "One of the chief lessons of the Salvadorean uprising is the great danger of putschist and 'left' sectarian tendencies against which we must wage the most energetic struggle," O. Rodríguez, "The Uprising in Salvador," *The Communist,* XI, No. 3 (March 1932), 251.

[9] For an account of relations between Sandino and the Communists, see Víctor Alba, *op. cit.,* pp. 208–210.

munist radicalism of the period was Cuba. In that country, during the struggle against the dictatorship of Machado (1928–1933), and later, with the triumph of the revolutionary government of Ramón Grau San Martín (September 1933–January 1934), the Communists made no distinction between the parties that supported the dictator, the traditional parties that opposed him, and the youthful groups that had emerged from the struggle (Directorio Estudiantil, ABC, Joven Cuba de Guiteras, the portions of Grau's party later called Auténticos). All were condemned as fascists, quasi-fascists, or instruments of Yankee imperialism. Thus the spectacle was offered of a revolutionary and nationalist government, to which Washington was refusing diplomatic recognition as a radical and Communist government, being fought, at the same time, by the Communists as a lackey of Yankee imperialism. As late as 1934, when this government had been overthrown and replaced by the more moderate one of Carlos Mendieta and Fulgencio Batista (immediately recognized by Washington), the Party still considered the greatest danger to the revolution to be that represented by the parties of the left (document 11).[1]

The Communist Party of Brazil, the majority of whose founders had been anarcho-syndicalists,[2] led a

[1] In 1937, the *Soviet Encyclopedia* declared: "The Government of Grau carried out a certain number of reforms—eight-hour working day, nationalization of a number of foreign companies. The directive of the Cuban Communist Party adopted incorrect positions toward this government and did not support it." *Bolshaya Sovetskaya Entsiklopediya* (Moscow, 1937), XXXV, 355.

[2] Says Leoncio Basbaum of the Party founders: "With the exception of Manoel Cendoa, a Spanish tailor who was already a Marxist, all the others came from the anarcho-syndicalist movement," *Historia sincera da república* (São Paulo: Edições LB, 1962), II, 313.

very limited existence until 1931, when Luís Carlos
Prestes with his prestige as a legendary hero[3] joined
them. But Prestes stayed in Russia from 1931 to 1934.
When he returned to Brazil, profound changes in the
radicalism of the Communist parties were already
being announced. The Seventh Congress of the Comintern was approaching; the Brazilian national situation, furthermore, was suffering alterations. The establishment in 1932 of a rightist party with fascist
trimmings, Ação Integralista, mobilized the left: various elements that were in opposition to Getúlio Vargas
in 1934 founded the Alianza Nacional Liberadora and
appointed Luís Carlos Prestes as honorary president.
The expansion of the political force of the Alianza,
its anti-fascist character, and the cooperation in it of
Socialists, Communists, and other left groups were
highly symptomatic. In 1935, the Comintern praised
the Alianza as a good example for Latin America.[4]

[3] Luís Carlos Prestes distinguished himself in 1924 by supporting the so-called "Lieutenants' revolt" and heading a rebel
column that for two years traveled about the interior of
Brazil, until it was forced to enter and surrender in Bolivia.
His official incorporation in the Party is a debated point.
According to Alexander, Communism in Latin America, op.
cit., pp. 1–8, Prestes did not join until 1934. As early as 1928
and 1929, however, during his exile in Argentina, Prestes was
openly acting together with the Argentine Communist Party.
See Jorge Amado, Vida de Luís Carlos Prestes (São Paulo:
Livraria Martins, 1945), p. 213. It is worthy of mention, as
proof of the precariousness of the Marxist penetration in Brazil,
that the first Brazilian Communist leader who approached
Prestes to win him to the cause was able to find Marxist books
only in French to give him, as Astrojildo Pereira reports in
Formação do partido comunista brasileiro (Rio de Janeiro:
Editorial Vitória, 1962), p. 107. For a history of the events
in Brazil during this period, see Helio Silva, A grande marcha
(Rio de Janeiro: Editorial Civilização Brasileira, 1965).

[4] VII Congress of the Communist International (Moscow:
Foreign Languages Publishing House, 1939), pp. 294–297.

The sweeping revision of the radical policy that had been followed by the Latin American Communist parties up to 1935 is clearly visible in the general survey that the magazine *The Communist International* makes of the situation of these parties in 1935 (document 12). There, although the traditional gamut of topics is insisted on, severe criticism of the inability to distinguish between the various bourgeois and petty bourgeois parties takes shape, as well as criticism of the underestimation of the influence of these parties on the rural population and workers of Latin America.

This criticism was amplified and ratified at the Seventh Congress of the Comintern, held in Moscow in August 1935. In the twenty-third session, Wang Ming generalized against the tendency to "exaggerate the influence exercised by the fascist movements" and stated specifically that "many of our comrades in Latin America have characterized nearly all the bourgeois and petty bourgeois parties as fascists, thus hindering the establishment of an anti-fascist Popular Front." [5]

A series of self-criticisms and admissions of error followed these words. The Cuban Communists held out their hands to the Auténticos and Guiteristas; the Argentines approached the Radicals; the Chileans allied themselves with the Socialists; and the Peruvians turned toward the Alianza Popular Revolucionaria Americana (APRA).

The hour of the Popular Front had come.

[5] *Ibid.,* p. 302.

From the Popular Front to the End of World War II (*1935–1945*)

Although the Latin American Communist parties played only a secondary role in the Seventh Congress and received a sound dose of criticism during it,[6] the new attitude of the Comintern toward other parties, the bourgeoisie, and nationalism,[7] represented a highly beneficial change for the Latin American parties. The 1935–1945 period marked, in general, a stage of notable advance. It was during this period that, for the first time, the Communist parties of various Latin American countries, such as Chile, Cuba, and Mexico, among others, became important political factors. Ironically, communism suffered its only serious loss in the country that had been most highly praised at the Seventh Congress—Brazil. The revolutionary hopes of the Alianza Nacional Libertadora, which apparently was planning a general uprising, were violently aborted by the Vargas government in November 1935.[8]

[6] "It must be noted that in most of the colonial and semi-colonial countries (with the possible exception of Brazil) the Communists underestimated the importance of united front and trade union tactics; they were unable to take the lead and organize the growing desire of the mass of workers . . . and have thereby surrendered the initiative to the reformist and even the national reformist government (namely Mexico)." *Ibid.*, p. 302.

[7] In his opening report, George Dimitrov said: "We Communists are the irreconcilable opponents, in principle, of bourgeois nationalism. . . . But anyone who thinks that this permits him, or even compels him, to sneer at all national sentiments of the wide masses is far from being a genuine Bolshevik. . . . Comrades, proletarian internationalism must, so to speak, 'acclimatize itself' in each country in order to sink deep roots in its native land." *Ibid.*, pp. 182–183.

[8] Apparently the Vargas government was on to the plans (the Party's secretary had been considered a "government agent") and provoked the insurrection before the date set. The strug-

The harsh repression and jailing of the principal leaders, including Luís Carlos Prestes, destroyed all possibility of achieving either the expansion of the Party or the creation of a Popular Front.

In the new phase, the Communist parties not only extended their hands to other political groupings but reduced their revolutionary radicalism,[9] unfurled national flags,[1] and sought to legalize their political activities.[2] Furthermore, this was happening at a time when the anti-North American tension had decreased considerably in Latin America due to the Good Neighbor Policy inaugurated by Roosevelt.

Without completely abandoning their old watchwords, in the period prior to the Nazi-Soviet Pact the Communists defended the necessity of tightening the

---

gle was limited, essentially, to the compromised military sectors. See Edgard Carone, *Revoluções do Brasil contemporáneo* (São Paulo: Coleção Buriti, 1965), pp. 144–147.

[9] In Cuba, for example, in an effort to win over Guiteristas and Auténticos, Blas Roca declared: "Such slogans as the self-determination of the Negro nation and the confiscation of the lands of the large estates have been withdrawn," *The Communist*, XIV, No. 1 (October 1935), 957. Later the Party adopted the emblem of the machete and the hammer, instead of the hammer and sickle.

[1] The nationalism of the Communist parties is a theme that has been maintained up to the present. From the wide range Marxist literature defending the revolution "a la colombiana," or "a la peruana," suffice it to quote this: "Today there is nothing more Uruguayan, more patriotic and democratic on the national stage than the Communist Party," from *El partido comunista: su política, su ideología, su organización* (Montevideo: Ediciones de la Sección Agitación y Propaganda, 1958), p. 32.

[2] Typical is the following declaration: "The Communist Party desires legality, in order to struggle more effectively against all coups, against all kinds of disorders." See "The Place of Venezuela among the Democratic Nations of Latin America," *The Communist*, XVIII, No. 10 (October 1939), 961.

bonds of Pan Americanism.[3] During the lifetime of
that Pact (1939–1941), they maintained a "neutralist"
line vis-à-vis the "imperialist" war. Later, after the attack on Russia, the Communists supported cooperation
with the Allies and the national war effort. This attitude, plus the resultant legalization of the Communist parties in nearly all Latin American countries
during World War II multiplied their propaganda possibilities and their capacity for influence in the labor
sectors. The results, however, were not uniform.

In Argentina, the Communist Party supported
Marcelo T. de Alvear, the candidate of the Radical
Party in 1937; after the triumph of the opposing candidate, Ramón M. Ortiz, the Party defended the government of Ortiz against the "maneuvers of the oligarchy" that were supported by the vice-president,
Ramon S. Castillo.[4] Continuing the anti-fascist line,
the Party condemned the military coup of 1943 and
then vehemently opposed the emergence of Juan Perón
and his electoral triumph of 1946.[5] At the beginning of
the Peronist decade, with all its new and radical social implications, the Popular Front had not yet jelled
in Argentina.

In Mexico, the years 1934–1940 marked a period of
development and recuperation for the Party. The favorable attitude of President Lázaro Cárdenas and the
alliance with Lombardo Toledano and his powerful
Confederation of Mexican Workers (an alliance

[3] In July 1939, the Communist parties of Canada, Mexico,
the United States, Cuba, and Venezuela signed a joint declaration entitled "Strengthen Panamerican Democracy." See *The
Communist*, XVIII, No. 7 (July 1939), 576–589.

[4] Ramos, *op. cit.*, pp. 113, 115.

[5] See *ibid.*, pp. 124–125; and Central Committee of the Communist Party of Argentina, *op. cit.*, p. 109.

marked by such dissensions that it required the personal intervention of Earl Browder) permitted a rapid Communist expansion. In 1939, the Party succeeded in enlisting nearly 30,000 members. Later, however, partly as the result of a change of attitude in the Mexican government, the Party entered a new stage of crisis and purges.[6]

The most spectacular, if not the most effective, triumph of the period was won by the Communists in Chile with the formation of a Popular Front in 1938.[7] This Front, formed of Socialists, Radicals, and Communists, won the victory of the Radical candidate, Pedro Aguirre Cerda, in the presidential elections. However, an adverse Congress, the heterogeneity of the group, and the death of Aguirre Cerda in 1941 prevented the Popular Front from doing much with regard to social transformations.[8] The electoral triumph coincided, moreover, with the neutralist line toward the war, which gave rise to friction between Socialists and Communists as well as to a greater radicalization in the tone of the Communist demands (document 13), which revived old alarms against the Party. The Communists, however, who had refused to participate in the government, effectively maneuvered in the labor centers and skillfully used the in-

[6] Karl M. Schmitt, *op. cit.*, pp. 18–19.

[7] A very personal but extremely interesting version of how the Communist Party succeeded in breaking the political isolation and forming the Popular Front is given by Eudocio Ravines, *The Yenan Way* (New York: Scribner's, 1951), pp. 164–186.

[8] Curiously, the Communists attribute part of the ineffectiveness of the Popular Front to the "penetration of the influence of Masonry in the highest spheres of the Party." See *Partido comunista de Chile, XI congreso nacional* (Santiago, 1959), p. 79.

ternal crisis of the Socialist Party to win over many labor leaders. In 1946, the Communists backed another victorious Radical candidate, González Videla, and this time, with three members in ministerial positions, they participated directly in the government. At a moment when international and national circumstances were less than favorable for them, the Chilean Communists controlled approximately 50 per cent of the organized worker movement.[9]

In Cuba, after the failure of the conciliatory gesture toward the opposition parties (Auténticos and Guiteristas), the Communists turned toward an alliance with Batista, whose political aspirations led him to seek all support possible.[1] In 1938, the Party obtained legal recognition. Joining with another Communist group, the Revolutionary Union Party of Juan Marinello, to form the Cuban Revolutionary Union, the Communists participated in the elections for the Constituent Assembly of 1940 and formed part of the political coalition that supported Batista in his triumphant presidential campaign in 1940. From this alliance, the

[9] Alexander, *Labor Relations in Argentina, Brazil, and Chile, op. cit.*, p. 260.

[1] The rapprochement was defended, not as a change of position of the Communists, but as a necessity imposed by the ideological variation of Batista and the Auténticos. Thus, in February 1938, Blas Roca stigmatized Batista as "the chief enemy of the democratic liberties of our people" who aspired "to establish a fascist regime." In March 1939, this same Blas Roca declared: "Toward Batista the Communist Party maintains a general attitude of support. . . . Trotskyists and pseudo-liberals to the contrary notwithstanding, the continued trend of Batista toward democratic reform has fully justified the Party's positive attitude toward him." *The Communist*, XVII, No. 2 (February 1938), 49, and XVIII, No. 3 (March 1939), 75. At the same time, the Auténticos, who had been considered a "progressive" party, began to be defined as a group "that was moving toward the right."

Communists obtained two great successes: the progressive control of the Cuban workers' movement, which was integrated in the Confederación de Trabajadores de Cuba (CTC), and a great expansion of the Party. In 1938, the Party had 23,000 members;[2] in 1944, it had 122,000 members.[3] Following the political line of the period, in 1944, when Grau San Martín won the presidential election, the Communist Party (then called the Popular Socialist Party) publicly confirmed its gratitude to Batista, at the same time that the possibility of cooperating with the new Auténticos government (document 14) was opening up.

In Brazil, the disaster of 1935 was followed by the persecution of the Party and the proclamation of the New State by Vargas. Under these conditions, the creation of a Popular Front was almost impossible. Despite all efforts to achieve a rapprochement with non-Communist groups,[4] the Party led a very precarious life.[5]

[2] *Por la victoria popular: informes y conclusiones* (Havana: III Asamblea del Partido Comunista de Cuba, 1939), p. 63.

[3] *Los socialistas y la realidad cubana* (Havana: Ediciones del Partido Socialista Popular, 1944), p. 225. But, at the same time as he offered this figure, Severo Aguirre complained that the magazine *Fundamentos* had a circulation of only 6,000 copies.

[4] "The Party is ridding itself of its old sectarian heritage and is entering into temporary alliance with all groups, classes, parties, and associations which agree to wage the anti-fascist struggle . . . the Party is fighting side by side with the bourgeois-democratic governments such as the U.S.A. and France. . . . The slogan, 'Struggle against every form of imperialism,' is a Trotskyite slogan." See F. Lacerda, "The Fascist Coup d'Etat in Brazil," *The Communist International*, XV, No. 1 (January 1938), 46.

[5] According to Osvaldo Peralva, in 1940 the leadership of the Party fell entirely into the hands of the police. On being reorganized in 1945, the Party, according to this author, had

It was not until 1945, when national opposition and the international situation were pressing heavily in favor of democracy, that Getúlio Vargas loosened his grip, freed Luís Carlos Prestes, and permitted the organization of national political parties. Following the line marked out, Prestes immediately proclaimed the necessity of proceeding with the nationalist democratic struggle and supporting the Allies and Pan Americanism (document 15).

From the End of the War to the Cuban Revolution (1945–1959)

At the close of World War II and with the beginning of the Cold War, international circumstances altered and influenced the situation and the policy of the Latin American Communist parties. These parties rejected the "Browder deviation," [6] and instead marshaled their propaganda against United States imperialism and in favor of international peace and the neutralization of Latin America. As early as the end of 1945, the Cuban Communist Party acknowledged that it had misinterpreted the results of the 1943 Teheran Conference and nourished false illusions as to the possibility of basic changes in the international behavior of capitalism. [7] A short while later, Rodney Arismendi, who was now emerging as one of the most outstand-

---

fewer than 4,000 members. Osvaldo Peralva, *O retrato* (Belo Horizonte: Editora Italiana Limitada, 1960), pp. 8–9.

[6] The previous excessive conciliation with capitalism was attributed to the influence of the United States Communist leader, Earl Browder, who was expelled from the Party in 1945.

[7] *En defensa del pueblo* (Havana: Ediciones del Partido Socialista Popular, 1945).

ing theoreticians of communism in Latin America, ratified the continental position against the United States and Pan Americanism (document 16).

This position did not, however, imply a return to hard-line radicalism. Russian ideological influence, exercised through the deliberations at the Soviet Communist Party congresses (the Comintern had been dissolved in 1943), provided another guideline. Of these congresses the most outstanding was the Twentieth, which was held in Moscow in 1956. The possibility of a peaceful victory of the socialist system, the nonexistence of a single formula that could be applied without differentiation in all countries, and the attacks on the "cult of personality," the most important themes of this Congress, were immediately incorporated into the discussions and programs of the Latin American Communist parties. None of them meant, however, that they were to go back to the radicalism of the earliest days.

Furthermore, the Cold War was also affecting the tone of inter-American relations. The Rio Treaty of 1947 confined hemispheric conflicts to the jurisdiction of the American nations; the United States strongly endeavored to make the Treaty the basis of a common front against the possibilities of international Communist aggression. In 1948, in the light of the flames of the Bogotazo,[8] the Ninth International Conference of the American States adopted a resolution urging member states to take measures to control the expansion of communism.

The suggestion quickly found an echo in Latin

---

[8] This is the popular name attached to the episode of violence that shook Bogota on April 9, 1948, after the assassination of the Liberal leader Jorge Eliécer Gaitán.

America. After 1947, beginning with Brazil, Chile, and Colombia, a number of Latin American nations broke diplomatic relations with the Soviet Union. In 1947, the Brazilian Communist Party was outlawed and its elected senators and deputies expelled from the Brazilian Congress. In 1948, the government of Chile declared the Communist Party to be illegal. In that same year, military coups took place in Peru and Venezuela and were followed by immediate anti-Communist declarations. In Cuba, the democratic government of Grau San Martín began a successful offensive against Communist control of the CTC. In Argentina, independently of continental policy, Perón forced the Party into illegality and seized control of the labor unions. In Colombia, the conservative reaction reduced the Party's possibilities of action to their lowest point.[9]

Certain factors, nevertheless, affected the situation. In the first place, the anti-Communist position of many governments that held power by force was more in response to international exigencies than to the actual state of affairs in the countries. Hence, on occasion, the Communists, or at least some of them, acted with a certain amount of freedom in the labor unions and universities, in exchange for supporting the government, or at least not fomenting disturbances. The cases of Manuel Odría in Peru, of Pérez Jiménez in Venezuela, and of Fulgencio Batista in Cuba (beginning in 1952, when he returned to power through a military coup) are examples of this situation.

[9] "The Colombian proletariat sank into a state of prostration comparable to that suffered by the Russian proletariat in the long years of the 'Stolypin' reaction." *Treinta años de lucha del partido comunista de Colombia* (Bogota: Ediciones Paz y Socialismo, 1960), p. 89.

In the second place, it was only after World War II that the Soviet Union really began to devote attention to its relations and influence in Latin America. Soviet policy not only strove to increase commercial relations;[1] culturally, Russia began to intensify its propaganda throughout the continent by means of publications, books, and radio broadcasts.[2]

Finally, the period following World War II also marked a new era of social and revolutionary insurgency in Latin America and a period of disillusionment with regard to the United States. The more or less favorable economic development of the first years of the postwar period began to taper off beginning in 1952. Beset with old agrarian, industrial, and social conflicts, Latin America considered itself neglected by its great northern neighbor, whose sole preoccupation seemed to be to assure anti-Communist postures.

In that period, therefore, more than the vicissitudes of the Communist parties, the important symptoms of the state of health of Marxism in Latin America are the profusion of studies with a more or less Marxist accent on the economic "exploitation" of Latin America, and the beginning of a phenomenon that was to grow more acute in the sixties: the fragmentation of the Marxist left.

How deeply the economic arguments against impe-

---

[1] Some pertinent figures (up to 1958) can be found in Robert Loring Allen, *Soviet Influence in Latin America: the Role of Economic Relations* (Washington: Public Affairs Press, 1959).

[2] In 1948, for example, the number of radio hours devoted by the Soviet bloc to Latin America was seventeen and a quarter a week. In 1961, the total was 219. See Dorothy Dillon, *International Communism and Latin America* (Gainesville: University of Florida Press, 1962), p. 16. See also Frederick C. Barghoorn, *The Soviet Cultural Offensive* (Princeton: Princeton University Press, 1960), Chapter VII.

rialism had penetrated and how receptive the environment was to Marxist criticism may be gauged, at least in part, from the studies of Communist authors, such as the Brazilian Caio Prado, Jr. (document 19), or of writers who had been influenced by Marxism, such as the Chilean Julio César Jobet (document 17) and the Colombian Antonio García (document 18).

The fragmentation of the Marxist left, although it was naturally related to the post-bellum crisis of world communism, was also a reflection of the revolutionary state of affairs that was shaking the continent. Indicative of the situation of the Communist parties in this period, and a key to the internal and external conflicts that were overwhelming them was their scant participation in the most important events of the moment. Not in Guatemala in 1944, in Bolivia in 1952, or in Cuba in 1959, nor in any of the other political convulsions in Venezuela, Argentina, Colombia, or Peru did the Communists play an outstanding role. The initiative, which fell instead into other hands, opened up political horizons to nationalist and democratic parties, which, like Acción Democrática in Venezuela, the Movimiento Nacionalista Revolucionario (MNR) in Bolivia, the Christian Democrats in Chile, Acción Popular in Peru, or Liberación Nacional in Costa Rica went on to become decisive forces in their respective countries.

This apparent absence of revolutionary dynamism intensified the Marxist criticism of the Communist parties and extended it to the new groups that now began to germinate on the continent. Up to 1945, it may be said that the basic and virtually exclusive nucleus of Marxism in Latin America was formed by the Communist parties. The Socialist groups had become extremely devitalized and the Trotskyites had long been isolated to mere ideological redoubts. After the war, the situation began to change. The Communists had to cope with the increasing attack of a more varied and extensive left, which censured them not for being Marxists but for not acting upon their own Marxist postulates.

To the Trotskyites, the Latin American Communist parties (always called Stalinists) are merely political machines maintained for the particular benefit of the Soviet bureaucracy in their tortuous rapprochement with capitalism. These parties, therefore, are not only incapable, in the Trotskyite view, of being the revolutionary vanguard, but also represent the principal obstacle to the achievement of the genuine proletarian anti-imperialist revolution. A good example of this type of analysis is the one published by the Socialist League of Bolivia (document 32).[3] With less virulence, a number of Socialists voiced similar criticisms,[4] which,

[3] There is scarcely any material published on Trotskyism in Latin America. Research is rendered difficult because nearly all the expulsions from the Communist Party are accompanied by the accusation of Trotskyism, in addition to which, on occasion, those expelled accuse those expelling them of being "Trotskyites." See, for example, Eugenio Gómez, *Historia de una traición* (Montevideo: Editorial Elite, 1960), whose author, expelled from the Party, accuses Rodney Arismendi and other leaders of "Trotskyism-opportunism." An idea of the Trotskyite posture with regard to the Bolivian Revolution can be seen in Guillermo Lora, *La revolución boliviana* (La Paz: Editorial Difusión, 1963). A Trotskyite evaluation of the Cuban Revolution, after Castro's attacks on Trotskyism, appears in J. Posadas, *Sobre la revolución socialista en Cuba* (Montevideo: Ediciones Revista Marxista-Leninista, 1966).

[4] This type of Socialist criticism can be found in Oscar Waiss, *Nacionalismo y socialismo en América Latina* (Buenos Aires: Ediciones Iguazú, 1961), p. 164, and Vivian Trías, *El Plan Kennedy y la revolución latinoamericana* (Montevideo: Ediciones El Sol, 1961), pp. 166–170.

in the new epoch, spread among such independent Marxists as the Argentine Silvio Frondizi (document 20). After the experience of Bolivia and Guatemala and particularly after the Cuban Revolution, young core groups of tremulous radicalism added their voices to the critical chorus.

In Bolivia, at the beginning of the fifties, the Marxists were divided into three groups: the Partido de Izquierda Revolucionaria (PIR), whose intellectual elite consisted of three professors—José Antonio Arze, Ricardo Anaya, and Arturo Urquidi;[5] the Communist Party; and the Revolutionary Worker Party, the only Trotskyite party of any importance in Latin America. The participation of the PIR in the military coup against the progressive government of Gualberto Villarroel in 1946, and its apparent support of the governments that succeeded it, contributed to its division and decline. It was dissolved in 1952.[6] For their part, neither the Partido Obrero Revolucionario (POR) nor the Bolivian Communist Party had sufficient force to counterbalance the formidable weight of the MNR. From the triumph of the revolution in 1952, up to the military coup of 1965, Bolivian policy circled around the actions and crises of the party of Paz Estenssoro.

The Guatemalan episode in 1954 cannot be fully understood without taking into account the international factors that affected the period. At its peak, the Guatemalan Communist Party had no more than 4,000

[5] Of the three, probably the best known is José Antonio Arze, author of the very superficial and poorly organized *Sociología marxista* (Oruro: Publicación de la Universidad Técnica, 1963).

[6] For a defense of the PIR's action together with a recognition of errors, see *Partido de izquierda revolucionaria y desarrollo nacional* (La Paz: Talleres Gutenberg, 1961).

members.[7] Despite the Communists' skill at infiltrating key positions, as well as supporting and radicalizing the most popular causes, and in spite of the anti-Communist tension of the moment—all of these factors that tended to throw out of focus the true nature of the role they were playing—it must be remembered that the Communists in Guatemala relied not so much on their own vitality as on their ability to influence a government that had been brought into being by non-Communist forces.[8] The inherent weakness of that situation became apparent in 1954, in view of the relative facility with which the government of Jacobo Arbenz was overthrown by the "invasion" of a small force commanded by Castillo Armas.

After Guatemala, a revolutionary shudder traversed the continent. In 1955, Perón was overthrown in Argentina; the same year, Rojas Pinilla was expelled from the government in Colombia. In 1956, General Odría in Peru was compelled to allow elections and the new government relaxed political repression and permitted the propaganda of the parties, including APRA. In 1958, the dictatorship of Pérez Jiménez was liquidated by an insurrection in Venezuela and Acción

[7] Ronald M. Schneider, *Communism in Guatemala, 1944–1954* (New York: Frederick A. Praeger, 1959), p. 55. According to Guillermo Toriello, *La Batalla de Guatemala* (Santiago: Editorial Universitaria, 1955), p. 160, the real force of the Guatemalan Labor Party (Communist) did not exceed 1,500 members.

[8] Neither in the 1944 revolution that deposed the dictator Jorge Ubico, nor in the 1945 Constitution, which opened the way for the Agrarian Reform of 1952, was there any considerable Communist influence. The agrarian reform, in fact, was largely copied from the Mexican one. A brief but excellent account of the Guatemalan process can be found in Mario Rodríguez, *Central America* (Englewood Cliffs, N.J.: Prentice-Hall, 1965), pp. 137–158.

Democrática, with Rómulo Betancourt at the head, returned to power. In January 1959, General Batista hurriedly left Cuba and the 26th of July Movement led by Fidel Castro burst forth triumphantly on the island.

It seemed as if the democratic forces of the continent were finally making a breakthrough. But not all of these forces were democratic. In Argentina, the army had been the principal anti-Peronist instrument and its shadow was to powerfully influence the country's future. In Cuba, the ruling team was very quickly to head in a new direction and significantly change the political panorama of Latin America.

The Cuban Revolution and Its Consequences (1959–1967)

One of the characteristics of the Cuban revolutionary process—and the most important feature of Latin American socialist field—is that the revolution did not take place under socialist banners.[9] The overthrow of Batista, the triumph of the 26th of July Movement, and, most of all, the transformation of the new government into a Marxist regime were events that were almost absolutely unforeseen at the time by Cuban and continental communism.[1]

[9] To support this point there is no need to resort to the many testimonials and pronunciamientos of the 26th of July Movement during the period of struggle. Suffice it to remember the words of Fidel Castro on May 8, 1959: "I don't know why the slanders against our revolution that it is Communist, that it is infiltrated with communism. Can anyone think that we conceal obscure designs? Can anyone say that we have lied at any time to the people?" Quoted by José Barbeito, *Realidad y masificación* (Caracas: Ediciones Nuevo Orden, 1965), p. 243.

[1] In November 1958, one month before the downfall of Batista, the Cuban Communist Party thus sized up the national

Despite this, the full importance of the changeover to Marxism-Leninism in Cuba was immediately grasped by the Communists. One of the conclusions most frequently repeated by the Marxists, in referring to the Cuban Revolution, was its continental symbolism. As the Mexican Alvaro Mendoza Díez (document 22), among many others, said, the survival of the Cuban regime indicated that the conjunction of international forces was tilting toward the socialist side. North American imperialism, the Communists concluded, could no longer reproduce the Guatemalan episode.

The Cuban situation, however, also brought its aftermath of headaches and contradictions. The Cuban guerrilla struggle had apparently triumphed at a time when the Communist parties of the continent were basically supporting a non-violent line. Not only in Argentina and Chile, where the Party had always defended the electoral and democratic way, but in countries that had been shaken by violence, such as Peru and, more specifically, Colombia, the Communist Party in 1959 showed a profound lack of faith in the possibilities of guerrilla warfare.[2] As in Bolivia, Cuba was

situation and its aspirations: "The tyranny has failed in its attempt to dominate and force the resistance and struggle of the masses *but it would be wrong to suppose that this alone implies the imminent possibility of its overthrow* since domestically its principal basis of sustenance is the disunity of the opposition forces. Hence, our effort to fight for national unity, to do away with tyranny, and *pave the way for a democratic coalition government* shall be unremitting." Message of the Partido Socialista Popular (Communist) to the Chilean Communist Party, in *Partido comunista de Chile, XI congreso nacional* (Santiago, 1959), p. 29 (italics mine).

[2] "The Seventh Congress approved the position taken by the Central Committee against the 'extreme left, venturesome and idealistic' line that was openly or tacitly manifested in the thesis that 'the principal form of struggle, in this stage and in

now, apparently, to prove the rightness of those who had maintained the wrongness of that lack of faith.

On the other hand, the victory of the revolutionary government in Cuba had been achieved despite the almost total non-participation of the Cuban Communist Party. The supposed vanguard of the proletariat—the only vanguard truly capable, according to the Marxists, of directing the peoples in their struggle—had remained in a secondary position.[3] The necessity of recognizing this passivity, the former relations with Batista, and the disguised or open criticism of the new revolutionary leaders, from the outset placed the so-called Communist "old guard" in an extremely delicate

Colombia, is armed combat.' The Seventh Congress denounced the 'guerrillaism' that was expressed in this venturesome orientation as a tendency openly opposed to the Party line." *Documentos Políticos,* No. 13 (Bogota, January–February 1959), p. 23. This position was later changed to open support for the thesis of "armed self-defense of peasants," a defensive position aimed at protecting areas held by the rebels (principally, the region of Marquetalia). The self-defense tactic—severely criticized by Ché Guevara, Regis Debray, and several other spokesmen for Cuba—ended in disaster in 1966 after Marquetalia was occupied by the Colombian army. For an exposition of the Communist position see *Colombia en Pie de Lucha* (Prague: Editorial Paz y Socialismo, 1966).

[3] "We once asked Blas Roca what in his opinion was the most important phenomenon of the Cuban Revolution, and he replied to us: 'It is the first socialist revolution that was not made by the Communist Party,'" Janette Hab and Fidel Castro, *Proceso al sectarismo,* Jorge Álvarez, ed. (Buenos Aires, 1965), p. 49. In the Conclusions of the Party plenum, held in May 1959, the non-leading role of the proletariat in the struggle was recognized and non-extremist tactics were recommended to the revolution. See Luis E. Aguilar, "El Comunismo y la revolución cubana," *Prensa Libre* (Havana, July 5, 1959), p. 2. A reply to this article, explaining the Communist position, was published by Blas Roca in *Hoy* (Havana, July 9 and 10, 1959), p. 1.

and vulnerable position.[4] Despite this, until March 1962, it seemed as if the Communist team was marching toward complete control of the Cuban regime. But then Castro accused one of its principal members, Aníbal Escalante, of "sectarianism," stripped him of his powers, and considerably reduced the political potential of the old guard.[5] Two years later, the public trial, condemnation as a traitor, and shooting of an insignificant member of the Party, Marcos Rodrígues, marked another severe weakening of this group.

The repercussions of these events naturally went beyond the Cuban sphere. It is evident that many of the arguments that were hurled directly and obliquely at the old Cuban Communist cadres—"the bachelors of Marxism," as they were disrespectfully called by Ché Guevara—could very easily be applied to nearly all the Communist parties of the continent. Hence, from the beginning, a certain coolness and reserve marked the relations of these parties with the Cuban government. The support of the revolution has always been explicit, but the speeches of Castro and other Cuban leaders have not always aroused the same echo in the "official" Latin American Communist press.

Finally, the position maintained by the spokesmen

[4] In an interview published in *Nueva Prensa* (Bogota, August 8, 1964), pp. 53–54, Ché Guevara declared: "We consider the Marxist-Leninist party to be the ideal one to make the revolution. In the specific instance of Cuba, for example, the Partido Socialista [Communist] did not see the problem clearly. The analysis by the Party, therefore, was mechanical. The Party regarded coldly the possibility of taking power."

[5] For a painstaking analysis of the relations between Castro and the Communists, see Theodore Draper, *Castroism, Theory and Practice* (New York: Frederick A. Praeger, 1965), and Andrés Suárez, *Cuba: Castroism and Communism: 1959–1965* (Cambridge: M.I.T. Press, 1967).

of the Cuban regime, and particularly by Guevara, its most outstanding theoretician (document 21), offered certain dangerous parallels with some Trotskyist arguments and, even more seriously, with the increasing radicalism manifested by China in its progressive challenge to Russia.[6] Guevara's theses—the peasantry as the instrument of liberation, the ability to override the limits of objective conditions by group audacity, the virtually absolute negation of the possibility of a peaceful transition to socialism in Latin America[7]—clashed in many aspects with principles that have been maintained as essential to Marxism-Leninism by the Latin American Communists. This explains a certain Communist ambivalence vis-à-vis the Cuban case: applauding the revolution, yet warning that the Cuban formula must not be copied "mechanically," or voicing tangential criticisms of the Cuban revolutionary position. The arguments of Rodney Arismendi against the Chinese line (document 25), for example, may be wielded with equal validity against Guevara's theses.[8]

[6] The initial influence of China on Cuba is described in Peter S. H. Hang and Joan Maloney, *The Chinese Communist Impact on Cuba* (Chestnut Hill: Research Institute on the Sino-Soviet Bloc, 1962).

[7] This last point is in Ché Guevara's Prologue to Fidel Castro, *El partido marxista-leninista* (Buenos Aires: Editorial Rosa Blindada, 1965).

[8] The following vague accusation by Roger Garaudy, an outstanding French Marxist, belongs to the same type of two-headed argument: "Contrary to the legend (*of Trotskyite inspiration*) which would have us regard the Cuban Revolution as a 'peasant' revolution . . . ," "El Marxismo y la revolución cubana," *Documentos Políticos*, No. 27 (Bogota, July–August 1962). In an interview published in the newspaper *Hoy* (Havana, March 9, 1963), p. 2, the Brazilian Communist Luís Carlos Prestes argues, "For Marxism-Leninism, revolution is not a synonym of violence, it is fundamentally a change of classes in power and this is possible, even in certain Latin

All this has produced a series of implications and complications among the Latin American Marxist groups that are very difficult to synthesize. Initially, Chinese propaganda and discussions on Cuba contributed to a large extent to increasing the fragmentation of the Marxist left inside and outside the Communist parties. In 1961, the Brazilian party split into two groups: the Brazilian Communist Party of Luís Carlos Prestes (pro-Russian) and the Communist Party of Brazil (pro-Chinese). The same thing happened in Peru, Colombia, Bolivia, and other countries. In Chile, the Communist-Socialist relations maintained by the Frente de Acción Popular (FRAP) were complicated by "ultra-leftist" tendencies inside the Socialist Party and by the appearance of various pro-Chinese groups that, like the "Spartacus" group, trained their best artillery against the electoral position of FRAP.[9]

Outside the parties, while some socialist and Trotskyite factions were taking advantage of the opportunity to redouble their attack against the ineptness of the Communist leadership, other groups, more or less identified with the Chinese or Cuban line, adopted a much more radical attitude and began to preach or practice the revolutionary theses of Guevara. After the weakening of the Russian leadership center, it seemed as if Marxism had become the collective patrimony of the most diverse individuals or groups, who adopted it, entirely or in part, in their combat programs.

Thus, for example, while in Argentina such authors

American countries in present conditions, without civil war and without armed insurrection."

[9] For the impact of the Chinese line and the Cuban example in Chile, see Ernst Halperin, *Nationalism and Communism in Chile* (Cambridge: M.I.T. Press, 1965), Chapter 3.

as Jorge Abelardo Ramos (document 23), Gregorio Bermann,[1] and José M. Aricó called upon Marxism to censure or disqualify the Communists, in Brazil the Peasant Leagues of Francisco Julião and student groups such as Política Operaria made their appearance with a more independent and revolutionary Marxism.[2] The Movimiento de Izquierda Revolucionaria (MIR), which favored guerrilla actions, sprang up in Chile and Peru with Luis de la Puente Uceda (document 28) and Guillermo Lobatón, and in Venezuela the Fuerzas Armadas de Liberación Nacional (FALN) joined in the armed combat. The 13th of November Movement, directed by Captain Jon Sosa (accused of being a Trotskyite by the Communists), rose up in the Guatemalan mountains at the same time as Movimiento de Liberación Nacional (MLN) took a revolutionary position in Argentina and Mexico. On a greater or lesser scale, the same phenomenon was duplicated in nearly all the countries of Latin America. On the fringe of the Communist parties, a new left, more radical in both theory and practice, had sprung up on the continent.

Once again, however, prudence must be exercised in the face of the multiplicity of names and organizations. The radical left, stigmatized by the Communists at times as "ultra-left," is still more an aspiration than a force, more a wish than a program. One of the few traits that identify radical left groups is their eagerness to extol results over theories, their proclaiming that

[1] Gregorio Bermann, *La crisis argentina* (Buenos Aires: Editorial Proceso, 1964), pp. 32–36.

[2] A good panorama of the situation in Brazil before the coup d'état is presented in Timothy F. Harding, "Revolution Tomorrow: The Failure of the Left in Brazil," *Studies on the Left*, IV, No. 4 (Fall 1964), 30–54.

the only possible means of achieving reforms in Latin America is through revolution "here and now." This is the line that usually distinguishes them from "official" Marxism-Leninism. On one side are the traditional Communist parties, with their hundred-times-repeated political thesis: The revolution cannot be risked by haste nor can it be based on isolated group actions. The revolution must be accomplished with the masses and when historical conditions are favorable. So long as the objective conditions are not favorable, the best path is not to renounce any means of combat, whether they be elections, political alliances, or "gathering strength." [3] All the rest is revolutionary "infantilism," which usually strengthens the most reactionary forces in the countries and results in the collapse of the progressive movements. On the other side are those groups which, in word or in deed, maintain that such a thesis is nothing more than a defeatist pacifism that indefinitely postpones the revolutionary eruption; that the true definition of a revolutionary is not his knowledge of Marxism but his capacity to act in a revolutionary way. The polemic goes deeper than the right moment or way for action. It is trying to decide who should be the leader of the revolutionary struggle—the Communist parties, whose basic force is usually in the cities, or the New Left, which usually

[3] Of particular interest are: Rodney Arismendi, "Algunos aspectos actuales del proceso revolucionario en la América Latina," *El centenario de la · I internacional*; Gilberto Viera, "Nuevas experiencias de la lucha revolucionaris en Colombia," *Nuestra Epoca*, No. 8 (Santiago, August 1965); "The Guerrilla Movement and Its Prospects in the Light of the Present Political Situation," Resolutions of the Twenty-First Meeting of the Central Committee IX, *Peruvian Communist Party Bulletin*, printed in *World Marxist Review*, No. 64 (January 28, 1966).

supports armed struggle in the country (see documents 30, 31).

Hence the permanent importance that the case of Cuba acquired for both groups. For Cuba, at least until very recently, like a revolutionary Janus, for a while turned a favorable face to all sectors: at the same time as it was proclaiming itself Marxist-Leninist in official fashion, it was insisting that the only way to victory was the revolutionary way and offered the myth of its guerrilla triumph as evidence. Countless factions invoked the name of Cuba in reproaching one another. "In Latin America, the Peaceful Road that you advocate stands in marked contrast to the Revolutionary Road of Fidel Castro and other comrades, who have led the Cuban people to victory," the Chinese sarcastically pointed out to the Chilean Communist Party in 1963.[4] During the same year, Russia was editing a volume very significantly entitled *The People of the U.S.S.R. and Cuba Will Always March Together.*[5]

However, the shadow of Cuba greatly influenced many other Latin American groups; inciting in some a desire for reforms, alarming others, encouraging in many a resistance to Marxism. In Chile, in the elections of 1964, the spector of the Cuban *paredón* was a very important factor in the defeat of FRAP.[6]

[4] Halperin, *op. cit.*, p. 113.

[5] *Los pueblos de la U.R.R.S. y Cuba marcharán siempre unidos* (Moscow: Ediciones Pravda, 1963). The book is made up basically of fragments of speeches by Castro and Khrushchev.

[6] A few days before the elections, to which I was an eyewitness, the walls, the newspapers, and the radio of Santiago were saturated with alarming anti-Communist illustrations of the Cuban process, always accompanied by the question: "Chileans, do you want this to happen in Chile?"

In other countries the reaction was more violent: the proclamation by the Cuban government of its intent to "convert the Andes into the Sierra Maestra of the continent" and the violent outbreaks of the radical groups were answered by a spate of military coups. Only a handful of democratic governments have survived the curtain of anti-Communist sabers that has fallen upon the continent. On the other hand, aware of the continental risk, the United States has, since 1961, demonstrated, with renewed economic aid to Latin America or through the landing of the Marines in Santo Domingo, how far its decision to avoid "another Cuba" extends.[7]

Accordingly, one of the most radical questions being asked by the Marxists today is the one voiced by the Guatemalan José Manuel Fortuny, "Has the revolution become more difficult in Latin America?" (document 27). That the reply tends to be affirmative is shown by the series of self-criticisms and confessions of error to which, in the face of multiple misfortunes, nearly all the Marxist groups ranging from the Communist Party of Brazil (document 35) to the Venezuelan FALN (document 34) have subjected themselves. While the Marxist left, despite a partial increase in votes, did not win electoral victories in Peru in 1962, in Uruguay in 1963 or 1967,[8] or in Chile in 1964, neither did the revolutionary groups see any decisive

[7] An analysis of the Santo Domingo experience from a Communist point of view is found in Partido Comunista Dominicano, *Triunfaremos* (Prague: Editorial Paz y Socialismo, 1966).

[8] For a study of the electoral vicissitudes of Socialists and Communists in Uruguay, up to 1963, see Aldo E. Solari, "Requiem para la izquierda," *Estudios sobre la sociedad Uruguaya* (Montevideo: Ediciones ARCA, 1965), III, 135–156.

success. In Peru, the deaths of Uceda, Lobatón, and other guerrilla leaders in 1965, as well as the reformist program of Fernando Belaúnde Terry, caused the violence to abate. In Colombia itself, the pacification of large areas, the electoral defeat of the MIR in 1966, and the death of padre Camilo Torres, who had dramatically joined the guerrillas, have shown the vitality of the present political system. In Venezuela, a state of conflict has arisen between the Communist Party, the MIR, and FALN,[9] which, with its inevitable flood of mutual accusations, has exposed to public view the at least temporary crisis of the action groups. In Guatemala, neither the 13th of November Movement (which suddenly, after Castro's accusations, disappeared from world news) nor the Fuerzas Armadas Rebeldes (FAR) under the new leadership of Major César Montes[1] has thus far won appreciable success. In Mexico, in July 1965, the Communist magazine *Política*[2] was complaining of the fragmentation and weakness of all the leftist groups vis-à-vis the economic might of the right. At the beginning of 1968, Cuba continued to be the only example of victory on the continent.

[9] A number of reports on the crisis appeared in the newspaper *La República* (Caracas), July 14 and 15, 1966, reproducing mutually accusatory documents of the Political Bureau of the Venezuelan Communist Party and the MIR. The crisis grew more serious and significant because the Cuban government backed the revolutionary position of the MIR, in the face of the so-called "Democratic Peace" defended by the Venezuelan Communist Party.

[1] Turcios Lima, the leader of FAR hailed by Castro at the Tricontinental Conference in Havana as the real representative of Guatemalan revolutionary spirit, was killed in a mysterious automobile accident on October 2, 1966.

[2] "La izquierda y las cadenas de oro y los soles," *Política*, No. 125 (July 1, 1965), p. 16.

However, the traits of the Cuban phenomenon or, more accurately, the Castro phenomenon, continue to be difficult to pin down. The vertiginous and multifarious nature of the internal process—from the humanist repudiation of communism[3] to the embrace of Marxism-Leninism; from the uninterrupted hymn over the progress of the agrarian reform and industrialization to the sudden recognition of monumental blunders in the economy[4]—have been matched by the seesawing of external affairs. In a temporizing balance in the face of the Chinese-Soviet conflict up to October 1962, Castro, after the withdrawal of the Russian rockets from Cuba, seemed to aim his applause at China, where the press emphatically exalted him while they were accusing Russia of having perpetrated a new Munich on Cuba.[5] Later, during and after the Tricontinental Conference held in Havana in January 1966, the pendulum apparently swung drastically in favor of the Russians: Castro attacked China and its government first in the economic, and then in the political, field.[6] To deduce from this, however, that the

[3] "Capitalism sacrifices man; the communist state sacrifices the rights of man, therefore we are not in agreement with one or the other." Words of Fidel Castro in the spring of 1959. Quoted by Luis Franco, *Espartaco en Cuba* (Buenos Aires: C. Dávalos y Hernández, 1965), p. 307.

[4] For one of the best analyses of the Cuban economy, both for its approval and for its criticism, see René Dumont, *Cuba, socialisme et développement* (Paris: Editions du Seuil, 1964).

[5] "The attempt to play the Munich scheme against the Cuban people is doomed to complete failure," *Peking Review,* 45 (November 9, 1962), quoted in William E. Griffith, *The Sino-Soviet Rift* (Cambridge: M.I.T. Press, 1962), p. 61.

[6] "What is involved is not the number of tons more or less of rice . . . but a much more important and fundamental question: whether in the world of tomorrow, which revolutionaries are fighting to achieve, powerful countries can assume the right to blackmail, pressure, attack, and strangle

Tricontinental was a victory for the Russian line as some analysts, among them the Trotskyites, did was a risky simplification.[7] Such is, at least, the impression of some of the participants in the Conference.[8]

In the Tricontinental, aside from the presence of a large Chinese delegation, the official Communist parties were in a minority and, with Cuban backing, it appears that the organizations of the New Left carried the day.[9] The Mexican Communist Party and the Popular Socialist Party of Lombardo Toledano were excluded from the Mexican delegation because of their attitude of support for the government of their country. The principal representation devolved upon the Movimiento de Liberación Nacional (Mexican). In all, eight Communist parties (those of Peru, Panama, Haiti, Mexico, Puerto Rico, and the three Guianas) were not officially represented at the Conference.[1] In other cases, such as Brazil and Bolivia,

small countries," *Gramma* (Havana, February 6, 1966, special English edition), p. 1. A more ferocious and direct attack against the Chinese leaders was made by Castro in his speech on the following March 13.

[7] See, for example, Adolfo Gilly, "A Conference without Glory and without Program," *Monthly Review*, XVII, No. 11 (April 1966), 21–34.

[8] José Vazeilles, "The Tricontinental: Concrete Internationalism," *Monthly Review*, XVIII, No. 2 (June 1966), 28–34.

[9] The Chinese, for their part, used the Conference to attack Russia. "At the Political Committee meetings, the Soviet delegate insisted on imposing on the Conference a resolution on so-called peaceful coexistence . . . by these maneuvers the Soviet delegation revealed to the Conference their true colors of sham anti-imperialism, sham support for the revolutionary struggles, and sham unity." *Peking Report*, January 16, 1966, quoted in U.S. Congress, Senate, Committee on the Judiciary, *The Tricontinental Conference* (Washington: U.S. Government Printing Office, 1966), p. 134.

[1] However, according to the *Informe especial para estudiar las resoluciones II, numeral I y VIII de la octava reunión de con-*

delegations from both the Russian and the Chinese factions were accepted. And there can be no doubt that at least the tone of the declarations seems to reflect the supremacy of the revolutionary accent.

The Cuban support of the New Left's thesis of violence has become more radical in the last year. Not only are Cuban propaganda media increasingly excoriating the "hesitant leadership," the "reformist attitude" of the "pseudo-revolutionaries" of the continent (Havana radio has a special program by Chileans called "Peoples' Revolution versus Reformism"), but Castro himself, in his speech of July 26, 1966 (document 29) defined the only true Latin American pathway as the revolutionary struggle. Since that speech, this hard and uncompromising line has become the official Cuban position, increasing the possibility of friction with several Communist groups in and out of Latin America.[2] Not only has Cuban propaganda repeatedly lashed every revolutionary group that does not accept the thesis of armed insurrection as the only way out for Latin America, but carrying the thesis to its ultimate conclusion Cuban spokesmen have also demanded that the guerrilla, as the real revolutionary vanguard, should be the practical leader

---

sulta de ministros de relaciones exteriores, relativo a la Conferencia Tricontinental (Washington: Unión Panamericana, November 1966), pp. 128, 135, several of the names of those who attended the Conference were actually pseudonyms of members of the supposedly unrepresented parties.

[2] The strain suffered by Cuban-Soviet relations became evident during the celebration of the fiftieth anniversary of the Russian Revolution (November 1967). The Cuban representative—a secondary figure of the government—was not invited to speak during the ceremonies. On October 27, 1967, *Pravda* published an article by Luis Corvalán praising the Cuban Revolution but refuting the Cuban revolutionary thesis.

of all movements for national liberation (see document 30). In support of this demand—aimed directly at the position of Latin American Communist parties—French writer Regis Debray, in his now famous little book *Revolution in the Revolution?*,[3] has proclaimed that the Cuban Revolution opened a new horizon for guerrilla warfare and thus forces a total re-evaluation of the objectives and methods of national wars for liberation. According to Debray, who tends to reduce the entire Cuban phenomenon to the correct application of the guerrilla formula, in the new era of "war to the death" in Latin America, the guerrilla becomes the only instrument capable of breaking the power of the army—"the backbone of the bourgeois state"—and of forging a new and superior type of revolutionary leadership. If the Latin American Communist parties are unable to learn the true lesson of Cuba, then history will not absolve them. Quoting Castro, Debray pronounces his sentence: "Who will make the revolution in Latin America? Who? . . . the people, the revolutionary with or without the party." [4]

In July 1967, Havana played host to another international gathering of supposedly fiery revolutionaries, the OLAS (Latin American Organization of Solidarity). The motto of the conference was also its program: "The duty of a revolutionary is to make revolution."

But Cuban war drums have not yet forced Latin American Communist parties into submission. Quite

[3] *Révolution dans la révolution?* (Paris: François Maspero, 1967). There is a good English version published by the *Monthly Review*.

[4] *Ibid.*, p. 103. For some debatable aspects of Debray's thesis see Luis E. Aguilar, "Regis Debray: Where Logic Failed," *The Reporter* (December 28, 1967), pp. 31–32.

the contrary, a tendency to openly reject Castro's role as revolutionary mentor has become evident. In March 1967, the Venezuelan Communist Party published a harsh answer to Castro's criticism. In August of that year, one month after the meeting of the OLAS in Havana, the Colombian and Venezuelan Communist parties issued a joint declaration ratifying their role as revolutionary vanguard and denying the possibility of a single formula for fighting to be applied in every country (document 36). Similar manifestations with overtones less clearly anti-Castro, have appeared in several other countries.

On the other hand, the Cuban hard line suffered two dramatic setbacks during the last months of 1967. In October, Ernesto "Ché" Guevara, the second great hero of the Cuban Revolution, the master tactician of the guerrilla, was killed by the Bolivian Army in a minor skirmish with a small rebel band. The following month, Regis Debray himself, the theoretician of the new and supposedly correct method of guerrilla fighting, who had been previously captured by the Bolivian Army, was sentenced to thirty years in prison. In spite of these severe and still unexplained disasters,[5] Havana's propaganda continues to insist that armed struggle and guerrilla warfare are the only Latin American ways for revolutionary victory.

If in the face of conditions that make revolution a very difficult task, the Marxist left, divided by so many

[5] On October 16, 1967, Castro officially confirmed the death of Guevara, but why a leader of Guevara's caliber was left alone for nine months in a remote area of Bolivia, fighting in the worst possible conditions, was not explained or even mentioned in Castro's lengthy speech. For a good analysis of these events see Norman Gall, "The Legacy of Ché Guevara," *Commentary* (December 1967), pp. 31–44.

positions, is going to follow the guerrilla path as the only way for union and victory, if it is going to basically support the line of "gathering strength," while awaiting a more favorable situation, or if it will continue with its present multiplicity of roads, only time, which passes anxiously and fast in Latin America, can tell.

The Impact of Marxism

It is unfair to talk of Marxism in Latin America without mentioning, at least briefly, its impact in political and cultural areas quite removed from militant communism. Marxism, as was pointed out earlier, did not reach Latin America in transcendental form until the twenties, when the atmosphere was charged with radical aspirations. That is why, overflowing the more or less dogmatic channels of the Communist, socialist, and Trotskyite groups, where theoretical expression does not seem to be vigorous, Marxism has penetrated deeply into the Latin American revolutionary cadres and has provided more than one rebellious generation with the terminology and the ideological arsenal that they needed to justify their attitude. The impact of a program that seemed to clarify history, to simplify the causes, and to identify the enemy explains why out of the Marxist quarry were hewn not only socialists and Communists but also such parties as the Peruvian APRA and such political leaders as Víctor Raúl Haya de la Torre in Peru and Rómulo Betancourt in Venezuela. Its presence, either as an affirmation or as a negation, as ally or enemy, makes itself felt in the most important political areas of the continent, from the universities to the governments. And even if it is true, as its leaders delight in repeating, that Christian Democracy would be defending the same positions even if Marxism did not exist,[6] it cannot be denied that the vast challenge of Marxism has helped to galvanize the forces of the Catholic Church, the Christian groups, and the democrats in general.

Its literary dimensions are also worth taking into account, although at times the "literature of commitment" exhibits more commitment than literature: in poetry, from the vaguely Marxist stance of the Chilean Pablo de Rochka, all the way to the definite stand of Pablo Neruda; from the metaphysical verse of the Peruvian César Vallejo, who never made literary concessions to his political convictions, all the way up to the social and sometimes overly condescending poetry of the Cuban Nicolás Guillén; in the novel, with the brutal protest of the Ecuadorian Jorge Icaza (*Huasipungo*) or with the more refined and intellectual protest of the Guatemalan Miguel Angel Asturias (*El señor presidente*) or the Mexican Carlos Fuentes (*La región más transparente*); and in the historical interpretations of the Argentine Ezequiel Martínez Estrada or the Mexican Jesús Silva Herzog. In all these and in many other authors, Marxism, either confused or clear, vague or firm, as a mere pretext for desperate protest or as a serious interpretive effort, as the superficial stridency of youth or as the radical belief of maturity, has contributed a fundamental trait to the ideological physiognomy of Latin America.

[6] "I declare this night that if the Communist Manifesto had never been written, we would have the same imperative duties of conscience and patriotism to do what we are doing for the same reasons that we are doing them," Rodomiro Tomic, *Con los Pobres de América* (Lima: Ediciones Fela, 1962), p. 21.

INTRODUCTION
TO THE REVISED EDITION

From the Death of Ché Guevara to Cuban Intervention in Africa (1967-1977)

In 1967 the Cuban hard line suffered two major set-backs: the April capture of Regis Debray, theorist of a new, supposedly proper method of guerrilla warfare, by the Bolivian army; and the October killing of Ernesto "Ché" Guevara, also by Bolivian troops, in remote Ñancahuazu, where his sick and isolated group had dwindled to seventeen men. The death of the second greatest hero of the Cuban Revolution had a profound effect on Latin America and the world. Eulogies, both usual and unusual, were heard throughout the continent, with even rightist publications praising Guevara's heroism (as nothing is safer than homage for a defeated opponent). Once the dust of rhetoric began to settle, however, some naked facts came to light. No Bolivian peasant had joined Ché's struggle; the Bolivian Communist Party had denied him aid; his guerrilla group had been plagued by antagonism between Cubans and Bolivians. Publication of these aspects of Ché's failure triggered apparently typical accusations and counter-accusations by the left, in the name of "true Marxism." Fidel Castro publicly denounced Mario Monje, secretary general of the Bolivian Communist Party, who had met with Ché in the mountains, and mining leader Oscar Zamora.[1] The Bolivian Communist Party in turn denied all accusations.[2] Maoist groups denounced both Castro and the Communists for sacrificing Guevara to obey their Soviet masters.[3]

Beyond the factional bickering, the true significance of the episode began to emerge; in the Bolivian mountains the basic issue which had divided the guerrillas and the Communists, the dilemma of leadership (see documents 30–32), had been put to a test. Loyal to its principles, the Bolivian Communist Party had demanded political and military control

---

[1]"Mario Monje," said Fidel Castro, "one of these specimens who are becoming typical in Latin America, branding his title of Secretary of the Communist Party, tried to challenge Ché's political and military leadership. . . . These "Communist leaders" are below the concept of "internationalism" held by the native tribes conquered by the Europeans. . . . Oscar Zamora [was] another Monje, who had promised Ché his support and later betrayed his promise and remained cowardly with his arms folded at the moment of action." Fidel Castro, "Una Introduccion Necesaria," in *El Diario del Ché en Bolivia* (Mexico: Siglo XXI, 1973), pp. 14–16.

[2]Spurning Castro's accusations and Ché's comments (taken from his diary), the Bolivian Communist Party reminded everyone that they "never invited Ché to Bolivia," and that Bolivian Communists "do not accept tutelage from anyone, no matter how revolutionary that person is or pretends to be." See "Refuta el Partido Comunista Boliviano las notas del Ché Guevara," in *ibid.*, p. 282.

[3]The pro-Chinese Communist parties of both Bolivia and Columbia issued similar declarations in July and August 1968. For a summary in English, see "Colombians Say Castro Left Ché to Die," *Washington Post,* August 19, 1968, p. 11. For a lengthier Maoist attack on Castro and Debray, picturing the former as a petty-bourgeois racist dictator under a Soviet thumb, see Antoine G. Petit, *Castro-Debray contre le Marxisme-Leninisme* (Paris: R. Laffont, 1968). The author is a Haitian who lived in Havana and later in Peking.

of the struggle. Faithful to his own theory, Ché
Guevara had remained adamant: he must be the
leader.[4] The break was thus unavoidable. Monje returned to La Paz and the Communist Party did nothing more than issue some vague declarations of
support;[5] unperturbed, Ché Guevara went on with his
guerrilla campaign, confident that he could win without Monje's support and that the most combative
elements of the Communist Party would eventually
rush to his aid.[6] Subsequent events demonstrated
how tragically wrong he was. The theory of the
"guerrilla focus" as a galvanizing center for revolution
suffered a devastating blow.[7] Two years after Gue-

[4]"On the second point," wrote Guevara in reference to Monje's
demand, "I could not accept it under any circumstances. I was
going to be the military leader, and no ambiguities could be
accepted. Here the discussion struck and turned into a vicious
circle." *El Diario del Ché*, p. 53. For Monje's defense and version of the events, see *El diario* (La Paz), February 5, 1968;
Daniel James, ed., *Complete Bolivian Diaries of Ché Guevara
and Other Captured Documents* (New York: Stein and Day;
1968), pp. 95, 227–228; Rolando E. Bonachea and Nelson P.
Valdes, *Ché: Selected Works* (Cambridge, Mass.: MIT Press,
1969), p. 33; and Richard Gott, *Guerrilla Movements in Latin
America* (New York: Doubleday, 1972), pp. 433–438.

[5]Allegedly, the leaders of the party did something worse; they
expelled from the party anyone who wanted to join the guerrillas. See Fidel Castro, *El Diario del Ché*, p. 14.

[6]"As I expected" wrote Guevara, "the attitude of Monje was
first evasive and later treacherous. The party is already taking
arms against us, and I don't know how far it will go, but that
won't stop us. Perhaps, in the long run, it will be beneficial (I am
almost sure of it). Those who are more honest and combative will
be with us." *El Diario del Ché*, p. 71.

[7]It is difficult to understand how a keen observer of the Latin
American revolutionary situation, Richard Gott, could make
this assessment of the Guevara-Monje meeting: "It was a historical meeting. It represented the final rejection by the Communists
of the thesis which had brought the Cuban revolutionaries to
power. And it marked the beginning of a new era, both in

vara's death, peasant guerrillas in Latin America had
been reduced to scattered groups, many of which had
accepted the prospect of a long and hazardous
struggle.[8]

With the decline of peasant guerrilla warfare and
the death or defeat of several other "guerrilleros" in
different parts of Latin America,[9] the debate around
the "focus" theory and the nature of the revolutionary
vanguard began to lose intensity. Reassured in their
convictions, the Communist parties occasionally recognized their own passivity as "vanguard" of the revolution (see document 32); but the dreamed-of

Latin America and world politics, an era which saw the end of
the Communist party's hegemony over the Left." *Guerrilla Movements*, p. 429. In the first place, it is quite debatable, and the
Communist parties had always made a point of it, whether the
guerrillas were the basic factor in Castro's victory. Secondly, the
defeat of the guerrilla peasants ratified the Communist thesis
that "guerrillaism" was a wrong approach to revolutionary victory.

[8]See, for example, the declaration of the Colombian ELN,
Ejercito de Liberación Nacional (National Liberation Army),
Continuidad y Desarrollo de una Concepcion Revolucionaria
(Colombia, 1969), where the subject of a "prolonged warfare"
is a basic point. For an excellent study on the Colombian rural
background, see Pierre Gilhodes, "Agrarian Struggles in Colombia," in Rodolfo Stravenhagen, ed., *Agrarian Problems and Peasant Movements in Latin America* (New York: Doubleday,
1970). An interesting insight into the guerrilla is Jaime Arenas,
La Guerrilla por Dentro (Bogota: Ediciones Tercer Mundo,
1971). Arenas was later killed by members of the ELN.

[9]The last casualty among the well-known leaders of the sixties, Guatemalan Marcos Yon Sosa was killed in May 1970 in
Mexico while trying to escape the persecution of the army. Yon
Sosa was an example of the ideological flexibility of some "guerrilleros." A former officer in the Guatemalan army, he founded
the November 13th Movement under Trotskyite influences; broke
with them to reach an accommodation with Turcios Lima of
the FAR, who held more orthodox Communist views, and finally,
after Lima's death, moved toward a pro-Chinese line.

unification of the left was by no means achieved. Quite to the contrary, new trends and issues very soon opened other areas of conflict and increased the atomization of the left.[10] Plagued by what a Mexican sociologist has termed "a voracious appetite for Marxist rhetoric," (see document 39), in the seventies the left was going to confront a fresh set of dilemmas.

Of all the issues facing the left in this period, four appeared to be the most important: (1) the rise and decline of the urban guerrilla, (2) the "revolution" of the Peruvian armed forces, (3) the failure of the socialist experiment in Chile, and (4) Castro's turn toward a pro-Soviet policy and Cuban intervention in Africa.

The Rise and Decline of the Urban Guerrilla

The first important emergence of the urban guerrilla in Latin America flared in Venezuela at the beginning of the sixties, but it was rather short-lived. In 1958, the military dictatorship of General Pérez Jiménez was toppled and, after a brief period of turmoil, Rómulo Betancourt, the leader of Acción Democrática (Democratic Action), was elected president of the

[10]"In Peru," wrote Jean Larteguy in 1967, "one can count nine parties, movements or fronts of the extreme left." Jean Larteguy, *Les Guerrilleros* (Paris: Raoul Solar, 1967), p. 330. For a view of the situation in 1970, see Luis E. Aguilar, "The Fragmentation of the Marxist Left," *Problems of Communism* (Washington D.C.), July-October 1970, pp. 1–11. The permanence of that situation can be glimpsed in the declaration of the Colombian revolutionary movement M-19, "La unidad: una necesidad revolucionaria," *Alternativa* (Bogota), No. 124 (July-August 1977), p. 11.

republic. He had the difficult task of ruling a nation still shaken by political unrest, whose army was not totally reliable and where the Communists had just demonstrated impressive political strength.[11] Very soon relations with Castro's Cuba deteriorated (Fidel Castro had paid a friendly visit to Caracas in 1959), and Betancourt was facing the opposition of the Communists and of the MIR, Movimiento de Izquierda Radical (Movement of the Radical Left), which had split from his own party.

By the end of 1960, MIR, which had proclaimed itself Marxist, was in open rebellion against the government. In March 1961, somewhat reluctantly, the Communist Party began to accept the necessity of armed struggle. In 1962, guerrilla groups, mainly under MIR's direction, began to appear in the countryside. Their actions, though, were limited. But in May 1962, a military rebellion took place in the naval base of Carúpano. Quickly suppressed, it nevertheless shattered the government and forced many of the defeated officers to join the guerrillas. Confronting an increasing official persecution and spurred by what appeared to be a deep crisis in the government, the Community Party took the path of insurrection in December 1962. Two months later, the MIR, the Communists, and the ex-officers formed the FALN, Fuerzas Armadas de Liberación Nacional (Armed Forces of National Liberation). At the insistence of the Communists, a supreme political instrument, the FLN, Frente de Liberación Nacional (National Lib-

[11]In the 1958 elections, the party's congressional candidates received 160,791 votes, as compared to 1,275,973 for Acción Democrática and 392,305 for COPEI (Christian Democrats). In the Federal District, which comprises most of Caracas, the Communists emerged as the second strongest party.

erating Front), was simultaneously created. Nevertheless, and perhaps as a concession to the ex-officers, the program issued by FALN had no Marxist overtones.[12]

In spite of the presence of peasant guerrillas, and probably under Communist influence, the center of the armed struggle shifted rapidly from the countryside to Caracas. Through a series of daring attacks and terrorist acts, the FALN quickly became famous in and out of Latin America. Their real force, though, did not correspond to their reputation. In addition, the political atmosphere was changing in Venezuela: the Betancourt regime had begun to implement some important progressive reforms. In December 1963, misjudging the national mood, FALN compromised its prestige by announcing an all-out offensive to prevent the holding of the upcoming presidential elections, which they termed "nothing more than another bourgeois farce." It suffered a stunning defeat. Not only were the elections held without major disturbances, but almost 90 percent of the registered electorate went to the polls. It was a massive rejection of FALN's propaganda and methods. In its self-criticism (document 49), the organization attributed the disaster to the efficiency of the repressive apparatus and to its own mistakes, but offered no explanation for that appalling lack of popular support.

The FALN never recovered from the blow. As early as 1964 important leaders of MIR and the Communist

---

[12]In the FALN proclamation of aims, the world socialism does not appear. Point one reads: "To enforce respect for national sovereignity and independence, the freedom and democratic life of the Venezuelan people." Point five: "To set up a revolutionary, nationalistic, and democratic government." The entire program can be found in Manuel Cabieses Donoso, *Venezuela okey!* (Habana: Editorial Venceremos, 1964), p. 285.

Party began to talk about abandoning the armed struggle and returning to legal methods. This change of tactics provoked, naturally, many internal discussions and polemics in both groups, weakening still more the cadres of the organization. By 1966 urban guerrillas had practically disappeared in Venezuela.

The failure of the FALN's urban guerrillas and the temporary survival of its peasant ones, plus the retreat of the Communist Party from the armed struggle arena, were to have many consequences for the left. The most important one was to increase factional conflicts on almost every level. Inside the Communist Party, the internal rift was publicly revealed in 1969–1970, when an important sector of the leadership, Pompeyo Marquez and Teodoro Petkoff among them, moved out of the party and formed MAS, Movimiento al Socialismo (Movement to Socialism). Petkoff became an outstanding critic of the ultra-left and the Communist Party (document 52). Externally, the party clashed with Fidel Castro, who was then an ardent support of the peasant guerrillas, and was forced to answer his accusation in a public declaration (document 51). This polemic, centered on Castro's support of guerrilla leader Douglas Bravo, whom he accused the Communists of betraying, ended in an odd, or perhaps typical, manner: by 1973, Douglas Bravo was denouncing both the Communists and Castro of abandoning and sacrificing the guerrillas to please the Soviet Union.[13]

As a second consequence, the collapse of urban resistance in 1964 caused many leftist and radical groups to transfer their attention and their hopes to the peasant guerrilla tactics. But, as we have pointed out, by 1968 the peasant guerrilla struggle was in full decline. Consequently, and because of the sudden emergence of radical groups operating successfully in some urban centers of Uruguay and Brazil, the urban guerrilla became again a central issue for the New Left.

One year after the death of Ché Guevara, while the prestige of the peasant guerrilla theory was ebbing, the names of Brazilian Carlos Marighela, founder of Acão Libertadora Nacional, ALN (National Liberation Action), and still more the Uruguayan Movimiento de Liberación Nacional, MNL (Movement for National Liberation), widely known as Tupamaros,[14] began to be in the forefront of the news. Once more, a non-Communist Marxist force seemed destined to play a decisive role in the revolutionary struggle.

Of all the new groups, the Tupamaros seemed to be the epitome of the New Left's dream. They were formed by several groups of leftists,[15] who relied more on direct action than on ideological programs. "The Tupamaros believe in the general principles of the

[13]Writing in France, Douglas Bravo reached what could be called a "revolutionary delirium"; he not only accused Castro of abandoning him, which was partially true, but demanded that the Cuban leader should have been ready to sacrifice the island to an American attack to continue the fight in the continent. See Douglas Bravo, "Cuba: rectificacion, tactica o estrategica?" quoted in Regis Debray, *Las Pruebas de Fuego* (Mexico: Editorial Siglo XXI, 1975), pp. 108–109.

[14]From Tupac-Amaru, an Indian leader who headed an unsuccessful rebellion against Spain in Peru in 1780.

[15]Raul Sendic, the best known of the founders, came from the Socialist Party, but the first cadres were formed by "groups coming from anarchism and from the myriad of leftist groups which had been in conflict with the Uruguayan left and leaned toward direct action." Antonio Mercader and Jorge Vera, *Tupamaros: estrategia y accion* (Montevideo: Editorial Alfa, 1969), p. 10.

Socialist Revolution, but avoid those concrete questions which usually either produce the sterility of too much "verbalism" or narrow a wide Marxist program of liberation which should attract leftists from all tendencies."[16] "Revolutionary action in itself, the mere fact of arming, of preparing and realizing actions which violate bourgeois legality, engenders revolutionary conscience and revolutionary conditions."[17] Thus spoke the Tupamaros in 1969.

As in Venezuela, the Tupamaros sprang into action at a moment when the political structure of Uruguay, the former "Switzerland of America," was breaking down under the pressure of a deep and long economic crisis which had begun in 1957 when the wool market collapsed. At th beginning of the sixties, with inflation and unemployment rampant, austerity programs failing, and a deteriorating economy, it was evident that the old liberal system designed by José Batlle y Ordóñez (1856–1929) could not cope with the crisis. Political unrest spread in Uruguay. It was the hour of the Tupamaros.

Formed in 1962, this small nucleus of the MNL (Tupamaros) hesitated initially between urban and peasant guerrilla tactics. After an analysis of Uruguayan geographical and social conditions (Uruguay is a small country with no remote or mountainous areas and with an urban population of about 83 percent) and impressed by the repeated failures of the peasant guerrillas in the continent (especially the annihilation of the Peruvian guerrillas in 1965), the Tupamaros decided in 1966 to concentrate their revo-

[16]*Ibid.*, pp. 24–25.
[17]Vania Bambirra et al., *Diez Años de Insurreccion* (Chile: Ediciones Prensa Latino-americana, 1972), p. 99.

lutionary efforts in the city of Montevideo.[18] Displaying an impressive sense of timing, secrecy, and
organization, aiming their first blows at discrediting
the regime rather than at spreading terror, the Tupamaros rapidly acquired international notoriety and a
myth of invincibility. Nevertheless, even in this period
(which has been called the "Robin Hood period"),
the Tupamaros were facing the dilemma of all urban
guerrillas: whether to rely on their own forces and
actions to destroy the regime or to become more
politicized, expounding programs and ideologies to
attract other sectors of the population (see document
34). Furthermore, the momentum gained by direct
action has its own inevitable course: sooner or later,
depending on when the established regime counter-
attacks, direct action has to turn into violent or terrorist actions. Perhaps because of their "petty-bourgeois" origins, as the Maoists claimed (document
53), or maybe because it is an inescapable fate of the
urban guerrilla (secrecy, isolation, self-intoxication),
the Tupamaros rejected a political opening and moved
swiftly to more violent methods: kidnapping, bombing, "executions" of opponents.[19] No measure of se-

[18]In a document published in January 1967, the Tupamaros
explained their decision. The central argument was that "the law
of concentration of capital is at the same time a law for the concentration of the population. It would be a strategic mistake to
isolate ourselves in the countryside, abandoning the unemployed
and hungry masses of Montevideo . . . where the population which
is the revolution waits." Antonio Mercader, *Tupamaros,* pp.
15–16.

[19]In May 1970, the Tupamaros made a raid on a naval training center in Montevideo and escaped with a large quantity of
arms. In June they attacked two banks and injured several persons. In July, Judge Daniel Pereira Manelly, who had tried most
of the captured Tupamaros, U.S. adviser to the Uruguayan
police Dan A. Mitrione, Brazilian diplomat Aloysio Dias Gomide,

curity, no repression, no police force seemed to be able to stop them. By 1971, staggering under much-publicized blows, the government of President Jorge Pacheco Areco appeared tottering toward collapse. The Tupamaros looked close to victory.

With hindsight it is easy to perceive that behind the appearances the reality of the situation was quite different. The current of events was moving against the Tupamaros, not in their favor. In the first place, terrorist acts had given the Tupamaros wide publicity, but not popularity. Their image had been tarnished by what appeared to many as indiscriminate terrorism.[20] Secondly, in 1971 elections were going to be held in Uruguay. Following what appeared to be a rising trend in Latin America—the establishment of a "revolutionary" military government in Peru in 1968; the electoral victory of Marxist Salvador Allende in Chile in 1970; the rise to power of leftist General Juan José Torres in Bolivia that same year—the Uruguyan Communist party succeeded in organizing a

---

and U.S. agronomist Claude Fly were kidnapped. When the government refused to release captured Tupamaros in exchange for the hostages, Mitrione was "executed." Dias Gomide was released after his wife paid the ransom the Tupamaros asked. The other two were released later.

[20]In 1975, analyzing the actions of the Tupamaros, Abraham Guillen, whose book, *Estrategia de la Guerrilla Urbana* (Montevideo: 1966) is said to have been a powerful influence among the Tupamaros, wrote a sharp criticism. "In a revolutionary war, every guerrilla action that has to be explained to the people is wrong: actions should be evident and convincing in themselves. . . . To kill a poor soldier in retaliation for the murder of a guerrillero is to descend to the same level as the reactionary army." See his "Lecciones de la guerrilla latinoamericana," in Donald C. Hodges and Abraham Guillen, *Revaloracion de la Guerrilla Urbana* (Mexico: Ediciones "El Caballito," 1977).

Frente Amplio, FA (Broad Front),[21] to challenge through electoral means the power of the traditional parties of Uruguay. Claiming that "it was the turn of Uruguay to join the progressive forces of the continent," the Frente called for the unity of all revolutionary forces to assure a democratic victory of the left. Although they had not been invited to participate and had been frequently if obliquely criticized by the Communists, the Tupamaros decided to proclaim a truce until the end of the electoral campaign,[22] thus giving a respite to the Uruguayan government.

[21]The FA (Broad Front) was formed by the Communist Party, the Christian Democrats, the Socialist Movement, and some other minor groups.

[22]So far, I have not found a reasonable explanation for the Tupamaros' decision to cooperate with the Communists. A reading of the speeches of the Communist leaders in the XX Congress of the Uruguayan Communist Party makes the conduct of the Tupamaros still less comprehensible. While the speakers ardently defended "mass struggle" under the direction of the CP as the only Marxist way, the tone of some of the speakers was obviously anti-Tupamaro. Rodney Arismendi, the Secretary General of the party said, for example: "Neither the 'feats' of 'heroes' or isolated groups, no matter how courageous or imaginative they might be, can endanger the stability of the system. As Lenin has taught us: 'Only new forms of struggle in the movement of the masses sparks in everyone a fighting spirit." Many of the speakers condemned the "ultra-left"; not one of them mentioned the struggles of the Tupamaros. See *Estudios* (Montevideo), No. 58 (January-February 1971) (the entire issue is devoted to the XX Congress of the CP). In his book *Castroism and Communist in Latin America* (Washington D.C.: American Enterprise Institute; 1976), William E. Ratliff states that in its program, the CP adopted the FA (Broad Front) program, of which point No. 1 was "the lifting of government security measures against the Tupamaros." As approved in the above-mentioned Congress, resolution No. 15 simply demands: "lifting of the security measures, restoration of public liberties, restitution of the workers to their jobs." There is no mention of the Tupamaros. Furthermore, according to one Tupamaro leader, in 1972, when many leftist groups were being crushed by the army, the Communists' news-

Finally, and probably much more decisively, by 1971 the Uruguayan regime had learned the Tupamaro's tactics and had improved his methods of repression. A paramilitary organization, the "Death Squadron," had been created, infiltrators had penetrated the Tupamaros, efficient propaganda was being used to distort the image of the guerrilleros, and the armed forces had been put on full alert.

When the FA of the Communists received less than 19 percent of the vote in the presidential elections (November 1971), the government felt more secure in its position. The new president, Juan Maria Bordabarry, who took office on March 1, 1972, had promised to stamp out guerrilla activity, and he immediately stepped up the offensive against the Tupamaros. On their side, the Tupamaros began to implement the so-called "plan Tatu," which involved expanding their operations to the interior of the country in order to force the army to disperse its forces. The crucial confrontation, though, came too soon. On April 14, 1972, applying their usual tactic of "executing" those persons who had been condemned by the organization, the Tupamaros killed four members of the Death Squadron (nine had been sentenced to death). This time the regime's reaction was swift and deadly. Proclaiming a "state of internal war" and suspending all constitutional guarantees, the government unleashed the armed forces against the guerrilleros. In three months the armed forces killed hundreds of Tupamaros, arrested many more, raided vital hiding places, and crushed every effort to rally the dispersed sur-

---

paper *El Popular* was "mounting an 'in crescendo' attack against the Tupamaros." See "Los tupamaros y las masas," *Punto Final* (Santiago de Chile), No. 163 (August 1, 1973), pp. 16–17.

vivors. By the end of 1973, the army was in full control of the government, Congress had been dismissed, and all leftist groups were in jail, in exile, or underground. At the price of democracy, the Tupamaros had been put out of action in Uruguay.[23]

After the eclipse of the Tupamaros in Uruguay, Latin American urban guerrillas kept a low profile and seemed anxious to establish contacts with labor organizations. It is quite symptomatic that the resurgence of the Colombian M-19 in the summer of 1977, with its sequel of executions and kidnappings, was accompanied by proclamation of a new phase in urban guerrilla tactics. According to M-19 the movement was now "an armed body of the proletariat," ready to strike in its behalf in any labor dispute. By seeking an alliance with the workers, M-19 is, perhaps, demonstrating that they have learned from the failure of the Tupamaros.[24]

The Peruvian Military "Revolution"

In few Latin American countries has the left been as quarrelsome and ineffective as in Peru, birthplace of

[23]Before the Tupamaros' defeat, the Brazilian urban guerrilla had been decimated. In May 1969, Carlos Marighela was trapped and shot to death by the police. In 1970, most of the leaders of ALN were killed. For an excellent if sympathetic account of the urban guerrillas in Brazil, Uruguay, and Argentina, see James Kohl and John Litt, *Urban Guerrilla Warfare in Latin America* (Cambridge, Mass.: MIT Press, 1974). The books of Debray and Gott mentioned before are also highly recommended.

[24]M-19 assumed responsibility for the "executions" of several Colombian labor leaders accused of "being sold to capitalism and imperialism." "From now on," the Movement proclaimed, "our political and military forces are at the disposal of the workers."

influential Marxist writer José Carlos Mariategui. Since its inception in the twenties the Peruvian left has never been a real threat to the status quo, either through political coalitions, labor power, or armed struggle. In popular support the Marxist left lags far behind its ancient and most criticized rival, APRA, and behind such hastily organized bourgeois parties as Fernando Belaúnde's Acción Popular, a reformist organization formed in the fifties which won its founder the presidency in 1962. The actions and movements of the left before the military coup help explain its reaction vis-à-vis the coup.

Until the fifties, the left's most important instruments were the Communist Party and some Trotskyite groups, although their influence was rather limited among workers and even more among peasants. For peasants in northern Peru, where the sugar industry is the basic structure, APRA was the main organizing force. Those in the south were left to their own initiative. Differing from the usual Latin American pattern, peasants in that region organized their early "sindicatos" without guidance from urban centers.[25] In 1954 these peasant organizations began appealing to the Communist-controlled Federacion de Trabajadores de Cuzco (Cuzco Federation of Workers) for advisors in their growing struggles with the landlords.

The pressure of peasant demands for land and justice was just beginning to be felt in southern Peru when, in 1958, a new leader appeared. Influenced by

---

See "Sorpresa y Temor por Reaparicion M-19," *El Espectador* (Bogota), August 21, 1977, pp. 1-A, 13-A.

[25]Eduardo Fioravanti, *Latifundio y Sindicalismo Agrario en el Peru* (Lima: Instituto de Estudios Peruanos, 1974), p. 146.

Trotskyite ideology, Hugo Blanco rallied peasants with the slogan "Land or Death!" and soon radicalized their campaign.[26] His impact, which prompted the "occupation" of lands by peasants, mobilized both the government and the Communists. The former's stern countermeasures were somewhat mollified by an Agrarian Reform Law in 1962, which limited itself to validating what the peasants had already done. The latter increased propaganda among peasants, formed their own organization, and began fighting Blanco's influence. In 1962 Blanco's expulsion from the Convencion-Laras region was requested of the army and police by thirty-two Communist-controlled "sindicatos," in order "to avoid the realization of violent acts which would endanger peasant organizations and lives."[27] A firm believer of peasants in a "militia" rather than "guerrilla" capacity,[28] Blanco was forced into a defensive war against increasing army and police pressure. Criticized by the Communists, attacked by government forces, abandoned by many peasants who feared repression or preferred the legality of the Agrarian Reform Law, Hugo Blanco was captured in May of 1963 and sentenced to twenty years in prison. Since his release in 1969, he has not played as significant a role in the struggles of Peruvian peasants, but his past revolutionary prestige and his struggles with

[26]Hugo Blanco studied in the Argentine University of La Plata, where he became a member of the Trotskyite group Palabra Obrera (Worker Word), organized by one of the professors, Hugo Bressano (he used the pseudonym Nahuel Moreno). Blanco returned to Cuzco in 1956 and joined the Partido Obrero Revolucionario (Revolutionary Workers Party), another Trotskyite organization.

[27]*La Prensa* (Lima), May 2, 1962.

the Communists created a new division in the Peruvian left.

Almost at the same time that Hugo Blanco was imprisoned, young Peruvian radicals of urban extraction began to make plans for guerrilla uprisings in Peru. The peasant guerrilla theory was then at its zenith. By 1964 Luis de la Puente Uceda, Guillermo Lobatón, Hector Béjar, and some others had organized MIR Movimiento Izquierda Revolucionario (Movement of the Revolutionary Left) (see document 28) and ELN, Ejercito de Liberacion Nacional (Army of National Liberation). In 1965, after proclaiming their aims and objectives, which included a fervent appeal for unity on the left, they began their campaign.

Once again, the underestimation of one basic factor, the condition of the army,[29] was to be fatal to the guerrillas. As many other Latin American armies, the Peruvian had studied guerrilla tactics, received "advice" from the United States and was ready to face the guerrilleros.[30] Insurgency actions began in

[28]The idea was to use effectively the peasants' attachment to their land and their unwillingness to fight in distant regions. "The majority of the peasants are willing to die, but not to abandon their houses," wrote Blanco. "For each hundred peasants that we find willing to be militiamen, we find one who accepts being a guerrillero." Fioravanti, *Latifundio,* p. 203. See also Hugo Blanco, *El Camino de Nuestra Revolucion* (Lima: Editorial Revolucion Peruana, 1964).

[29]Forgetting the total lack of military capacity of Fulgencio Batista and the demoralization and corruption of his army in Cuba, which rendered it incapable of mounting any serious offensive, the "Cuban model" of guerrilla warfare took for granted that all Latin American armies were going to react with similar inefficiency. It was, to say the least, a very dangerous assumption.

[30]The army's version of the operations is found in *Las Guerrillas en el Peru y su Represion* (Lima: Ministerio de Guerra, 1966).

June 1965; seven months later the guerrillas had been surrounded, isolated, and annihilated. Both the pro-Soviet and the recently organized pro-Chinese Communist parties of Peru (the pro-Chinese Party had been formed in 1964) had more or less condemned the action of the guerrilla groups.[31] The usual wave of mutual recrimination and splitting groups followed the collapse of armed struggle.

Even in the Latin American context, by 1967 the fragmentation of the left in Peru was somehow dazzling. Besides the pro-Soviet and pro-Chinese Communist parties, there existed the already mentioned MIR and ELN; the FIR, Frente de Izquierda Revolucionaria (Left Revolutionary Front), organized by Hugo Blanco; VR, Varguardia Revolucionaria (Revolutionary Vanguard); FLN, Frente de Liberacion Nacional (National Liberation Front); the Trotskyite LSR, Liga Socialista Revolucionaria (Socialist Revolutionary League); and POR, Partido Obrero Revolucionario (Revolutionary Workers Party), plus several other insignificant "revolutionary" groups.

On October 3, 1968, while the left floundered in this rather appalling confusion, the Peruvian armed forces deposed President Fernando Belaúnde Therry and installed a military government under General Juan Velasco Alvarado. Initially, the more important leftist groups rejected what appeared to be another reactionary attempt by the army to save the oligarchy. Declaring its intent to alter Peru's socio-economic structure for the popular majority, the self-proclaimed

---

A more general military study is in General Carlos Soto Tamayo, *Inteligencia Militar y Subversion Armada* (Caracas: Ministerio de Defensa, 1968).

[31] Richard Gott, *Guerrilla Movements,* pp. 381–389.

"revolutionary" government's first announcements were met with scorn by the left.[32]

Soon, however, the military regime began taking steps which appeared radically nationalistic and anti-oligarchic. The Army occupied oil fields of the American firm International Petroleum Corporation and diplomatic relations were established with several Socialist nations, including Cuba; an Agrarian Reform Law was enacted "to give the land to those who toil it"; the Industrial Reform Law gave workers a share not only in profits but also in management; social security was reorganized and modernized.[33] Scarcely more than a year after the coup, the regime's unexpected policies had created a different image, and the Peruvian "revolution" became a topic of international dimensions.

Predictably, this situation posed a dilemma for the Peruvian left. Many of its ideas and programs were now apparently being enacted by the army, a traditional enemy. Should the regime be supported? How far should that support go? Was this a real revolution or merely a modernization process? Essentially the question was an old Leninist one: What is to be done?

[32]For the speeches and ideological position of Velasco Alvarado, see *La Revolución Nacional Peruana* (Lima: COAP, 1972).

[33]For a better understanding of the Peruvian situation, see Abraham F. Lowenthal, ed., *The Peruvian Experiment: Continuity and Change under Military Rule* (Princeton, N.J.: Princeton University Press, 1975), and Henry F. Dobyns and Paul L. Doughty, *Peru, a Cultural History* (New York: Oxford University Press, 1976). The different reactions of political parties toward the revolution are offered in Hernando Aguirre Gamio, *El Proceso Peruano* (Mexico: Ediciones "El Caballito," 1974). Two very useful books are Henry Pease Garcia and Olga Verme Ynsua, *Peru 1968–1973: Cronología Política* (Lima: Centro de Estudios y Promocion, 1974), and Jose Matos Mar et al., *Peru: Hoy* (Mexico: Siglo XXI, 1975).

The fragmented left could only give a diversity of answers such as Ismael Frias' total support for the government (document 35); the pro-Soviet Communist Party's near-total support (document 37); the skeptical, almost negative answer of Anibal Quijano (document 36); as well as the total rejection of pro-Chinese Communists and the MIR. Reacting to Fidel Castro's comment that the Peruvian military government was developing a genuine revolution, the pro-Chinese groups described the Peruvian government as "bourgeois imperialist" and termed Fidel Castro a "petty-bourgeois traitor to the revolutionary cause of Cuba and Latin America."[34]

The peculiarities of the Peruvian process became increasingly evident with passing years. The "revolution" was dictated from above by a government seemingly torn between desire for popular support and fear of mass participation. SINAMOS, Sistema Nacional de Apoyo a la Movilización Social (National System to Support Social Mobilization), a political instrument for mobilizing the masses, had been created, but was forced to play a passive role in gathering support for government initiatives. Consequently, in spite of all official efforts, the regime's popularity remained low. Economic and political difficulties, on the other hand, continued to mount, as rising public debt, lack of international credit, and inflation hit Peru. Growing tension inside the armed forces was noticeable in 1975. In Lima, on February 5 and 6, dozens of per-

[34]*Unidad* (Lima), June 4, 1970; quoted in William E. Ratliff, *1971: Yearbook on Latin American Communist Affairs* (Stanford: Hoover Institution Press, 1971), p. 139. A Maoist indictment of the Peruvian government and its allies is in *Propicdad Social: Una Nueva Estata* (Lima: Ediciones "Patria Roja," 1973).

sons were killed and more than a thousand arrested when the army crushed a strike by police and subsequent civilian rioting. The episode saw the beginning of a political crisis which ended on August 29, when President Velasco Alvarado was deposed by his military commanders and replaced by General Francisco Morales Bermudez.

Beginning a policy of moderation, the new government gave guarantees to private enterprise, cooled its relations with Cuba, and promised elections for a constituent assembly in 1978, to be followed by general elections in 1980. What for many was a necessary return to democratic and logical policies was for the left a turn to the right. While the pro-Soviet Communist Party expressed growing concern (document 38), the vast majority of leftist groups and individuals offered complete opposition. By the end of 1977 it appeared that Peru's regime was involved with calming the national unrest and restoring the economy rather than saving its revolutionary image.

The Failure of the Chilean Socialist Experiment (1970-1973)

Although the complex process of events in Chile cannot possibly be explained or studied in such brief space, certain basic points help clarify the general course and disastrous end of the socialist experiment.

It is essential to recall some reasons for Salvador Allende's electoral victory in 1970. A fundamental cause of previous defeat by Christian Democrat Eduardo Frei was Frei's support by centrist and rightist elements in Chile. In 1964, Chilean conservative and moderate groups. fearing a Socialist victory and lacking confidence in their own political candidate,[35] voted for Frei as the lesser of two evils. By 1970, however, the political situation was quite different. Christian Democrats had lost considerable popularity, their candidate, Radomiro Tomic, displayed an increasingly leftist position, and traditional parties thought their candidate, ex-president Jorge Alessandri, capable of defeating both Socialist and Christian Democrats. Consequently, where FRAP, Frente de Acción Popular (Popular Action Front), the leftist coalition backing Allende, once confronted a powerful alliance of Christian Democrats, conservative, and moderate elements, the left, reorganized as Unidad Popular (Popular Unity), now faced a divided opposition. Allende's marginal victory (he received only 36.3 percent of the votes) was made possible not by a powerful up-- surge of the left but by the division of its opponents.[36]

Since Allende could not act with the assurance and unquestionable power of a president elected by sweeping majority, his initial efforts were to expand the bases of popular support. Allende was not leader of a disciplined party but head of a heterogeneous political coalition including the Communist, Socialist, Radical, and Social Democratic parties, API, Alianza Popular Independiente (Independent Popular Alliance), and MAPU, Movimiento de Acción Popular

[35]Chile's traditional Liberal and Conservative parties decided to support Frei when in March 1964 their candidate was defeated in the municipal elections of Curicó, a little town which was supposed to be a stronghold of conservatism.

[36]Actually, in 1970 Allende received a lower percentage of the votes than what he got in 1964, when he obtained 38.9 percent. In an extremely interesting analysis of the situation of the Chilean left before the elections, Socialist Raul Ampurro forecast its electoral defeat in 1970. *La Izquierda en punto muerto* (Santiago de Chile: Edit. Orbe, 1969).

Unida (Movement of United Popular Action), a group of ex-Christian Democrats. Balancing these bickering allies to avoid splitting the coalition would consume much of the president's energy. Making things worse was a radical leftist group, MIR (Movement of the Revolutionary Left), not part of the coalition which, even while supporting Allende, believed armed struggle the only revolutionary road and mistrusted the use of bourgeois legality to achieve socialism. Bitter and at times bloody confrontations between MIR members and Communists defending moderation (see document 41) were to have disturbing implications for the Chilean government and people.

Despite Allende's victory, the left had actually gained only one position of power—the government. Other political structures remained virtually intact. Congress, the judiciary, political parties, labor unions, the press, and (most significant) the armed forces retained their independence and their capacity to blunt the menace of a Socialist president.[37] In Marxist terminology, Chile was one of those bourgeois societies mentioned by Italian socialist Antonio Gramsci, where behind the fortress of the state lies a series of trenches, barricades, and defenses which are far more difficult to conquer.

A rough chronological approach divides Chile's Socialist process into four phases: offense, stalemate,

[37]This is not retrospective wisdom. Many analysts of the Chilean situation agreed with this statement, written barely six months after Allende took office: "Chile's armed forces still have the means to oust Allende if they choose to do so, and the regime might trigger such a decision at any time." See Luis E. Aguilar, "Chile: Traditions and Perspectives," *Problems of Communism* (Washington, D.C.), May-June 1971 pp. 62–69.

recession, and collapse. In November 1970, with a divided, seemingly paralyzed opposition,[38] an elated Allende (see document 40) took office and the government began its programs of reform. Three economic "areas" were to be created;[39] banks and private enterprises were expropriated by the government; relations with Cuba were re-established; copper nationalization was announced and wages increased. In April's municipal elections the ruling coalition received almost 50 percent of the votes. Jubilant leftist spokesmen even suggested calling a plesbicite to overcome congressional resistance.

The summer, however, brought signs of change. Christian Democrats and traditional parties forgot past antagonisms and moved toward political alliance. Accusations and actions by the "ultra-left" helped consolidate a potentially dangerous coalition.[40] In July, when a candidate backed by the Christian Democrat and National (a fusion of Liberal and Conservative) parties won elections in Valparaiso, the opposition gained courage and began finding ways to check the government offensive.

The second half of 1971 saw a stalemate, of sorts,

[38]In a desperate attempt to stop Allende from becoming president, some ultra-rightist group assassinated General Rene Schneider in October 1970. The assassination, however, repudiated by all political parties, discredited the opposition and reinforced Allende's position.

[39]The idea was to create a state-owned area, which would include all major industries; mixed areas, with the majority ownership in the hands of the state; and a private area of small- and medium-sized enterprises.

[40]Indiscriminate and virulent attacks on all Christian Democrats forced even Tomic's group to close ranks around the party. The assassination in July of ex-Minister Eduardo Perez Zujovic, a Christian Democrat leader, by an extremist leftist organization, VOP (Organized Vanguard of the People), convinced many re-

in Chile. The government won some victories such as
a law nationalizing copper, but the opposition produced a constitutional amendment checking executive
power to take over private business. Street fighting
became common, and Christian Democrat candidates
gained the support of several peasant organizations.
A visit by Fidel Castro at the invitation of President
Allende increased tension and hastened polarization.[41]
On December 1 thousands of women poured into
Santiago's streets beating their empty pots in an open
sign of defiance. As a Chilean analyst wrote, "carrying
its fight to traditional leftist territory, the opposition
even moved to the streets."[42]

Although these demonstrators were dispersed, the
government was forced to proclaim a state of siege.
The stalemate broken, enemies of the regime took the
initiative.

From January to October of 1972, the forces of the
opposition increased pressure on almost every level,
while the unity of the regime began to crumble. Aided

luctant Christian Democrats of the urgent necessity of forming a
general political alliance against the government.

[41]Fidel's lengthy visit was a mixed blessing for Allende. He
gave some "revolutionary" prestige to the government, but he
also exacerbated the criticism of the opposition. Similarly, in his
numerous speeches he seemed at times to defend a radical stand,
while at other times he recommended moderation. In his last
meeting, Fidel sounded somehow disappointed with the reduced
numbers of Chileans who bade him farewell: "In Cuba," he said,
"we can gather in ten minutes as many persons as are here and
in two hours ten times as many! In two hours! And our capital
has only two thirds of Santiago's population." For all Castro's
speeches, see *Cuba-Chile* (Habana: Ediciones Politicas, 1972).

[42]See the excellent study by Fernando Castillo, Jorge Larrain,
and Rafael Echeverria, "Etapas y Perspectivas de la lucha ideo-
logica en Chile," *Cuadernos de la Realidad Nacional* (Santiago
de Chile), No. 13 (July 1972), pp. 114–152.

by external forces (Allende termed American economic action "the invisible blockade") and improving their tactics, enemies of the government helped to accelerate inflation, spread all kinds of rumors, and fought government initiative.

Besieged by a multitude of forces including the growing disunion of his allies, Allende was forced to fight on too many fronts (see document 40). An alarmed Communist Party encouraged rapprochement with Christian Democrats and tried to calm opposition by a "stopping to consolidate" program, a moratorium on radical measures. MIR and the Socialist Party's left wing bitterly criticized that position (document 42) and demanded "weapons for the people."[43] In October, a series of strikes almost paralyzed the country. This was for many leftists the "moment of truth," a time to call up the masses and break the strikes. Fearing civil war and sticking to his legalistic principles, Allende avoided that road and took a momentous decision by appointing top-ranking officers as ministers. Once the army had stepped in, the essential question was how long the armed forces would remain neutral.

By the first half of 1973, the end of the Socialist regime was already in view. Inflation had risen to 300 percent; street demonstrations and fights occurred daily; food shortages were constant; the opposition

---

[43]Regis Debray, *La Crítica de las Armas* (Mexico: Siglo XXI, 1975), pp. 268–270, makes a devastating criticism of this demand: "Only a glorious frivolity, typical of chamber revolutionaries, . . . could accuse Allende of not giving weapons to the proletariat. . . . What weapons?; which proletariat? . . . how long does it take to train men in the use of weapons? . . . was the army going to wait patiently while the workers learned how to fight?"

was talking about winning municipal elections in March with sufficient numbers to impeach the president. Although Allende escaped that fate by getting 43 percent of the vote, the violence and tension did not subside. On June 29, an ill-prepared military putsch failed but did not diminish the menace of military intervention. Interpreting these signs, MIR and the Socialst left wing began preparing for a confrontation with the armed forces, circulating propaganda among soldiers and workers to paralyze possible action by the officers. In August, Allende's last shield, General Carlos Pratt, commander in chief of the armed forces and a personal friend of the president's, was forced to resign by subordinates. On September 11, the expected coup took place. As tanks rolled the streets and airplanes bombarded any center of resistance, the regime collapsed. Allende was killed in the presidential palace and a military curfew imposed. The dreaded event that had haunted Chile for more than two years had become a reality: Chile was no longer a Socialist experiment or even a democracy. As in many other Latin American areas, the saviours wore boots and helmets.[44]

[44]The extensive bibliography on Chile's Socialist experiment is less than objective. A few of the many books that can be recommended are: for a non-leftist view, Robert Moss, *Chile's Marxist Experiment* (New York: John Wiley & Sons, 1973); to the left, but rather objective, Alain Labrousse, *El Experimento Chileno* (Barcelona: Ediciones Grijalbo, S. A., 1973); leftist—Troskyite oriented, Les Evans, ed.), *Disaster in Chile* (New York: Pathfinder Press, 1974); a good Marxist discussion on the subject, Paul M. Sweezy and Harry Magdoff, *Revolution and Counter-revolution in Chile* (New York: Monthly Review Press, 1974); excellent anthologies, *Marxismo y Revolucion* (Santiago de Chile), No. 1 (July-September 1973); and from a different point of view, *Chile: The Balanced View* (The University of Chile: 1975); a typical attack on American imperialism, Fer-

Once more, the left was reduced to licking its wounds and analyzing the causes of disaster. But not even defeat had produced significant changes in the ideological positions of most important leftist groups. To continue the fight against dictatorship in Chile, MIR reaffirmed its radical position and the credo that armed struggle is the only revolutionary road to power.[45] Modifying his extremist position, Socialist Carlos Altamirano now stressed the necessity of union with the Communists, "in spite of existing discrepancies," to form an anti-fascist front;[46] and the Communists proclaimed that Allende's failure demonstrated the viability of "popular front strategy" and the pernicious errors of the "ultra-left" (see document 43).

The "Sovietization" of Cuba and Intervention in Africa

During the first half of 1967, a defiant Fidel Castro, confident that guerrilla warfare would transform the Andes into the Sierra Maestra of the continent,[47] criticized the Soviet Union's lack of revolutionary zeal and its dealings with oligarchic, pro-imperialist

nando Rivas Sanchez and Elizabeth Reimann Weigert, *Las fuerzas armadas en Chile: un caso de penetracion imperialista* (Mexico: 1976). The book by Debray, *La Critica de las Armas,* devotes one very useful chapter to Chile.

[45]The best collection of MIR documents that I have been able to find is in Herausgegeben Von Voiker Petzoldt, *Widerstand in Chile: Aufrufe, Interviews und Dokumente des MIR* (Berlin: Politik 54, 1974).

[46]See Carlos Altamirano, *Dialectica de Una Derrota* (Mexico: Editorial Siglo XXI, 1977).

[47]The Sierra Maestra is the Cuban mountainous zone where Castro fought his guerrilla campaign (1956–1959).

countries. On March 13, Castro said: "We have irrefutable proof for those governments' lack of independence in the recent case of Colombia, where the secretary general and all Communist Party leaders were recently arrested because of some guerrillas who attacked a train. At the time they did not pay the least attention to the presence of a delegation of high Soviet officials who had come to sign a commercial agreement with the government. . . Not everything is rose colored in the revolutionary world. . . We shall not aid financially any oligarchy to repress the revolutionary movement in blood. And whoever gives aid to those oligarchies where they are fighting against the guerrillas is helping to repress Revolution."[48]

By year's end, however, the tone of the leader of the Cuban Revolution began to change. Among other factors, two realities were bending his revolutionary stand: Cuba's poor economic condition, and guerrilla failure as dramatized by the death of Ché Guevara in Bolivia. The first made Cuba increasingly dependent on Soviet economic help; the second deprived Castro of his continental image as leader of a new revolutionary crusade.

Fully aware of this situation, the Soviet Union tightened economic control over the island. By January 1968, Castro's government denounced a "microfaction" of Cuban Communists headed by Aníbal Escalante, who with Soviet officials had attempted to discredit the regime. Perhaps reflecting his country's view of the situation, a Soviet diplomat implied that to paralyze the Cuban government[49] it was enough to stop sending Soviet ships from the oil port of Baku for three weeks.

[48]*Gramma* (Havana), March 14, 1967.

On March 13, a somber Castro told the Cuban people to prepare "to sell our lives very dearly, without expecting anyone to come to our defense."[50] In retaliation Cuba had sent no delegate to the meeting of Communist parties in Budapest the previous month. But such action could not change the situation: Soviet assistance was essential for the revolution's survival, even if the price were political submission. On August 28, 1968, Fidel Castro capitulated, supporting the Soviet invasion of Czechoslovakia in a speech that marks a turning point in his political career (see document 33).

With that speech, relations between Cuba and the Soviet Union began improving rapidly. As a sign of growing alignment with Russia, Castro began to downplay the role of guerrillas and to show a friendly face toward non-revolutionary governments such as Peru's military regime and Venezuela's Rafael Caldera. While praise for the Soviet Union showered daily in the Cuban press, attacks on China increased in virulence.

In 1970, in a possible effort to gain some measure of economic independence, Castro mobilized almost the entire island population to obtain a record crop of ten million tons of sugar. After disrupting many other sectors of Cuban economy, the effort failed; total sugar production was barely eight and a half million tons. On July 26, Castro acknowledged the failure and the numerous mistakes of his leadership.

[49]The quotation was attributed to Rudolf P. Shliapnikov, Second Secretary of the Soviet Embassy. See the lengthy report of Raul Castro in *Gramma* (Havana), English edition, February 11, 1968.

[50]*Bohemia* (Havana), March 15, 1968, p. 56.

In September, the Soviet Union set up a submarine servicing facility in Cienfuegos.[51]

By 1973, moral incentives for workers had been replaced by material incentives,[52] the Cuban army had been reorganized according to a Soviet model, and the road toward "institutionalizing" the revolution followed Soviet patterns. In 1975, Havana played host to a gathering of Marxist parties. This time, however, there were no radicals, no dissidents; the delegates were disciplined members of Latin American Communist parties. Their decisions were firmly pro-Soviet (see document 44). Expressive of the situation, the Cuban Constitution of 1975 begins by proclaiming eternal gratitude to the Soviet Union. According to the acid comment of a Peruvian Maoist, Cuba had moved from the Platt Amendment[53] to the Plattoff yoke.

Fidel Castro's display of loyalty to Cuba's sovietization alienated not only Latin American pro-Chinese groups but virtually all elements of the New Left who had been staunch defenders of Cuba's revolution in the sixties. But in the Latin America of the seventies, the wind was blowing from the right. With few exceptions, the armed forces controlled the continent.

[51]A clear analysis of this historical process can be found in Edward Gonzalez, *Cuba under Castro: The Limits of Charisma* (Boston: Houghton Mifflin, 1974).

[52]For a favorable point of view on the subject of moral incentives, see Robert M. Bernardo, *The Theory of Moral Incentives in Cuba* (The University of Alabama Press, 1971). Subsequent events have proved that Mr. Bernardo's conclusions were less than accurate.

[53]The Platt Ammendment, giving America the right to intervene in Cuba, was imposed on the Constitution of 1901. Abolished in 1934, it was for many years the symbol of American imperialism in Cuba.

Havana was no longer expecting a continental revolution and the Soviet Union did not appear too eager to foment one. Judging by Cuban and Soviet actions, their new tactics seemed to encourage and support any military or civilian government which tended to be anti-imperialist—that is, anti-American.

With a continent closed to his initiative, dependent on Soviet support for any revolutionary venture, Fidel Castro had to look beyond Latin America.[54] In 1975, with Soviet approval and logistical support, thousands of Cuban troops were sent to Angola to help the Soviet-backed Popular Movement for the Liberation of Angola (MPLA). It was the first time in Latin American history that an armed expedition had been sent from rather than to the continent. The intervention regained international attention for Castro. After the MPLA's victory in April 1977, Castro explained his intervention in Africa, "the weakest link in the imperialist chain," and Cuba's Socialist duty toward all exploited countries (see document 46). In the meantime, Castro had opened the doors to a re-establishment of diplomatic relations with the United States, apparently trusting in his ability to balance anti-imperialist views with his need for the American market.

At the end of 1977, however, the African adventure was apparently becoming more complex, tying Cuban troops to an anti-guerrilla campaign (it is ironic that anti-government forces in Angola had stated that "Cubans do not know how to fight guerrillas")[55] and

[54]To understand Castro's interventions in Africa, one should remember that he began his revolutionary career by participating in a frustrated invasion of the Dominican Republic back in 1947.

[55]See the series of articles in the *Washington Post* (Washington, D.C.), "A Long March in Angola," August 7–11, 1977.

posing serious obstacles to Castro's desire for an understanding with the United States. At any rate, the tenth anniversary of Ché Guevara's death found a Cuba involved in international affairs quite different from those dreamed of by the fallen guerrilla hero.

Part I

Background

1890–1920

CHRONOLOGY

OF

IMPORTANT EVENTS

*

1862   Bartolomé Mitre becomes the first president of a unified Argentina.
The French invade Mexico.

1864   The First International is founded in London.

1867   Emperor Maximilian is shot in Mexico.

1876   Porfirio Díaz begins his long rule of Mexico.

1889   Brazil becomes a republic.
The Second International is founded in Paris.

1890   Unión Cívica (predecessor of the Radical Party) attempts a revolt in Argentina.

1891   President José Manuel Balmaceda is deposed in Chile, and the Congress takes over: beginning of the Parliamentary Republic.

1895   Cuba begins a second uprising against Spain.
José Martí dies.
Juan B. Justo founds the Socialist Party of Argentina.

1898   The Spanish-American War erupts: Puerto Rico and Cuba are occupied by American troops.

1902   Cuba becomes a republic.

1903   José Batlle y Ordóñez is elected president of Uruguay: an era of reform begins.
The Republic of Panama is created.

1904 The Socialist Party of Uruguay is founded.

1906 Second American intervention in Cuba begins.

1908 Second American intervention in Cuba is terminated.
Juan Vicente Gómez seizes the presidency of Venezuela.

1910 The Mexican Revolution begins.

1911 End of Porfirio Díaz's dictatorship of Mexico.

1912 The Socialist Labor Party of Chile is founded.

1914 World War I begins.

1916 Hipólito Irigoyen of the Radical Party is elected president of Argentina.

1917 Russian Revolution takes place.
The Mexican Constitution is promulgated.

1918 Reform is instituted at the University of Córdoba, Argentina.
World War I ends.

1919 The Third International is founded in Moscow.

1920 Arturo Alessandri is elected president of Chile.

1

Marx and Engels on
Latin America

*

Marx's article on Bolivar is remarkable for its lack of objectivity and valid data. Apparently Charles Anderson Dana, the editor of The New American Cyclopedia, *was shocked by Marx's complete lack of recognition of any of Bolivar's virtues.*

Marx on Bolivar

FROM *The New American Cyclopedia**

. . . [Bolivar] established a choice corps of troops under the name of his body-guard, and surrounded himself with the show of a court. But, *like most of his countrymen, he was averse to any prolonged exertion,*[1] and his dictatorship soon proved a military anarchy, leaving the most important affairs in the hands of favorites, who squandered the finances of the country, and then resorted to odious means in order to restore them.

. . .

---

* Reprinted from Karl Marx's article "Bolivar y Ponte," in George Ripley and Charles A. Dana, eds., *The New American Cyclopedia* (New York: D. Appleton and Company, 1858), III, 441–446.

[1] Italics mine throughout selection [ed.].

The skirmishers of Morales having dispersed his advanced guard, he lost, as an eye-witness records, "all presence of mind, spoke not a word, turned his horse quickly round, and fled in full speed toward Ocumare, passed the village at full gallop, arrived at the neighboring bay, jumped from his horse, got into a boat, and embarked on the Diana, ordering the whole squadron to follow him to the little island of Buen Ayre, and leaving all his companions without any means of assistance."

. . .

Piar, the conqueror of Guiana, who once before had threatened to try him before a court-martial as a deserter, was not sparing of his sarcasms against "the Napoleon of the retreat," and Bolivar consequently accepted a plan for getting rid of him.

. . .

His sudden withdrawal of the foreign legion, which *was more dreaded by the Spaniards than ten times the number of Colombians,* had given Morillo a new opportunity to collect reenforcements.

. . .

In the year 1827, from which the decline of his power dates, he contrived to assemble a congress at Panama, with the ostensible object of establishing a new democratic international code. . . . What he really aimed at was the erection of the whole of South America into one federative republic, with himself as its dictator.

. . .

As soon as he became aware that Paez meant serious fighting, his courage collapsed. For a moment he even thought to subject himself to Paez. . . .

FROM A *Letter of Marx to Engels**

. . . With regard to a longer article on Bolivar,[1] Dana has second thoughts because it is written in a "partisan style," and he demands my sources. Naturally I can give him those sources, even though it is a curious request. As for the "partisan style," I must admit that I relinquished the encyclopedic tone a little. To see the most cowardly, ordinary, wretched rascal decried as though he were Napoleon I was really too absurd. Bolivar is the true Soulouque.[2]

On the War Between Mexico and the United States

FROM ENGELS' *The Events of 1847* †

In America we have witnessed the conquest of Mexico, and we are happy about it. For a country which until now has been busy exclusively with its own affairs, perpetually torn by civil war and impeded in every development, a country whose highest prospect was to come under the industrial vassalage of England—for such a country to be dragged into historical activity by force is indeed a step forward. It is in the interests of its own development that hence-

* Translated from a letter of Marx to Engels, February 14, 1858, in Karl Marx, Friedrich Engels, *Werke* (Berlin: Dietz Verlag, 1963), XXIX, 280.

[1] Marx is referring to the article "Bolivar y Ponte" excerpted above.

[2] Faustin Élie Soulouque (1785–1867) was a Haitian general and politician who was elected president of Haiti in 1847 and proclaimed himself emperor in 1849. He was deposed in 1858 and exiled.

† Translated from Friedrich Engels, "Die Bewegungen von 1847" (1848), in Karl Marx, Friedrich Engels, *Werke* (Berlin: Dietz Verlag, 1959), IV, 501.

forth Mexico should be placed under the tutelage of the United States. It is in the interests of the development of all America that the United States, in taking possession of California, gains control of the Pacific Ocean. . . . In California and New Mexico the North Americans acquire new land with which to beget new capital, that is to say, to call into being a new middle class and to enrich the one that already exists; for all capital that is produced today falls into the hands of the bourgeoisie. . . .

FROM A *Letter of Marx to Engels**

. . . Among the Yankees the feelings about independence and individual ability are perhaps stronger than among the Anglo-Saxons. The Spaniards are indeed degenerate. But a degenerate Spaniard, a Mexican, that is the ideal. All the vices of the Spaniards— boastfulness, grandiloquence, and quixoticism—are found in the Mexicans raised to the third power, but they no longer have the substance that the Spaniards possess. Mexican guerrilla warfare is a caricature of Spanish warfare, and even the deserters from the regular army are infinitely outdone. But then again the Spaniards themselves have produced no such genius as Santa Anna.

---

* Translated from a letter of Marx to Engels, December 2, 1847, in Karl Marx, Friedrich Engels, *Werke* (Berlin: Dietz Verlag, 1963), XXVIII, 417.

2

JOSÉ MARTÍ

On the Death
of Karl Marx*

*

*A man of numerous talents—critic, poet, orator, and
one of the best prose writers in the Spanish language—José Martí (1853–1895) sacrificed his life
and his work for Cuba's freedom. Exiled for many
years in New York, he always found time to write
about the events that crossed his intellectual horizon.
Martí's life, from his imprisonment at fifteen to his
death in combat, was always a ratification of the
thought that was dearest to him: "Only love con-
structs." Here, in recalling an act of homage to Marx
in 1883, Martí offers us a glimpse of his own idealistic roots.*

Here we are in the great hall. Karl Marx is dead.
Because he sided with the weak he deserves honor.
But he who yearns arduously for a remedy and only
points out the injury does no good; the good lies in
exercising a gentle remedy for the injury. The task of
throwing men against men is a frightful one. The

---

* Translated from José Martí, "Escenas Norteamericanas,"
Obras completas (Havana: Editorial Lex, 1946), I, 1517–1518.

forced brutalization of some men for the benefit of others evokes our wrath. But to stop it we must find a way out for our wrath without provoking any rush or stampede. Karl Marx studied ways to place the world on new foundations. He awoke the sleepers and showed them how to cast down the broken pillars. But he walked in a hurry and somewhat in the shadow. He could not understand that no child can be born either at home from the womb of a woman or in history from the womb of a people without a natural and laborious gestation.

Here they are, the good friends of Karl Marx who was not only a titanic arouser of the European workers' anger, but also a profound analyst of the reasons for human misery and of human destiny. A man consumed by the desire to do good, he projected into everything that which was actually inside himself: rebellion, a way forward, struggle.

Here they are, a Lecovich, a man of the press. Listen to him: He carries reflections of the tender and radiant Bakunin. . . . He begins to speak in English; addresses others in German; "da, da!" his countrymen answer enthusiastically when he speaks in Russian. The Russians are the whip of the reform. But these impatient and generous men, darkened as they are by anger, are not the ones who are going to lay the foundation for the new world! They are the spur, and they come in time as the voice of man's conscience. But the steel that makes a good spur will not do for the builder's hammer.

3

DIEGO VICENTE TEJERA

————•◦•————

The Future
Cuban Socialist Party*

❋

*Poet and writer, Diego Vicente Tejera (1848–1903)
was one of the few fighters for Cuba's independence
who expressed concern about the social problems
that would appear in the island's future.¹ Prevented
by his frail health from bearing arms, he made,
while in exile, propaganda for separation from Spain
and later, in Cuba, founded the very short-lived
Cuban Socialist Party. We present here part of a
speech to the Cuban workers in Key West, Florida,
in 1897, expounding some of the socialist ideas he
had acquired during his travels through Europe.*

But for now, we have only one thing to do: the simple task of preparing. However just and noble our
forthcoming fight against the exploiters of labor, we

---

* Translated from Diego Vicente Tejera, "Los futuros partidos
políticos de la república cubana," *Razón de Cuba* (Havana:
Municipio de la Habana, 1948), pp. 32–42.

¹ One of the few other fighters concerned with social problems was Carlos Baliño (1848–1925), who much after the war
for independence was one of the founders of the Cuban Communist Party in 1925.

face today a battle that is more urgent, more vital, more "holy," if you will, and which requires the complete dedication of all our energies: a battle in which we are engaged for the purpose of eliminating from Cuba, along with Spanish domination, the old regime; a struggle that will inevitably lead us to a homeland, that is, to a ground upon which to build the foundations for our most cherished dreams. On this point we must remain firm. . . . so that no one can cunningly accuse the workers of Cayo[2] of lacking in patriotism, or of being ignorant of it, or of allowing their own selfish interests to place obstacles in the path of the revolution that will liberate us and give us dignity. No! The Cuban laborer, long before he considered his miserable condition as a worker, had already sensed the misery of Cuba as a colony, and his first efforts in public life have been directed not toward the attainment of his rights within Cuban society itself, but rather toward the establishment of his primordial right to be recognized as a free man before the nations of the world. Because of this political instinct, which is manifesting itself admirably, he has understood that, above all and before everything else, a homeland must be created, and he has quelled his resentments for the time being in order to devote himself more vigorously to protesting his position as a despised colonist.

But with our impending triumph close at hand, let us begin to speak out and to take stands.

In all probability, we shall have in Cuba two main political parties, which will each represent both progressive and reactionary tendencies, and which will

---

[2] A reference to the Cuban workers of Key West, whom Tejera was addressing [ed.].

join together in undertaking the gigantic task of drafting a good constitution and good laws. This is just and natural. The laborer, the worker, can then, according to his tastes, affiliate himself with one side or the other, but it would be more desirable if he were to join ranks with the liberals.

But the Cuban laborer must keep in mind that neither the liberals nor the conservatives will be able to solve his specific problem, nor will they attempt to do so. He must be mindful that the two parties, engaging wholeheartedly in the more or less elevated struggle for control, will align themselves with the proletariat only in order to use it as a platform from which to make power-gaining promises, which are as deceitful as they are alluring.

The worker has to wage his own battles, openly, in broad daylight, whenever and however he can. Even the most superficial knowledge of the history of the European labor movements will substantiate that fact. Halfway through this century, when the age-old conflict between capital and labor reached its peak, the inexperienced laboring classes began to entrust their claims to the more powerful of the existing political parties. They even began to imagine that with the substitution of the republic for the ancient monarchical feudal systems, the redemption of the laborer would automatically become a reality, and the sun of paradise would once more shine upon the land. But the republic emerged, and it re-emerged in France, and it appeared in Spain, and radical parties seized control in other countries . . . and yet the worker continued to be dominated by the capitalist, just as persecuted and exploited as before, but made even more bitter, more wrathful by his new disappointments.

It would be, then, both feasible and extremely beneficial for the Cuban laboring class to form an independent party among those future parties that will attempt to direct and model the Cuban republic after their own designs. Such a group would have their own clearly defined platform, with carefully thought out procedures, and aspiring to nothing more or less than the attainment of justice. Its broad, generous standard would be easily adaptable so as to include the demands for the rights of others. It would become involved along with the other parties in contributing toward the betterment of the homeland. In other words, such a party's rise to power could not be regarded as anything less than a completely natural and plausible occurrence.

Tomorrow in Cuba, then, organize the great Socialist Party. Organize wisely and strongly; begin—by means of the press, public speeches, repeated excursions to villages and towns—an intense, tireless propaganda campaign. Clasp to your bosom all those on this lovely island who are in any way hemmed in by or shamefully dependent upon foreign capital: the industrial workers, the field hands, the wretched craftsmen and lesser employees—the dependent ones —all those who, in the midst of Cuban plenty, are without their just rewards. And from the beginning, faithfully maintaining the battle on strictly legal grounds, formulate your platform, support universal suffrage, send representatives to the houses of legislature, give equal attention both to your specific interests and to the general interests of the nation, demonstrate your ability to govern—and aspire to leadership!

But while the party is taking all this overt, public action, do not overlook the vast underlying task of moral and intellectual education. Do not forget that, during this transformation that is to take place in our society, it is important, in striving to maintain equality, that we do not merely allow those who are now on a higher plane to step down, but instead insure that those who are now below will move ever upward.

Who shall see in us the sullen demagogues of the decrepit European societies, products of age-old misery, saturated with the hatred of twenty oppressed generations, ready to fire their deadly arms at the first group of their fellowmen who cross their path? No! Cuban socialism will not and should not intimidate any person. The bourgeoisie must feel called upon to deal with this party cordially and courteously, and then perhaps, through mutual respect, we will achieve the final victory of justice.

4

SANTIAGO IGLESIAS

———•◆•———

Ideological Background of the Workers' Socialist Party of Puerto Rico*

✳

Santiago Iglesias' (1872–1939) role as a tireless fighter in workers' struggles began in his early days in his native Spain. While still very young, Iglesias emigrated first to Cuba and next to Puerto Rico, where he became an active organizer of labor groups. A member of the Senate of Puerto Rico from 1917 to 1933, he was elected Resident Commissioner in the United States and held that position until his death in Washington, D.C. This selection is from his book of recollections of his early struggles with labor and social problems.

The Spanish labor movement suffered intensely the consequences of the differences that arose between Marx and Bakunin on an international level. Inevitably, the labor organizations were drastically split between Anarchists and Socialists.

* Translated from Santiago Iglesias, *Luchas emancipadoras* (San Juan, 1958), pp. 36–38. Printed by permission of Igualdad Iglesias Vda. de Pagan.

And so proceeded the story of labor in Spain, and in Italy and France as well, while England, Germany and the United States were building the labor organization into a powerful political and economic tool that would give the masses personality and strength, vigorous organization, and the support of public opinion. Our Spanish and Latin American philosophers, revolutionary in spirit, altruistic and poetic, very intelligent, quixotic in their ideas, preached and taught as their basic tenet individual devotion to the emerging labor organizations, in order to bring about a soon-to-come social revolution. This almost suicidal tactic gave the governments the best weapon they needed to destroy men and organizations that were founded on romantic and pure idealism but which had no economic strength. For years progress was held in check.

The Socialist Labor Party was organized in San Juan on June 18, 1899. . . . The Socialist Labor Party became directly affiliated with the U.S. Socialist Labor Party, from which it received its credentials as the Socialist organization of the "State of Puerto Rico."

In accordance with this, the Socialist Labor Party came out frankly in favor of the international program of Karl Marx—not knowing much about it, never having had an opportunity to analyze it. They had not seriously considered these principles nor had they read and studied these ideals. In those days, socialism was for the workers of Puerto Rico a doctrine much like the doctrine of emancipation preached by Jesus Christ. For them it was an intuitive idealization of justice and well-being. It meant more bread for the hungry, higher wages, and fewer hours of work. It meant civil, social, human liberation and, thus, a greater spirit of democracy.

In order to appreciate the extraordinary significance of the idealistic and platonically revolutionary declarations that were made by the Free Federation and the Socialist Party of Puerto Rico at the time of their organization, one need only contrast them with the actual intellectual and social conditions of the workers of that time. Nothing illustrates those conditions better than a cable sent out by the Associated Press, and published by *The New York Herald,* which describes most pathetically the deplorable conditions of that period:

SAN JUAN, PUERTO RICO, Feb. 27, 1899. The first important labor strike in Puerto Rico began yesterday morning when 500 men who were working on the new military highway between Ponce and Adjuntas entered the latter city bearing flags and signs with these words: *"We workers demand 5 cents per hour."* The present salary paid to these men is 3 cents per hour, and the workers protest they are forced to work from sunup to sunset.

5

JUAN B. JUSTO

———————

Argentina and the Problems of Socialism

*

Juan Justo (1895–1928), a doctor by profession, was the founder and guide of the Socialist Party of Argentina. He always had a fondness in his socialist programs for practical applications and for concrete objectives, and he also encouraged his followers to study the adaptation of theoretical formulas to the concrete conditions of his homeland. The first selection appeared in 1910; the second was written after Justo returned from an international socialist congress held in Bern in 1920.

*The Beginning of Socialism in Argentina**

By around 1885 there were a million European immigrants in Argentina of different nationalities and tongues, men disciplined to work, with regular habits, with aspirations for a better life. Some became promoters, but many more remained wage-earners and

———————

* Translated from Juan B. Justo, *Socialismo* (Buenos Aires: Editorial La Vanguardia, 1920), pp. 101–107.

displaced the less able workers of the country, at the same time increasing the viability of the *criollo* proletariat.

They had also brought with them their socialistic education, which led to the general practice of mutual aid among the immigrants—a practice little known to the people of Argentina. Many of those who came from the more advanced countries arrived with their new social ideas already shaped and were used to superior political forms.

On January 1, 1882, the Germans in Buenos Aires formed the *Vorwärts* club with the objective of cooperating "for the realization of the principles of socialism." It was the first agitational group to be formed, and from 1886 on, it placed itself at the disposal of the workers in the few small conflicts with which the fight between capital and labor was begun in this country. In December of that same year the weekly *The Worker* appeared, the first herald of the fight of the proletariat.

It was truly an international movement. The public meetings were conducted, in turn, in Spanish, Italian, French, and German. The committees chose to call themselves "international," and they sought to allow equal representation from each of the diverse tongues and nationalities. The very style of *The Worker* reflected the German origin of the engineer Ave-Lalleman and of the workers who printed it.

It was more or less during this epoch that anarchism began to appear, with its honest extremism, its violence and its ambiguous procedures; opposing all serious organization within the laboring class, and preaching absolute disregard for the law.

But circumstances were changing. *La Vanguardia,*

put out primarily by Argentines, appeared in April 1894. In July the first local socialist group began to take shape, supported by men who spoke the language of the country. This gave new incentive to union agitation. In 1895 the first executive committee of the newly founded Socialist Party resolved that its members would all be citizens, native or naturalized.

It is not necessary to expound here the increasing activity of the party from its origin till today.

Economic evolution has been the basis of Argentine history and the key to an understanding of its bright and dark phases. The most efficient political groups in our history are those who have represented the more general and best understood economic interests.

We have managed to break away from the simple formula and the schematic doctrine, and we are developing a popular method of historic action, vast and complex enough to meet the demands of circumstances. The problem of socialism is not, in this country or in any other, a matter of putting a definite, perfect plan of social organization into practice, as those who wish to see the people with their heads forever in the clouds suppose it is, and as those who are too lazy and cowardly for the necessary historical action say it is. Such people interpret the problem in this way in order to excuse their inability to find a solution to the real problem. Here and everywhere, socialism presents a problem that is infinitely more common and, hence, more transcendental: What types of individual and collective activity are needed to step up the physical and intellectual development of the masses? How can the tangible well-being of the workers be increased? I say "tangible" in order to exclude from consideration the glories of the homeland, the pride of being governed by heroes, etc. . . . Only those changes that are statistically evident and which can be shown in diagrams should be considered: increased consumption, wage increases, more schools, a decrease in the rate of mortality.

Socialism is thus the coming of science to politics, the most advanced of all politics—not for what it foresees or promises, but for what it does. Socialism leads the people to the conquest of political power as an essential prerequisite to economic liberation—to gain control of the State in order to check capitalist exploitation up to its final abolition.

A Program of International Socialist Action*

Socialist international declarations on the colonial problem, with the exception of a few remarks about the destiny of the natives, have been generally insincere and meaningless. The subconscious imperialism of many European socialists becomes apparent when, in dealing with the goals of international trade and world supply, they separate and distinguish between food and raw materials on the one hand and manufactured products on the other. At the recent congress in Bern I was forced to oppose, without being heard, the idea that the declaration about the society of nations refers only to the control "of the production and distribution of foodstuffs and raw materials." Why not also international control of coal and petroleum, iron and steel, tanned leather and textiles, etc.?

---

* Translated from Juan B. Justo, "Fundamentos del programa de acción socialista internacional," *Internacionalismo y patria* (Buenos Aires: Editorial La Vanguardia, 1933), pp. 56–60.

The Moscow Communist International also lacks an all-inclusive plan for international political action. The Twenty-One Conditions for admission almost all refer to the composition and internal management of the parties. In Moscow's small program of international action, everything that is not negative is subversive, and it is only applicable at certain moments and under exceptional circumstances, such as those that existed in Russia at the time of the Revolution.

The Socialist Party of Argentina is in a favorable position for formulating a plan of international socialist action and for presenting it to sympathetic bodies. An American community in formation, intimately linked with the world market by its principal imports and exports; a tributary of the oligarchy of landowners, of the newly born capitalism and of foreign capital; accustomed by the spectacle of our national politics to have no great faith either in "order" or in "insurrection"; without a colonial empire and with no desire to have one, the Argentine working people are eagerly receptive to the impressions of world politics and, seasoning them with their own experience, they can establish for themselves a standard of international action that should be worthy of acceptance by the Socialist parties.

6

EMILIO FRUGONI

———•◦•———

Socialism Is More than Marxism*

✳

One of the most respected political figures in Uruguay, Emilio Frugoni (1880–   ), in 1904, founded the Karl Marx Study Center and, in 1910, the Uruguayan Socialist Party. Poet and several times a Deputy, and until very recently his country's ambassador to the Soviet Union, Frugoni has always represented a moderate and independent socialist view.

We are disciples of Marx and pride ourselves on our adherence to the most vivid and indestructible aspects of his method of interpreting history. But following the example of Marx, who said he was not a Marxist, we can say that our Socialism is not exclusively Marxist.

Socialism includes Marxism, and not the reverse, as some tend to believe—certainly those who give the strictest interpretation to Marx, violating all truly scientific spirit by reducing his assertions to dogmas.

* Translated from Eduardo Jaurena, ed., *Frugoni: Una vida dedicada al ideal* (Montevideo: National Executive Commission for Homage to Dr. Emilio Frugoni, 1950), pp. 67–70. Printed by permission of the editor.

Socialism is more than Marxism, because it is not just a point of view or a historical, sociological, philosophical, and economic criterion. It is also a movement which answers needs that are far removed from any theory, a current of anxiety, of hopes, of desires for social and human justice. For these things, Marxism is a channel, and as such it acts as a guide, but certainly a channel is not the whole river.

Socialism is an orientating and regulating element in class struggles. It makes clear to the laborers just what their real interests are and how they can best be defended. It repudiates forms of destructive violence which are unpleasant, if not abominable and useless, above all in societies where other, more practical and more efficient action is possible, which does not reduce the spirit of the masses to brutality, but which instead lifts and educates it.

For this reason we Socialists do not speak, as other revolutionaries do, in terms of class war, but rather in terms of class struggle. War presupposes hatred of the enemy and the use of any means to reach an end; struggle is possible between mere adversaries. Socialism takes action against institutions, not individuals, because rather than an action of a class versus individuals, it is an action of class versus class.

The fight against capitalism, economic privileges, and social inequalities should never reduce the political horizon of the people, confining it to a precinct where the State eliminates all those liberties which are the oxygen of civic lungs.

Socialism deviates from its high mission as an instrument for the liberation of the masses if it underestimates those fundamental liberties and follows the foolish line of calling them "bourgeois," when it is precisely the bourgeoisie who denies these liberties and the blood of the working people that has fertilized them.

Part II

The Emergence of the Communist Parties and the "Hard Line" Period 1920–1935

CHRONOLOGY
OF
IMPORTANT EVENTS

*

1924   The Peruvian Alianza Popular Revolucionaria Americana (APRA) is founded in Mexico by Haya de la Torre.
The *tenentes* revolt in Brazil.

1925   Army coup takes place in Chile; the Constitution of 1925 is promulgated; the Parliamentary Republic ends.

1927   Leon Trotsky is expelled from the Communist Party.

1928   Hipólito Irigoyen is elected president of Argentina for a second time.
Carlos Ibáñez becomes dictator in Chile.
Gerardo Machado becomes dictator in Cuba.
Sixth Congress of the Third International meets in Moscow.

1929   The National Revolutionary Party, later the Partido Revolucionario Institucional (PRI), is formed in Mexico.
General Augusto César Sandino fights in the mountains of Nicaragua against American intervention.
The Congress of Latin American Communist Parties meets in Buenos Aires.
The Congress of Latin American Labor Unions meets in Montevideo.

1930 Getúlio Vargas becomes ruler of Brazil.

Army coup succeeds in Argentina: Irigoyen is deposed.

1931 Ibáñez is overthrown: political turmoil breaks out in Chile.

1932 The Chaco War between Paraguay and Bolivia begins.

Political anarchy follows proclamation of a Socialist Republic (duration—one week) in Chile.

1933 Good Neighbor Policy is inaugurated.

Machado is overthrown, and the revolutionary government of Ramón Grau San Martín comes to power in Cuba; Fulgencio Batista is named head of the army.

Seventh Pan American Conference (Seventh International Conference of American States) is held in Montevideo; principle of non-intervention is accepted at Conference.

Arturo Alessandri is elected president of Chile: anarchy ends.

1934 Batista and the army depose Grau in Cuba.

Abolition of the Platt Amendment.

Alfonso López, a Liberal, is elected president of Colombia.

Lázaro Cárdenas becomes president of Mexico.

A semi-fascist constitution is proclaimed by Vargas in Brazil.

1935 The Chaco War ends: a period of social awakening begins in Bolivia.

Juan Vicente Gómez, dictator of Venezuela since 1908, dies.

7

LUIS EMILIO RECABARREN

The Dawn
of Social Revolution
in Chile[*]

*

A typographer and self-taught man, Luis Recabarren (1876–1924) very early entered into the workers' struggles, writing and organizing labor unions in northern Chile. He was elected Representative to the Chamber of Deputies and in 1908 was a prisoner for eight months. Recabarren founded the Socialist Labor Party in 1912 and in 1922 was the prime mover in its transformation into the Communist Party. Elected Deputy (also in the Chamber) in 1921, he openly defended his socialist convictions, as can be seen in this portion of a speech that he gave in the Chamber of Deputies in 1921.

In the Chilean congress a persistent effort has been made in recent years to prove that any disturbances that occur in this country are the work of professional

---

[*] Translated from Luis Emilio Recabarren, "Los Albores de la revolución social en Chile," *Obras escogidas* (Santiago: Editorial Recabarren, 1965), I, 21–56.

agitators, the products of theories imported from abroad—as if the working-class sector of the Chilean population had no capacity for such actions.

What agitators there are in this country are authentic Chileans—we are workingmen and not intellectuals. All the agitational movements that have taken place in this country during the last twenty years have actually been the work of the Chilean proletariat. The assertion that we in Chile have copied Communist and Soviet doctrines from Russia is grossly untrue. A study of those doctrines was started in Chile as early as fifteen or twenty years ago.

I have here an article published in 1903 in *El Trabajo* [Work], a periodical put out by the Tocopilla Workers' Union. One worker writes: "The revolution will continue on its course without fear; peacefully, if sheltered by liberty; with violence and terror, if someone tries to stop its march. It is evident that the twentieth century will be one of profound social transformation, and all your efforts to avoid it will be useless." Take note, gentlemen, of the date and of the writer's social condition.

In 1912, the workers in the north were already speaking of taking over industry—an action that we customarily describe as "socialization." The Socialist Party was founded that same year in Iquique.

Some years later we developed the concept further, and before long the workers in the various towns of the republic were already professing Communist ideas and clearly conceiving of Socialism, as is evident from the program of the Socialist Party in 1912.

I wish to make it known that we believe we also have the right to seize political power. And it is not true that no one, as has been said here, is denying us that right. What, then, is the object of political fraud? of corruption? What are the dominant vices of the bourgeois regime for? If we see fraudulence and deceit being used against our rise to political power, what shall we do? Remain idle?

On the contrary, in the face of such illegal means we must fight staunchly until we come to possess all our rights—first, by legal means; but then, if that course is closed to us, we will resort, you may be sure, to revolution.

And no one in this legislature can deny us the right to revolt! You yourselves have done it! For the liberation of this country from Spain a revolution was effected; in 1891 you resorted to revolution[1] in order to change the political regime in this country! If you do not accept our thesis, does that not mean that the right to revolution belongs to only one sector of our population?

I say with all sincerity that I do not want revolution, at least not as you understand it—with guns and bloodshed. . . . I see that you are smiling, wondering, perhaps, where we would be able to obtain weapons.

I have always maintained that our revolution must be a revolution of folded arms, a general strike to force the powerful classes to be moral and just in all aspects of social life, but principally in their dealings with the workingmen, with those who desire to better themselves culturally, with those who want to become more useful, better citizens, an integral part of society.

We have witnessed the misery of the workers, as

---

[1] Revolution against President José Manuel Balmaceda, which brought into being the Parliamentary Republic in Chile (1891–1925) [ed.].

well as the brutal oppression to which they are subjected. This condition is what has developed their capacity and has made them ask: Is this life? Is this what we live for? To be slaves unto eternity?

Capitalist society blames us for the fomentation of these ideas, when the truth is just the contrary. It is you of the capitalist regime who have nourished revolutionary thoughts in the minds of the workers.

No capitalist can criticize our internationalist sentiments, since nothing is more international than capital. Capital has no homeland, no flag—none, that is, aside from the pound sterling.

You who are so patriotic, you should be proud of the fact that there is within this country an intellectual development among workers that is genuinely Chilean, not provoked by foreign theories, except to the extent that such doctrines normally affect our thinking.

Since life is so short, why shouldn't we live well? Why should you, who represent the people, want to hinder the aspirations of the people, who only want to live well?

I shall close by saying that I will speak of the Russian Revolution at some other time, if the honorable legislature so permits. . . . Have you not defended the French Revolution, the fight for independence, and all the revolutions that have taken place in this country? Be logical then; permit a worker to defend what other workers have achieved in other parts of the world.

8

JOSÉ CARLOS MARIÁTEGUI

———◆◆◆———

Yankeeland and Marxism*

✻

Born into a poor family and crippled in early childhood, José Carlos Mariátegui (1895–1930) was self-educated and self-trained as a typographer. Founder of the literary magazine Amauta *and always concerned with social problems, Mariátegui traveled to Europe after World War I and established contact with the Italian and German Socialists. On his return he wrote the most important Latin American Marxist work,* Siete ensayos de interpretación de la realidad peruana. *In the following article, written in 1927—two years before the economic crash of 1929—Mariátegui, more alert than most Latin American Socialists to world events, tries to explode the legend that the postwar economy of the United States might refute the laws of Marxism.*

The economic potential of North America has a spectacular effect on the more impressionistic and superficial critics, inducing them to put their faith

*Translated from José Carlos Martiátegui, "Yankilandia y el marxismo," Defensa del marxismo (Lima: Biblioteca Amauta, 1959), pp. 135–139. Printed by permission of Dr. Javier Mariátegui.

blindly in a Yankee formula of capitalist renaissance that, if it could, would place the laboring masses forever out of the reach of Marxism. Not infrequently a writer who is well versed in literature and philosophy, but largely ignorant of economic principles, will, after reading Henry Ford's book, announce boldly in some large newspaper that socialism is a school or doctrine which is greatly overshadowed by the remarkable strides that North American economists are making. Drieu La Rochelle, for example, a writer of no mean talent, in venturing to describe the contemporary scene, makes such statements as the following:

> The theories that are still talked about in socialist and Communist circles emerged from England in 1780, from France in 1830, from Germany in 1850—from countries that witnessed the coming of the machine, just as Russia is doing today. But the Russians know how to move toward North American capitalism, which is itself aware that it is merely a stepping-stone to something greater. Ford and Lenin are two powers stumbling toward each other in the same dark passageway.

The author of *Mesure de la France,* like any good Frenchman and European, does not believe that the task of defending Western civilization falls to the United States. Rather, he sees it as the mission of a European confederation led by France. And yet, for the present, he looks to Ford rather than to Poincaré and Henri Massis as the leader of the bourgeoisie and as the master capitalist strategist.

A study of the effective factors involved in North American prosperity shows, among other things, that Yankee capitalism has not yet arrived at the crisis which European capitalism is facing. Thus, it would be premature to discuss whether or not the United States is capable of surmounting such a crisis.

Until recently, industrial development in the United States depended entirely on the vigorous rate of consumption of the American population. But ever since production began to exceed consumption, this development has come to depend heavily on the conquest of external markets. The accumulation of the larger part of the world's gold supply in the Yankee reserves has created the problem of the exportation of capital. It is not enough for the United States to dispose of its excess production; it also needs to dispose of its gold surplus. The country's industrial development can no longer absorb all of its financial returns.

Before the war, Yankee industry was a good target for European investors. Profits from wartime production, however, made it possible for Yankee industry to become completely independent of European banking. The United States was transformed from a debtor to a creditor nation. During the postwar period of economic crisis and revolutionary agitation, on the other hand, the United States was forced to discontinue its loans. The European nations had to organize their financial affairs before they could apply for credit to the New York banks. Likewise, with regard to private investments, the threat of the Communist revolution, toward which poverty-stricken Europe seemed to be heading, warned the North American capitalists to exercise utmost care. For this reason, the United States did its best to put the Dawes Plan[1] into effect in Europe. It did not succeed until Poincaré suffered his political defeat in the Ruhr in 1923. From then on,

[1] Dawes Plan. A plan to ease the payment of reparations by Germany after World War I [ed.].

under stipulated conditions governing the payment of German reparations and the Allied debt to the Yankee treasury, Yankeeland has extended numerous credits to Europe. It has made loans to countries to help them stabilize their exchange rates; it has lent funds to private industries for the reorganization of their plants and policies.

A great number of stocks and titles have passed into Yankee hands. But such investing has its limits. United States capital cannot be used to finance European industry without creating the risk of European production cutting into the United States-controlled markets. On the other hand, these investments help the European economy in a manner that is beneficial to the North American economy. The Dawes Plan and its sequel of financial agreements and settlements have put Europe into a period of capitalistic—and democratic—stability, which the reactionary apologists call the work of fascists. But, as the last Economic Conference demonstrated, Europe has not yet reached her equilibrium.

Trotsky has made a singularly penetrating and objective study of Yankee capitalism today. "Gold inflation," observed the Russian leader, "is as dangerous to an economy as currency inflation. One can die of overeating as well as of starvation. A superabundance of gold prevents an increase in profits, reduces the interest on capital, and in this way brings about an irrational increase in production. Producing and exporting for the purpose of hoarding gold in cellars is tantamount to dumping merchandise into the sea. For this reason, America finds it necessary to expand more and more, that is, to convert her excess funds into investments in Latin America, Europe, Asia, Australia, and

Africa. But this course causes the European economy as well as other economies to become more and more an integral part of the United States economy."

If the United States were willing to be satisfied with ensuring the indefinite growth of her capitalism by solving her internal production problems, then the rosy predictions and hopes of Henry Ford might, perhaps, constitute the undoing of the Marxist thesis. But North America, by feats of historical strength that are superior to the will of its own people, has set out upon a vast imperialistic adventure, from which it cannot turn back. Spengler, in his famous book on *The Decline of the West,* maintained, some years ago, that the final stage of civilization is that of imperialism. His Germanic patriotism led him to hope that this mission would fall upon Germany. Lenin, a few years earlier, in the most fundamental of his books, was more advanced than Spengler, in that he considered Cecil Rhodes to be a representative figure of the imperialist spirit, and gave us, furthermore, a Marxist definition of the phenomenon, understood and envisioned as an economic phenomenon. With his usual precision he wrote:

> Economically, the main thing in this process is the substitution of capitalist monopolies for capitalist free competition. Free competition is the fundamental attribute of capitalism, and of commodity production generally. Monopoly is exactly the opposite of free competition. . . . Monopoly is the transition from capitalism to a higher system. If it were necessary to give the briefest possible definition of imperialism, we should have to say that imperialism is the monopoly stage of capitalism. Such a definition would include what is most important, for, on the one hand, finance

capital is the bank capital of a few big monopolist banks, merged with the capital of the monopolist combines of manufacturers; and, on the other hand, the division of the world is the transition from a colonial policy which has extended without hindrance to territories unoccupied by any capitalist power, to a colonial policy of monopolistic possession of the territory of the world which has been completely divided up.

The empire of the United States assumes, in accordance with this policy, all the responsibilities of capitalism. And, at the same time, it is faced with all its contradictions, which are precisely from what socialism gains its strength. The destiny of North America can be considered only on a worldwide plane. And on this plane, North American capital, still internally vigorous and prosperous, ceases to function as a national, autonomous phenomenon and is converted into the culmination of a world phenomenon, subordinated to an inescapable historical destiny.

9

ANÍBAL PONCE

————•◦•————

The Gaucho Legend
and the Spirit
of Our Revolution*

✳

Aníbal Ponce was born in Buenos Aires in 1898 and died in exile in Mexico in 1938. Interested in psychological questions and greatly influenced by the Argentine Marxist thinker José Ingenieros (1877–1925), Ponce marks the shift from positivism to Marxism in Argentina. As in others who underwent the transition, old-school conceptions survived in Ponce. In the following article, written in 1928, he gives us an interpretation of the gaucho that departs from both the usual once in his country and from current Marxist thought.

Mestizo of Spanish and Indian blood—doubly mestizo, because of the African impurities in the paternal bloodstream—the gaucho represented, during the

* Translated from Aníbal Ponce, "La legenda del Gaucho," *El viento en el mundo* (Buenos Aires: Librería y Editorial Ateneo, 1939), pp. 21–25.

colonial period, feudal servitude in its strictest form. Irresponsible, because of his ignorance, and obedient to his master's will, like a good servant, he followed him into the wars of independence and, in so doing, allowed his master's sentiments to become his own. For the most part, he was a warrior of the revolution, although at times he showed himself to be an enemy of the rebels.

Compared to the small number of pure or almost pure Europeans who fought the revolution, the gaucho made up an overwhelming majority of the population, and it was he who carried on the habits and customs of the colony. The conservative elements of the country found in him a natural ally, and in the face of the civil society that was defended in battle from Vertiz to Rivadavia, the gaucho savagery laid the foundation for a militaristic society: *caudillismo* and tyranny. Incapable of working, because of his inveterate indolence, quarrelsome and anarchistic by habit of war, he could make nothing more out of the nation than a conglomeration of small estates.

The fall of Rosas, and the wave of immigration that followed, aroused anew the impulse of the revolution. The gaucho came to be a living symbol for the conservative society that was in retreat, and that bastardized being—whom Ribot has described in his books as an eloquent example of contempt for voluntary effort—was transformed, by the grace of the same men who never ceased to exploit him, into something akin to a sullen, hunted knight whose land is being ravished by alien gods. . . .

An extremely copious literature sprang up, which almost converted him—a common criminal, a cheat, and a killer—into a demigod. The poem, the novel, and the theater contributed immensely to the curious formation of the legend, but in the sorrowful verses and picturesque narrations one can strongly detect the broken spirit of the colony, the undisguised bitterness of the mestizo against Europe.

In spite of indifference and ridicule, however, the foreigner brought us the railroad and the telegraph, wire fences and books, machines and hygiene. Within a short time, hard-working, honest men transformed the face of the nation. Perhaps more significant is the fact that the predominance of his blood brought about the gradual extinction of the gaucho. With the gaucho gone, or hiding in those regions that are a disgrace to the country, the conservative classes—forced to treat subordinates with a clearer consciousness of their rights—made the lost race into a sort of ideal archetype. All the homage paid to the memory of this race, then, is deeply rooted in anti-Argentine sentiment.

We, Europeans, altered by the bloodshed of many races, feel a new hope welling up within us. We are not Indians, nor Spaniards, nor gauchos, nor Frenchmen, either. Without compromising the dominant strains with which we have identified ourselves since the revolution, we accept and meet all kinds of populations with the hope of forging them into a new kind of unity.

Faced as we are with a past of vigorous feudalism, the present organization of our homeland represents a significant stage in our destiny—one that must be surmounted. The principles of the May Revolution[1] have not yet been fully realized. . . . The mode of thinking that was born on a rainy morning in May

[1] The Argentine revolutionary war for independence of May 1810 [ed.].

continues to thrive. Companion to the men of the First Junta, it remains our companion today, and will remain so until the none-too-distant day when popular rule ceases to be a myth and social justice reigns triumphant.

Ten years ago, amidst the horrors of the European war, a people in the grip of a barbarous and alien hand succeeded in overthrowing the greatest of the feudal empires and began, with exemplary heroism, to lay the foundations of that city about which they had dreamed so long. Were the determining causes of the Russian movement peculiar to that people alone? . . . The answer is no.

In words that have only one possible interpretation, Marx and Engels asserted that modern socialism was nothing more than the ultimate development and consequence of the fundamental principles of the eighteenth century. This is also the case with us; the ideals of the Russian Revolution are, in the strictest sense, the same as those of our May Revolution of 1810; and if Echeverría[2] had been able to witness their coming, he would have viewed it with the same joy with which he recognized, seventy years before, in the socialist movement of [18]48, "one of those great revolutions that initiate a new era in the life of humanity."

[2] Esteban Echeverría (1809–1851), radical Argentine poet and author of *Dogma socialista,* was a founder of the Association of May [ed.].

10

THE CONFEDERATION
OF LATIN AMERICAN
LABOR UNIONS

———•◆•———

The Organization and
Immediate Claims of Forestry
and Agricultural Workers*

✳

Despite their errors of judgment, both the Congress of Latin American Communist Parties (Buenos Aires, 1929) and the Constituent Congress of the Confederation of Latin American Labor Unions (CSLA) (Montevideo, 1929) represented the first great efforts toward continental coordination of Communist groups. We present one of the resolutions of the Congress of Montevideo devoted to the much debated question of the organization of the peasants and their relations with the proletariat.

I INTRODUCTION

The Constituent Congress of the Confederation of Latin American Labor Unions finds that the Latin

* Translated from "Resoluciones sobre organización y revindicaciones inmediatas de los trabajadores agrícolas y forestales latino americanos," *Bajo la bandera de la C.S.L.A.* (Montevideo: Imprenta La Linotipo, 1929), pp. 65–74.

American countries, despite their diverse economic structure and unequal economic development, fall into the category of agricultural countries. Agriculture is their principal endeavor and plays a dominant role in the economies of a majority of Latin American countries.

One of the characteristics we find in these countries is the existence of a series of systems going all the way from pre-capitalist systems (natural economy, vestiges of the system of feudal clans, communities, and large ranches) to a well-defined type of capitalistic economy, which accounts for a large part of the forestry and agricultural proletariat (plantations, large cattle ranches, forest industries, etc.).

In spite of all this diversity in agrarian relations, both in different countries as well as in different regions of the same country, the status of the agricultural proletariat is quite similar everywhere. Hundreds of thousands of agricultural proletarians and semi-proletarians are the victims of the most inhuman exploitation. A complete system of norms which are not very different from those of servitude and semi-slavery are directed against the agricultural proletariat: Obligatory work for all members of the family, the handing-down of debts from father to son, the payment of salaries through vouchers exchangeable only at company stores, deceitful hiring systems, etc., are common phenomena in the majority of Latin American countries or in different regions of the same country. Oppression by native exploiters is reinforced by pressure from foreign capital which has amassed enormous tracts of land and great plantations; it has converted Latin American agriculture into an economic appendage of the imperialist countries who mercilessly exploit the agricultural proletariat and the semi-proletarians, economically ruining the large peasant masses. All this leads to a constant sharpening of the class conflict which, if we bear in mind the considerable weight exerted by the agricultural proletariat, makes its role very important in the revolutionary movement. As shown by strikes in Colombia and elsewhere, the agricultural proletariat is bound to play an extremely important role in the struggle against imperialism and in the use of the proletariat as an influence on the huge masses of exploited peasants.

This important role can be played by the agricultural proletariat provided that it is organized into powerful horizontal labor unions under the leadership of a revolutionary union center.

Nevertheless, the agricultural proletariat, to which history has given an extremely important role, has not understood till now the need to organize horizontal labor unions. Thus we find hundreds of thousands or millions of wage-earners in the fields of agriculture, cattle raising, and forestry (on ranches and plantations, in mills, etc.) who are completely disorganized in almost every country.

Existing organizations, with few exceptions, are not really horizontal organizations, but rather, vertical organizations that include salaried workers as well as communal-farm workers, and small landowners or tenant farmers, etc. This leads to confusion in the proletarian nature of the agricultural workers' (peons) movement, and hampers the latter's movement and fulfillment of tasks that should be carried out.

II LABOR UNIONS FOR AGRICULTURAL AND FORESTRY WORKERS SHOULD BE HORIZONTAL ORGANIZATIONS OF AGRICULTURAL PROLETARIANS

Agricultural and forestry workers' unions should be horizontal labor organizations that bring together salaried workers in all fields of agriculture and forestry, both steady and seasonal workers, without distinction as to nationality, citizenship, race, and political or religious affiliation.

The Latin American Congress of Labor Unions feels that the basic task is to create organizations that will bring together workers on the large cotton, coffee, sugar, tobacco, rubber, banana plantations, etc., as well as workers on cattle ranches and in the forest industry. These workers should constitute the basic framework of the unions, with workers scattered over small enterprises filling out the whole.

In addition to basically proletarian elements, the labor union should include semi-proletarians; that is, small-property owners for whom the principal means of existence is still wages. The sharecropper is not considered a wage-earner, and should generally not belong to labor unions but rather to farmers' leagues.

III STRUCTURE OF LABOR UNIONS

Agricultural and forestry workers' unions should be organized in the following way: on plantations, large ranches, and other agricultural or forestry enterprises, workers' committees should be created through election by union members for each of these plantations, ranches, enterprises, or group of small enterprises. These committees form the basic organization of the unions. Unions may have, according to existing conditions, a twofold structure: the central committee and the workers' committee; or a threefold structure: the central committee, the regional or district organization, and the workers' committee. Agricultural and forestry workers' unions should be the backbone of industrial-proletarian labor organizations. The organic shape that relations between agricultural and forestry workers' unions, and parallel labor unions in other fields (whether union, national, or regional centers) will take, is determined by conditions in each country, based on the principle that agricultural-proletarian organizations are the continuation of union organizations of industrial centers.

IV BASIC AND IMMEDIATE TASKS OF AGRICULTURAL WORKERS' UNIONS

The basic and immediate task of the labor union is to defend the economic, union, and legal interests of agricultural and forestry workers by means of a revolutionary class struggle, by raising the political and cultural awareness and class consciousness of the workers, by educating, organizing, and preparing them for the overthrow of capitalism.

V RELATIONS WITH PEASANTS

The organization of agricultural and forestry workers' horizontal unions should in no way imply the separation of the agricultural proletariat or of the revolutionary peasant masses. Based on the assumption that peasants are the natural fighting allies of the agricultural or industrial proletariat in the struggle against landowners or capitalists, closer ties must be assured between labor unions and the peasant revolutionary movement, but in such a way that they may—without weakening the horizontal independence of agricultural and forestry workers' unions—strengthen their proletarian influence on the agrarian movement.

It is not out of place to recommend, according to local conditions, the signing of pacts of solidarity, the creation of committees, or of a worker-peasant bloc for the common defense of proletarian claims and agrarian revolutionary demands, and for the struggle against reaction and imperialism. Collective joining of Unions of Peasants' Leagues is possible only if the horizontal nature of labor unions is preserved, and if the managing circles of the labor movement are guaranteed proletarian leadership.

The establishment of fair relations with revolutionary peasants on the basis of the slogan "hand over the land to the one who cultivates it through confiscation without indemnification" is one of the most important, basic requirements for the success of the agricultural proletariat's struggle and of the labor movement in general.

VI PROBLEMS OF UNITY

The increase in the number of strikes in recent times throughout almost all of the Latin American countries is proof of a sharpening of rural class struggles. In a majority of cases, however, the strike movement of the agricultural proletariat takes place in complete isolation, without finding due support from the industrial proletariat or from revolutionary peasants. In view of the fact that the struggle of the agricultural proletariat is an integral part of the general struggle by the working class and the peasant class against their exploiters, the struggle of the agricultural proletariat must be assured the widest possible support by the industrial proletariat and the revolutionary peasants.

If necessary, this struggle should be widened by attracting the working class and the huge masses of exploited peasants.

The success of the agricultural proletariat's struggle depends solely on the unity between urban and rural proletarian forces. For this reason, agricultural and forestry workers' unions should give as much support as possible to the struggle of industrial workers and should take part, as active combatants, in the struggle for labor unity. They should fight for the unity of the labor movement on a national scale, for the adherence of horizontal unions to the Latin American Confederation of Labor Unions, for the formation of an international militant organization of agricultural and forestry wage-earners, for the creation of one international union center for all labor unions involved in the class struggle, both those adhering to the Red Labor Union International as well as those who are not members of the international centers of the labor movement.

The fight of the agricultural proletariat for its claims and demands is at the same time a struggle against foreign capital. This struggle is more than a struggle against domestic capitalists. That is to say, it becomes a political and anti-imperialist struggle. Revolutionary agricultural and forestry workers' unions should, for this reason, take an active part in the anti-imperialist movement, together with industrial-proletarian unions and with the large masses of exploited peasants.

VII   MAXIMUM ATTENTION SHOULD BE GIVEN TO ORGANIZING THE AGRICULTURAL PROLETARIAT

In those countries where there are still no horizontal unions for agricultural and forestry workers, special commissions must be created within the revolutionary labor centers, whose tasks should consist of drawing up plans and directing the work of organizing agricultural and forestry workers' unions, the reorganization of those already in existence, and the transfer of salaried workers from vertical organizations to newly created horizontal unions.

Within the industrial labor union and its local organizations, it is essential to create commissions to aid in the work between agricultural workers, designating a special worker (agrarian secretary), these commissions being related to the union center. The creation of a special fund to strengthen work between agricultural and forestry workers is indispensable. In addition to collecting funds, it is recommended that industrial labor unions take under their wing those districts containing large masses of agricultural workers or separate enterprises. The Congress calls the attention of all revolutionary labor unions in Latin America to the need of giving as much force, means, and opportunity as possible to the organization of agricultural and forestry workers.

The Congress entrusts the Latin American Confederation of Labor Unions with the task of finding concrete ways to ensure the successful organization of the agricultural proletariat on the basis of this resolution.

The Congress declares that the creation of revolutionary organizations of the agricultural and forestry proletariat, closely linked with the unions of the industrial centers and the establishment of fair relations with revolutionary peasants, in order to assure the proletariat of leadership in this struggle, is one of the most important basic requirements for the final triumph of labor over capital.

11

THE COMMUNIST PARTY OF CUBA

The Communist Party and the Cuban Revolutionary Situation[*]

∗

In order to explain the recently concluded revolutionary period in Cuba and its own rather lackluster actions during it, the Communist Party of Cuba was obliged to do some dialectical tightrope-walking. At its second congress (held in Havana in mid-1934), the Communist Party of Cuba, maintaining the radical international Communist line, insisted on the formation of soviets on the island and attacked all the non-Communist revolutionary groups. It seems remarkable that in 1934, when the international situation was totally unfavorable, the Cuban Communist Party was defending a radical line and a soviet government in Cuba, something they did not do in 1958 when the international situation appeared much more favorable for it. The following resolutions were drawn up by the second congress.

All the governments which have succeeded one another in power since the overthrow of Machado

* Reprinted from "The Present Situation, Perspectives and Tasks

have demonstrated equally their incapacity to solve even a single one of the problems created by the crisis.

The bourgeois-landlord government of Grau San Martín, who was placed in the presidential chair on the fourth of September, 1933, by the petty bourgeoisie, principally the students, by workers who were under the influence of the petty bourgeoisie, and by the army, failed because it could not fulfill its mission of curbing the revolutionary movement of the masses. It failed because it could not solve the problems of the crisis, having subsequently lost the support of the petty bourgeoisie, and because, although a government which defended the interests of the bourgeoisie, the landlords, and the imperialists, as well as their dictatorship, against the masses, it did not gain the confidence of Yankee imperialism nor the native ruling classes, precisely because it could not curb the developing revolution.

The advent to power of the Mendieta–ABC–Batista government on January 18, 1934, is a factor tending to deepen the crisis. It signifies the triumph of the policy of Yankee imperialism by setting up a government of concentration whose mission is to unleash a decided offensive, through methods of violence and terrorism, against the revolutionary movement of the toiling population.

The Mendieta government, faithful executor of the Yankee plans of slavery, not only puts them into practice, but is making enormous expenditures for its apparatus of repression in preparing for war to help

in Cuba" (Resolutions of the second congress of the Communist Party of Cuba), *The Communist,* XIII (1934), 875–887 and 1157–1169.

Yankee imperialism in the next imperialist slaughter.

Our Party has made great and unquestionable progress since its birth and development during the eight years of the Machado dictatorship, living under the most difficult conditions of white terror.

Our Party was able to convert itself from a group of Communists centered in Havana in 1925, struggling against ferocious persecution, imprisonments, tortures, and assassinations, into a national Party with organizations throughout the country, having thousands of members and leading hundreds of thousands of workers.

On the road toward this development the Party has had to combat and conquer alien class influences which filtered into our ranks. The Party has dissipated the influence of the anarchists and liquidated the opposition to the Party, purging itself of Trotskyite elements and strengthening its own ranks with the enrollment of new members and the forging of better discipline. The Party has liquidated the serious mistakes which were committed in the trade union field, especially relative to the liquidation of the united front tactic, and the policy of "joint committees" which were the expression of the united front from the top and not from below.

But there are also weaknesses. . . . As yet the Party has not completely liquidated the opportunist and anarcho-syndicalist influences which were in evidence during the general strike of August and which blinded our Central Committee to the perspective that the general strike opened up the road toward the agrarian anti-imperialist revolution and to the overthrow of Machado.[1]

[1] The government of Machado fell under the impact of a

Since the recognition of these mistakes by the Central Committee, with the help of the Comintern, a persistent struggle has been carried on against the consequences of those errors, but we must redouble our efforts to liquidate the causes which gave rise to them and to strengthening the Bolshevik leadership of the Party.

Of all the groups and parties in Cuba, the most dangerous for the revolution are the parties of the "left," chiefly the Cuban Revolutionary Party of Grau. The principal danger for the revolutionary movement in the present situation are these groups of the "left," which, not being systematically and energetically unmasked so that their influence may be broken, can analyze the mass discontent and use it for their own purpose, which is to divert the masses from the road of revolution in order to safeguard the bourgeois-landlord-imperialist domination.

Present Tasks of Our Party

The Party must have the perspective of establishing Soviet power on a local scale in exact proportion to the maturing of the revolutionary situation.

It is necessary to loose a systematic and implacable struggle against all the measures of the counter-revolutionary concentration government, particularly against the white terror.

We must advance a simple program which will convince the masses of the possibility of maintaining

---

general strike in August 1933. The role of the Communists in that strike is not clear. This paragraph seems to support the accusation, often repeated in Cuba, that at the last minute the Communists reached an agreement with Machado to break the strike [ed.].

a soviet government in Cuba. We must take advantage of the example of Soviet China, whose Red Army has driven back the sixth offensive of the Kuomintang.

We must convince the masses that there is no other way out except the agrarian anti-imperialist revolution, that is, the overthrow of the power of the exploiters, the complete independence of Cuba, the immediate withdrawal of armed Yankee forces from Cuban waters and from Guantánamo naval base; the confiscation and nationalization of all the means of economic power in the hands of foreign capitalists; the confiscation of the land of the *latifundistas* and their delivery without cost to the peasants; the establishment of a government based on soviets (councils) of delegates of workers, peasants, soldiers, and sailors; the arming of the broad masses and the formation of a Red Army of Workers and Peasants.

We must show the masses that the revolution in Cuba is not an isolated event, but constitutes part of the world revolution and develops in conditions marked by the growth of the world revolutionary crisis.

The Cuban soviet government will recognize and enter into negotiations with the U.S.S.R., exchanging sugar for wheat, oil, machines and other products. The Cuban soviet government will organize the economic basis of Cuba, stimulating the production of products that will assure the feeding of the population in spite of a possible economic blockade from the outside.

For winning the masses, the fundamental danger lies in the influence of bourgeois-landlord parties of the "left" and their reformist, anarchist, and Trotskyite agents. We must expose the role of the Auténticos and Guiteras [the left wing leader of the Auténticos] after coming to power, and their policy in favor of imperialist domination.

We must strengthen the work in the army and navy and other armed forces. The Party must seriously begin to penetrate the mass of soldiers and sailors. At the same time, we must unmask the betrayal of their struggles by Batista and the new officers, and popularize the instances of fraternization.

The Party will not be able to face these great tasks if it does not undertake serious work for its Bolshevization, for its conversion into a mass Communist Party, endowed with an iron discipline and with a strong sense of responsibility on the part of each active member.

We must liquidate the danger of right opportunist tendencies expressed in the lack of faith in the revolution, in defeatism and irresponsibility.

At the same time, we must combat the leftist tendencies to set a fixed time for the revolution, to talk loosely of taking power while we are isolated from the daily struggles. It is necessary to liquidate through merciless struggle all the alien class influences in the Party.

Only with iron discipline, Communist strategy, and correct tactics, forged in the fire of struggle, with a Bolshevik line, will the Party be able to lead the masses along the road of the agrarian anti-imperialist revolution.

12

THE COMMUNIST INTERNATIONAL

The Situation of the Latin American Communist Parties on the Eve of the Seventh Congress of the Comintern[*]

✳

A good standpoint from which to judge the effects that the "hard line" had produced on the Latin American Communist parties is provided by this general, but not at all brilliant, panorama offered by the Communists themselves on the eve of the great shift toward the Popular Front. Special notice should be taken of the sharp criticism of the Communist Party of Cuba's attitude.

During the period that has elapsed since the Sixth Congress of the Comintern (1928), the Communist movement in Latin America has achieved considerable success. At the time of the Sixth Congress, there

[*] Reprinted from "Struggles of the Communist Parties of South and Caribbean America," *The Communist International,* XII, No. 10 (May 20, 1935), 564–576.

were Communist parties and Communist groups in twelve countries in Latin America, while at the present time they exist in nineteen countries. Communist parties have been founded in Peru, Paraguay, Venezuela, Costa Rica, Panama, Puerto Rico, and Haiti, and Communist groups in Bolivia and Santo Domingo. In 1933 the Communist Party of Paraguay, which ceased to function in 1930, was reorganized. The Communist Party of [El] Salvador, which arose in 1930 and in 1932 was crushed by the government, at the present time is also being rebuilt. The Communist Party of Guatemala, which was formed prior to the Sixth Congress, had practically collapsed by 1932. It is also now being revived. Thus the only countries without Communist organizations in 1934 were Nicaragua, Guiana, and the West Indies.

The sharpening of class contradictions accelerated the bankruptcy of those petty bourgeois organizations that had tried to lead the mass revolutionary movement. Thus the petty bourgeois elements in the Mexican Revolution displayed their inability to solve the revolutionary tasks and slid into the camp of bourgeois national reformism, which is irreconcilably hostile to the agrarian revolution. In 1930 the process of disintegration of "Prestism" in Brazil led to the situation where the greater part of the leaders passed over to the side of various landlord parties, while the minority, headed by Prestes, came into the ranks of the Communist Party. In Nicaragua, where the rebel bands of Sandino had since 1927 carried on the struggle against the armed intervention by the United States, in 1933 the struggle ended by the capitulation of Sandino and his passage over to the side of the counter-revolutionary government of Sacasa.

The rapid radicalization of the masses and the sharp intensification of the class struggle accelerated and deepened the process of disintegration of the traditional parties, and the differentiation of the liberal bourgeois landlord parties and the petty bourgeois groups. Their upper ranks, openly leaning on imperialism, support the reactionary governments (e.g., the support of the Justo government by the Alvearist wing of the Argentine Radicals, the support of Benavides in Peru by the top leaders of the APRA [Alianza Popular Revolucionaria Americana], etc). At the same time a considerable part of these parties are striving to widen their influence on the masses by resorting to national reformist maneuvers, and even the "socialist" camouflage (the declaration of a "Socialist Republic" by the Grove government in Chile). Finally, petty bourgeois trends arose in the traditional parties ("Radical Bolsheviks" in Argentina, "Left" Batllistas in Uruguay, Socialist groups in Brazil, "Apro-Communists" in Peru, "Guiteristas" in Cuba, etc.) wavering between national reformism and the anti-imperialist and anti-feudal revolution.

Since the Sixth Congress the influence of anarcho-syndicalism within the working-class movement in Latin America has considerably decreased. In some countries, the best elements came over to the Communist movement as in Argentina, Brazil, Paraguay, and Cuba, where the revolutionary trade-union amalgamation, which is under the leadership of the Communist Party, has taken in a considerable majority of the former anarcho-syndicalist workers. In other countries the weakening of anarcho-syndicalist influence is accompanied by a strengthening of the Socialist and reformist organizations (Argentina), the national reformist parties (National Revolutionary Party in Mexico; "Revolutionary Party" of Grau San Martín in Cuba).

In spite of the successes that have been attained, the main reason that the development of the revolutionary crisis in Latin America is being delayed is the fact that the Communist parties continue to lag behind the big tasks that are called forth by the level of development of the mass movement, and that the proletariat is poorly organized. The Communist parties are not sufficiently ready for decisive revolutionary struggles for power.

In some countries (e.g., Colombia, Ecuador, and Panama) the Communist parties are still greatly contaminated with hostile class elements, and their activity is not yet of a consistent Communist character. In a number of countries, the Communist parties still very weak contacts with the masses and have by no means eliminated their sectarian tendencies (especially in Mexico).

Even the strongest and most firmly welded Communist parties are characterized by more or less considerable fluctuation of membership, inadequate ideological maturity of the leading cadres, insufficient ability to consolidate successes organizationally. Work in the mass organizations, especially in the reformist and anarcho-syndicalist trade unions, is weak in most cases. In some countries regression is even to be observed. In the vast majority of the countries, our opponents, the leaders of the reformist, anarchist, governmental, and other trade unions still succeed in carrying with them the vast majority of the organized workers. At the same time the majority of the Communist parties still carry on poor work in the countryside, especially among the Indian peasants.

Not a single Communist party has yet adapted itself

sufficiently to illegal conditions and at the same time has not been able to make full use of legal possibilities.

The basic weakness of the Communist parties of Latin America have made themselves particularly sharply felt in the carrying out of the united front. The work in the opponent mass organization is very weak and divorced from the struggle for the united front. In a number of cases the adoption of the tactics of a united front has met with direct resistance from various elements and units of the Communist parties and was subjected to the grossest right and left opportunist distortions. When carrying on joint activities with reformist organizations, the Communist parties and the revolutionary trade unions often prove to be incapable of keeping the leading role (e.g., in Mexico in 1932).

On the question of national reformism, the inability of these parties to correctly distinguish and differentiate the role of the various bourgeois and petty bourgeois parties in the growing anti-imperialist and agrarian revolution led occasionally to the revolutionary perspectives being toned down and to an overestimation of the forces of the counter-revolution. The bourgeois and petty bourgeois parties, which differed in the political role they played, in their class character and social composition, were regarded as a simple reactionary front which would inevitably take action against the anti-imperialist revolution. The Communist parties underestimated the special importance of bourgeois national reformism, which has great influence over the petty bourgeoisie, peasantry, and even over the working class in Latin America. As a result of this, they frequently adopted a "neutral" position when big mass struggle took place, fell into a passive attitude, and isolated themselves from the masses of the toilers at times when big political events took place.

At the very moment when a very wide revolutionary upsurge of the people was taking place, accompanied by a tremendous strike struggle waged by the proletariat and directed against American imperialism and its local reactionary agents, the Communist Party of Cuba absolutely incorrectly raised the question of differentiating between the camp of counter-revolution and the camp of the national liberation struggle, characterizing the national reformist party, the Auténticos, the national revolutionary Guiteras group, as parties moving in the direction of fascism.

Part III

The Popular Front and World War II

1935–1945

CHRONOLOGY

OF

IMPORTANT EVENTS

*

1936   The Spanish Civil War begins.

1938   The Popular Front wins in elections in Chile.
Falange Nacional (later called the Christian Democratic Party) is organized in Chile.

1939   The Spanish Civil War ends; many Republicans emigrate to Latin America.
Germany and the Soviet Union sign a non-aggression treaty.
World War II begins.

1940   A new constitution is promulgated in Cuba: Fulgencio Batista is elected president with the support of the Communists.
Lázaro Cárdenas is succeeded by Avila Camacho as president of Mexico.

1941   Germany attacks the U.S.S.R.
The Japanese bomb Pearl Harbor: the United States and many Latin American countries enter the war.
Acción Democrática is organized in Venezuela.
Movimiento Nacionalista Revolucionario (MNR) is founded in Bolivia.

1942   Alfonso López is elected president of Colombia for the second time.

1943   Army officers of the Grupo de Oficiales Unidos (GOU) depose the government in Argentina:

Juan Domingo Perón is named secretary of labor.

Gualberto Villarroel, supported by the MNR, takes over in Bolivia.

1944 A revolution in Guatemala overthrows dictator Jorge Ubico.

Ramón Grau San Martín is elected president of Cuba.

1945 Acción Democrática and other forces revolt in Venezuela: Rómulo Betancourt becomes provisional president.

President López resigns: political tension mounts in Colombia.

José Luis Bustamante, with the support of the Alianza Popular Revolucionaria Americana (APRA), is elected president of Peru.

Perón emerges as the most important political figure of Argentina.

Juan José Arévalo is elected president of Guatemala.

World War II ends.

Getúlio Vargas is forced to resign the presidency in Brazil.

13

THE COMMUNIST PARTY OF CHILE

A Program of Action for the Victory of the Chilean Popular Front*

*

In 1938, Gustavo Ross, the presidential candidate backed by the most traditional parties and the Alessandri government, was defeated by Pedro Aguirre Cerdá, the candidate of a very heterogeneous Popular Front, whose basic strength came from the Radical Party. By not participating directly in the government, and thus both sharing the applause and inciting criticism, the Communists missed no opportunity the moment afforded them to pass severe judgment on the Chilean oligarchy and to expand its combat program.

The discovery of the scandalous frauds perpetrated by the Alessandri-Ross government in the manipulation of stock certificates—constituting the most brazen transaction ever known on this continent—should

---

* Reprinted from "A Program of Action for the Victory of the Chilean People's Front," *The Communist*, XX, No. 5 (May 1941), 452–457.

serve as the beginning, even though a belated one, of a course of legal action against the guilty parties, such as the Popular Front and the people as a whole have been demanding ever since the present administration took office. The embezzlement of some tens of millions of pesos now under investigation in the courts is little more than an episode in the long string of crimes committed by the ringleaders of the recent regime, headed by Gustavo Ross, whom the people have rightly dubbed "the last pirate of the Pacific."

It has been established—as our Party has repeatedly pointed out—that Ross and his gang, in the course of the year 1938, received tens of millions of pesos from a group of foreign banks and corporations engaged in exploiting the basic resources of Chile, by way of financing the presidential campaign of the rightists and carrying out a project of wholesale bribery.

The banks and corporations in question are the following: the North American Guggenheim-Morgan-Rockefeller group, represented by the National City Bank, Lautaro Nitrate, the Anglo-Chilean, and other companies; and the British Rothschild group, represented by the Bank of London and South America, by the Tarapacá and Antofagasta Saltpeter Company, the Gente Grande Cattle Corporation, Williamson Balfour, and others.

It has been proved that Ross, upon receiving the money for his presidential campaign, contracted, among other things, to hand over the rich pampas of Pissis and Nebraska to the company which is headed by Señor Osvaldo de Castro, who likewise is deeply involved in the stock swindle.

Ross, head of the oligarchic-liberal-conservative outfit, stands charged, therefore, before the people, with the crime of high treason to the fatherland; with plotting against the dignity, sovereignty, and independence of the nation; with having schemed to sell the presidency of the republic to the foreign enemy; and with every variety of crime against the monetary stability of the country and the national economy, particularly as regards the enormous increase in the price of commodities.

The accused, then, is the entire oligarchy, a social caste that is inimical to the people and to the nation, one which, for more than a hundred years, has held power for the advantage of imperialism and its own enrichment, and which, in the course of its political degeneration, has descended to the very lowest depths of abject venality and corruption.

It is this oligarchy which has sought to hide its true face behind the hypocritical mask of "anti-communism," attributing to the Communist Party all its own crimes, even as the petty robber cries "Stop, thief!" in order that he may make good his own escape.

Facts have subsequently shown the correctness of the Popular Front policy. They show that the Popular Front movement, which triumphed in the presidential campaign of 1938, was and continues to be a great national crusade to preserve the independence and unity of Chile, to defend the democratic regime, to improve the working conditions and living standards of the toiling masses, and to safeguard peace.

The Popular Front victory spared Chile the ignominy of falling into the clutches of Ross and those who paid him for his unpatriotic labors. Thanks to the Popular Front, Chile was saved from being reduced to a mere colony of imperialism, and Chileans were saved from being slaves subject to the lash of a foreign master.

The only way to free Chile from the crimes of the oligarchy is to liquidate the latter's material base, that is to say, by putting an end to its key positions and economic privileges, and by adopting all those measures with respect to its property holdings which may be deemed necessary in bringing it to an accounting.

MEASURES THAT IT IS NECESSARY TO ADOPT

In view of these facts, the Communist Party calls upon the people to organize and to mobilize, and to demand of the government and state authorities the adoption of the following measures:

Establishment of an effective control on the part of the state over the operations of all banks in the country, with the object of preventing new frauds and utilizing the credit for the benefit of the independent industrial development of Chile, to the advantage of the small farmers, miners, merchants, and industrialists.

Nationalization of those foreign enterprises which are involved in the stock swindle and which are accused of having meddled in internal affairs, to the detriment of the people and of democracy.

Maintenance of the act prohibiting the return of the fascist conspirators Ibáñez and Herrera.

Support of the president of the republic in his veto of the rightist plot to outlaw the Communist Party and, in general, to limit the free expression of political opinions, in order to prevent the throwing of light upon the crimes of the oligarchy. Defense of the election of the Communist members of Parliament.

Formation of a true Popular Front government through the elimination of those ministers who display a conciliationist, anti-Popular Front tendency, and their replacement by men who are disposed to support the Popular Front by speeding the realization of an immediate plan of economic and social action, based upon the Popular Front program.

The Communist Party calls upon the people to organize and mobilize in order that they may obtain these measures of national salvation. Once again, the Communist Party addresses itself to the workers, peasants, professionals, and honest intellectuals, to all those progressive individuals who are devoted to the fatherland and who are desirous of seeing Chile freed of the shameful scars inflicted upon it by the landowning oligarchy; they are urged to group themselves in committees with a Popular Front base, in shop, commune, city ward, and on landed estate, with the object of struggling for the adoption of the measures indicated, for their own demands, and for the effective and rapid fulfillment of the 1938 program.

On the sixth day of April next, all the people of Chile will be called upon to pass judgment on the forces that confront them. The people will have to choose between the rightists (and their Schnakite[1] lackeys) and the Popular Front, between reaction and progress, between swindlers in the service of foreign interests and a struggle for the liberation and national dignity of Chile.

The Popular Front will triumph, and the people of each commune, organized in committees of struggle, will remain vigilant in seeing to it that the Popular Front program is carried out.

---

[1] Oscar Schnake was a Chilean socialist leader of moderate tendancies [ed.].

14

BLAS ROCA

———·•••·———

Batista, Grau, and the Roads to National Unity[*]

✳

If this selection is compared with document 13, it can be seen how great the change was in the Communists' attitude during the Popular Front. Whereas before nearly all the political groups and individuals were regarded as enemies, now the conciliatory attitude is extended simultaneously to such antagonistic figures as Batista, the outgoing president-dictator, and Grau, the incoming Auténticos president. In addressing the National Assembly of the Partido Socialista Popular (PSP) in 1944, Blas Roca, its general secretary, opens the doors to an understanding with the new administration and takes pains to ratify emphatically the positiveness of the Communist alliance with General Batista.

The Assembly has given the greatest attention to the matter of national unity, and in particular to the basic problem of our relations with Grau.

[*] Translated from Blas Roca, *Los socialistas y la realidad cubana* (Havana: Ediciones del Partido Socialista Popular, 1944), pp. 51–75.

It is quite natural that this should be so, because the fate of national unity depends to a considerable degree on the attitude of the next government toward us and toward the popular movement, and on our relations with this government.

Comrade Carbajal has sought to raise the question, and he has today explained it again, of whether our relations with Grau would be the same as those we have maintained with Batista, on the ground that Batista had been more sincerely appreciative of our efforts and our collaboration. Carbajal maintained, and has reiterated, his feeling that Grau does not want to collaborate with us; hence his references to the subjective and the objective.

I believe in all honesty that Grau has no plan to neutralize us, to annul us, once he is in full control of the government. Since we are sincerely prepared to work with Dr. Grau, since we are offering him our full, enthusiastic, and staunch support, what justification could he have for carrying out the plan that Comrade Carbajal attributes to him?

Comrade Joaquín[1] recalled the days when we first began to collaborate with Batista. It is well that he has reminded us of these things that, while they seem so natural to us today, provoked a crisis in the Party in 1938. The Unión Revolucionaria and the Communist Party were two independent parties at that time. There was very little doubt in the Communist Party concerning the line of support for Batista. On the contrary, in the Unión Revolucionaria we had a crisis that caused us to lose the active participation of

---

[1] Joaquín Ordoqui, an old militant of the Communist Party, now in disgrace and stripped of all of his duties under the Castro regime [ed.].

highly esteemed and valuable comrades who were unwilling to follow us in those confused days.

The first resolution I propose is that the National Assembly send a letter to the president of the republic, General Batista. His term is now drawing to a close. We have given him our support for four years. I believe that this collaboration has been productive and, since our Assembly will not meet again before he leaves the presidency, I think that we ought to take this opportunity to write a letter to him reviewing the results of our collaboration.

I propose the following as the text of the letter:

General Fulgencio Batista y Zaldívar
The Honorable President of the Republic
Presidential Palace
Havana

HONORED PRESIDENT AND ESTEEMED FRIEND:

The National Assembly of the Partido Socialista Popular, which will not have another opportunity to meet in the short period remaining before your term of office expires, wants to take advantage of the occasion of its meeting today to address a letter to you in that connection.

In a few days, General Batista, you will step down from the presidency of the Republic after having held that post, the highest in the land, for four years and will cease to be the most decisive voice in the leadership of the nation.

At this time, as you relinquish the presidency, our Party wants to declare that it is satisfied with the collaboration we have maintained and the support we have given you in your task of governing.

We began our collaboration with you in the middle of 1938, when you were still chief of the constitutional army, in those difficult and uncertain days for our country when the world was living through the prologue to the great war that is now drawing to a victorious conclusion for the United Nations. We, who as late as half a year before, had considered ourselves your political enemies, who had violently opposed many of the measures taken by the government you headed, who had—from the illegality in which we lived at that time—criticized you personally, offered you our cooperation so that you might formulate a broad, democratic, and progressive program in which the first step would be the convocation of a free and sovereign constituent assembly.

Today, in recalling those beginnings that seem far in the past, we are proud to declare our conviction that Cuba and the Cuban people have gained the very greatest benefits by your action and with our collaboration.

The free and sovereign constituent assembly, the political amnesty that wiped out all of the tumultuous proceedings of 1934–1937, the solution of the critical phase of the university problem and the pacific spirit with which, despite all this, it was possible to reintegrate all parties into the legal civil battles and to restore institutional normalcy, were the first fruits achieved by your action, with our most enthusiastic collaboration. These first steps can be viewed today as the antecedents and the foundation on which your program as president from 1940 would be developed, and which would, in four years, bring about public order, individual liberty, political democracy and the gradual improvement in the living conditions of the people.

In 1940, in one of the most strenuous and heated electoral campaigns our country has ever experienced, we contributed to your election to the presidency by our enthusiastic support, by the mobilization of our Party, and by our votes.

Since 1940, our Party has been the most loyal and unswerving supporter of your governmental measures, the most energetic promoter of your inspiring platform of democracy, social justice and defense of national prosperity.

We have fought at your side for the mortgage moratorium, for higher salaries and wages, for the extension of social security benefits to agricultural workers, for understanding of the principle of equal pay for equal work, for establishment of the forty-four hour work-week with forty-eight hours' pay, for expanding and consolidating maternity benefits, for a halt to evictions of farmers, and for so many other practical benefits for professional, farm and industrial workers and all of the people.

We have fought at your side for a declaration of war by our country against the criminal Axis powers, and together we have worked to eliminate enemy spies and agents, to place our moral and material force at the service of the United Nations' war effort. Together we have worked for national unity, for the union of all Cubans in the common task of leading our nation in this crucial hour for the entire world along the path of dignity, progress and freedom. Together we have defended Cuban interests against all evil designs. Together we have battled to contain speculation, to increase national production, to raise the living standard of the salaried and professional worker, of peasant and laborer. Together we have fought for a respect for democracy and a climate of freedom that have made possible this unparalleled example of the last general elections.

In the record of your acts as president, the public works, the progressive measures, the democratic declarations shine with such luster that they obscure and reduce any stains that might have tarnished your administration as a legacy of the past.

Although not all of our hopes have been fulfilled, we are satisfied with our collaboration and proud of the support we have given you—collaboration and support that were not determined, or even conditioned, on any petty considerations of favors from the government, or of any other type.

Today, as you leave the presidency, we want to reaffirm that you have our affection and our respect and esteem for your principles as a democratic and progressive leader.

Tomorrow you will be one of us as a private citizen. We are sure that neither your political party nor its conditions, nor your concern for the destiny of our country will permit you to remain aloof from the civil struggles of the troubled and fateful days ahead. We hope that tomorrow, as has been the case yesterday and today, we may collaborate with the same determination for the benefit of our country and our people.

We send you our cordial greetings.

The National Assembly
of the Partido Socialista Popular

Juan Marinello   Blas Roca
CHAIRMAN   SECRETARY GENERAL

(*prolonged applause*)

15

LUÍS CARLOS PRESTES

─── •••• ───

Brazilian Communists
in the Fight
for Democracy*

*

*During World War II, Communist cordiality was
not limited to governments and national parties, but
was opened up into broad support of Pan Americanism and the Allied nations. Here, Luís Carlos
Prestes, the leader of the Brazilian Communist Party
who had only recently been released from prison,
extols these objectives and points out the need to
create a Communist Party more in accord with the
present situation.*

The economic and political consequences of Nazi-
fascist advances throughout the world were equally
noticeable in Latin America. In those years when
fascism was spreading over the world, countries that
were still backward dependencies of imperialism, and
generally under the rule of governments that were

─────────

* Translated from Luís Carlos Prestes, *Os comunistas na luta
pela democracia* (Rio de Janeiro: Edições Horizonte, 1945), pp.
6–12.

always disposed to capitulate to foreign capital, in order to benefit the narrowest and most selfish interests of small cliques in the ruling classes, were victims of the most brutal exploitation by agents of fascist imperialism and by terrorist police suppression on the part of their rulers—those well-known dictators in South America whose names succeeded one another after the 1929 depression in a series that is unhappily not yet ended: Machado, Gómez, Ibáñez, Uriburu, Terra, Sánchez Cerro, Ubico, etc. With the support of such people, the Nazis gained ground on our continent, and did everything possible to organize their murderous bands (as invariably happens everywhere) for the purpose of exploiting our peoples, liquidating any remnants of organization in the movement of workers and progressive peasants, dissolving the Communist parties and, generally in the name of the fight against British and American imperialism, wiping out in each country any authentic movement for freedom and national independence.

However, none of this could conquer the anti-fascist hatred of the peoples of this continent who, led by their best and most enlightened sons—patriots who emerged both from the masses of the workers and from the progressive national bourgeoisie—were always able to defend democracy and progress and to carry on an unremitting battle for the great cause of freedom and independence for all peoples.

In this critical period, Roosevelt's Good Neighbor Policy was unquestionably a positive factor that made it possible to strengthen Pan American solidarity, one of the most effective political and economic weapons in our people's struggle against Nazi subversion and in defense of democracy. Equally outstanding was the role of the CTAL [Confederation of Latin American Workers], under the leadership of Vicente Lombardo Toledano, a champion in the fight for democracy throughout the hemisphere that made its defiant anti-Nazi voice heard even across frontiers that had been closed by the police and by the censorship imposed by the dictators, who eventually came to oppress the people in every one of our countries.

The war against Nazism served to strengthen the bonds of Pan American solidarity, especially after the Japanese attack on Pearl Harbor, which presented us with the imperative obligation and necessity of joining in the defense of the hemisphere alongside the great American nation. Despite subversive defeatism and the infamous fifth column activities of the reactionaries and the fascists (who carried on the most insidious campaigns, attempting to revive old injuries and distrust of British and American imperialism), the Latin American governments were bringing their countries into the United Nations bloc one by one, and into the war against the Nazis, with the full support of their people, and to the extent permitted by their material capabilities and the level attained by the anti-fascist working class organizations and the masses in each country.

Without going into a really critical analysis of our Party activities over the last ten years—a task, as we have noted, that can only be undertaken by a future Party congress—let us nevertheless attempt to make a summary evaluation of our political action in those years, specifically during the war years and those following our national conference in August 1943, when the subsisting state organs of the Party were restructured. The effects of the 1935 defeat on our Party are well known. In the fire of events, our Party was revealed in its true nature—a small party, only feebly linked to the masses, infiltrated by alien ideologies that employed ill-chosen methods of organization, and therefore incapable of surviving the brutality of reaction, which brought it to almost total extinction. But the very struggle revealed what there was of courage and self-sacrifice in a small number of Party cadres. These were elements that had been forged during the years of reaction and terror, and that had succeeded in maintaining their links with the masses, rebuilding the Party and, in practice, fighting against "liquidationism" and other forms of enemy infiltration into the ranks of the revolutionary movement. They succeeded in gradually restoring the Party to its legitimate role as the organized vanguard of the working class, and more specifically as the leaders of our people in the war on Nazism and the fifth column in our country.

Our Party's legal activity is itself a new factor in accelerating political definitions. Reactionaries and leftists of all shades are tearing off their masks, to reveal in their hatred of our Party the real value of the democracy they pretend to defend. In the very same newspapers, they accuse us of being Communists, the enemies of God, country and family, and at the same time, through the spokesmen of the Trotskyite rabble, of not being Communist enough, or of having betrayed Marxism-Leninism. . . . What they all want, it is clear, is to divide the people, to set up obstacles to their progress to democracy, to turn Brazilian against Brazilian once again to the benefit of the worst exploiters both inside and outside the country, the fascists and their fifth column within the country.

There are still many patriots under the malevolent influence of the enemies of national unity. Accordingly, it is up to us to redouble our efforts to enlighten the largest possible number—not only among the rural and urban workers but also among the intellectuals, who are the favorite target of the leftists and the Trotskyites.

Instead of the small, illegal party that carried on agitation and spread the general idea of communism and Marxism, we now need a great party, authentically linked to the working class and the decisive forces in our country, a party that will include the best, the most advanced, the most honest intellectuals, a party that will draw in the best elements of the rural masses, a party that by virtue of its broad social composition will in fact have the necessary power and ability to lead our people in the fight for progress and independence, for liberty and social justice, for popular democratic government.

Finally, we need a party quite different from our old and glorious Party, in which we old militants became the better and more valuable fighters the more we succeeded in resisting persecution by the police and in living incognito among the masses of the people. Today, we need a new-style party, a great party closely linked to the masses; and all of us need to adapt ourselves to the new conditions, to develop the new qualities that our Party, now expanded and legalized, is going to demand from each of its militants.

Our success is going to depend on the capacity we develop to carry out the Party's political line, on our ability to fight for national unity without sacrificing the Party's class independence, to defend its role of leadership in the struggle of the working class and the broadest possible spectrum of workers in the country. Our Party, the vanguard of the working class, must lead; it must not let itself be swept along by the spontaneous movement of the popular masses, by "public opinion," which is in general nourished by the bourgeois press in order to drag the masses in the direction of its class interests. Those who "preach *seguidismo* [tailism] are the carriers of that bourgeois policy which condemned the proletariat to the role of an instrument in the hands of the bourgeoisie," as Stalin has said.

This is the great peril that threatens us in the period through which we are now passing. If we let ourselves be carried along by the spontaneous movement of the masses—whose discontent, as a result of the economic crisis and after so many years of reaction was, and still is, readily exploited by fascism and its fifth column—we would unconsciously serve their ends and would be guilty of the greatest of all crimes against our people.

This is what is being done by all those who allow themselves to be swept along by events and who, however much they claim that they are Communists, are still under the influence of ideologies alien to the proletariat, not to mention those who employ leftist arguments and are nothing more than mouthpieces of the Trotskyite rabble. We must therefore make the most vigorous efforts to steer our Party cadres through these shoals—which will only be accomplished by resolutely and speedily raising the political and theoretical level of the entire Party, and above all, of its more responsible cadres.

Part IV

Cold War and New Crisis

1946–1959

CHRONOLOGY

OF

IMPORTANT EVENTS

✳

1946 Juan Domingo Perón is elected president of Argentina.

Ospina Pérez, a Conservative, becomes president of Colombia: tension mounts between Conservatives and Liberals.

The Christian Democratic Party (COPEI) is founded in Venezuela.

The government of Villarroel falls in a reactionary coup in Bolivia.

1947 The Truman Doctrine of containment of communism is announced.

Rómulo Gallegos is elected president of Venezuela.

1948 The Liberal leader Jorge Eliécer Gaitán is assassinated in Bogota: violence erupts in Colombia.

A military coup in Venezuela deposes Gallegos.

General Manuel Odría comes to power by a military coup in Peru.

1949 The Movimiento de Liberación Nacional (MLN) of José Figueres leads a successful revolt in Costa Rica.

1950 Jacobo Arbenz is elected president of Guatemala.

Getúlio Vargas triumphs in elections in Brazil.

1951 Uruguay abolishes the office of president.

1952 A military coup is mounted against the Auténticos

government in Cuba: Fulgencio Batista seizes power.

A victorious revolution led by the Movimiento Nacionalista Revolucionario (MNR) makes Paz Estenssoro president of Bolivia.

Eva Perón dies.

1953 General Gustavo Rojas Pinilla takes control of the government in Colombia.

José Figueres is elected president of Costa Rica.

A force led by Fidel Castro attacks the military barracks in Santiago de Cuba.

1954 The Inter-American Conference, meeting in Caracas, issues a Declaration against communism.

The government of Arbenz is overthrown in Guatemala.

Vargas commits suicide in Brazil.

A military coup in Paraguay puts Alfredo Stroessner in power.

1955 Perón is deposed in a military revolt in Argentina.

Juscelino Kubitschek is elected president of Brazil.

General Odría's dictatorship ends in Peru.

1956 Manuel Prado is elected president of Peru.

The Frente de Acción Popular (FRAP), a Communist-Socialist coalition, is formed in Chile.

Castro's forces land in Oriente Province, Cuba.

1957 Rojas Pinilla falls in Colombia: Liberals and Conservatives agree to form the Frente Nacional Democrático (FND) and rule Colombia; Lleras Camargo is elected president.

1958 A civil-military revolt deposes Pérez Jiménez in Venezuela: Rómulo Betancourt is elected president.

Arturo Frondizi is elected president of Argentina.

Batista flees Cuba.

16

RODNEY ARISMENDI

The End of the War and the New American Imperialism[*]

*

In 1945 the war had ended and, as a Spanish novelist puts it, "peace had broken out." The honeymoon with the United States, along with Pan Americanism, was ending because of the increasing tensions of the Cold War. Rodney Arismendi, a leading member of the Uruguayan Communist Party and an outstanding spokesman for Latin American communism, delineates the sharpness of the change by drawing attention, in drastic contrast to the preceding document, to the weaknesses of Pan Americanism and to the insurmountable racial and economic distances separating the United States and Latin America. United States imperialism, mere mention of which by the Trotskyites had been castigated by some Communists during the war, is now revived as the eternal and basic enemy.

The war is over and it is time for us South Americans to ask ourselves this question: And now what?

---

[*] Translated from Rodney Arismendi, "El Fín de la guerra y el nuevo imperialismo norteamericano," *Para un prontuario del*

We have come out of a great liberating and anti-fascist war, fought to destroy the monstrous financial oligarchies of the Rome-Berlin-Tokyo Axis.

. . .

This feature of the war has put its stamp on Anglo-American foreign policy, in that it allows for the possibility of coming to an understanding with the Soviet Union—a power that, because of its internal economic and social structure, is able to follow and does follow a policy of peace without contradictions. The war had made a new line of conduct possible in the foreign relations of the two great capitalist nations, Great Britain and the United States. But the smell of gunpowder was still contaminating the air when the secret conclaves of Anglo-Yankee financial oligarchies were starting to dynamite the foundations of the newly laid peace.

. . .

In spite of the fact that historical circumstances led the peoples of Latin America, in their determination to save themselves from Nazi aggression, to collaborate closely with the Roosevelt government (justifiable, under those conditions), this particular instance does not justify the general concept of Pan Americanism, based as it is on supposed historical ties, as postulated by the obliging lawyers of imperialism. There is a fundamental incompatibility between American monopolies and the basic tendencies of national sovereignty and liberty of the Latin American countries. These represent two conflicting—in fact, irreconcilably antagonistic—trends in contemporary historical development.

dolar (Montevideo: Ediciones Pueblos Unidos, 1947), pp. 16, 198, 205, 245.

American transactions in Latin America during World War II offer a typical example. In most of the trade agreements signed during the conflict, the United States managed to assure itself the control of Latin American raw materials, as well as a future advantage in the markets of these countries. These raw materials, under apparently reciprocal agreements, were and are still at the disposal of American monopolies. Since all these raw materials fall under the heading of "strategic," the Truman Plan, for example, would make America's exclusive position in this regard definitive.

British and Yankee monopolies are converging on the Latin American market. The United States is profiting from this vying for power, from advantages obtained during the war, and in particular from commitments and agreements made under the Pan American system. There is, therefore, no Pan American economic combination that does not lay South America at the feet of Yankee industry.

. . .

So-called Pan American brotherhood, it is clear, lacks social and economic foundations of any kind; only effervescent charlatans, unprincipled Quislings, and the power-hungry can unabashedly assert that the downtrodden Indian or Creole of Latin America has a communion of interests with the limitless wealth of Wall Street or the millionaire set on Park Avenue. The historical control that monopolies have exerted on us Latin Americans ranges, just as it does for Asians and other oppressed peoples, from dependency to semi-colonialism, and from semi-colonialism to outright colonialism.

If this inference can be drawn from an objective

study of the economic reality of Latin America, it is easy to deduce that the national destiny and social development of our countries cannot be fulfilled by a dismembered hemisphere ruled by Washington. Rather, these goals must be realized on a worldwide level: by carrying out a planned economic and political program together with all peace-loving forces and independent peoples.

17

JULIO CESAR JOBET

Consequences of Imperialist Penetration in Chile*

*

Imperialism is fundamentally an economic phenomenon. Hence its resurgence as a subject of continental debate, accompanied by a battery of figures and economic data that claim to show the incessant "exploitation" to which Latin America is subjected. In the following selection, Julio César Jobet, a well-known Chilean economist of Marxist leanings, describes the gloomy balance that imperialistic penetration has produced in his country.

The data that we have studied show us that foreign investments have come to Chile as a form of Anglo-American capitalist expansion, exploiting the working classes on a vast scale, and subjugating and impoverishing the whole country. Chile is an economic

* Translated from Julio César Jobet, "Consecuencias de la penetración imperialista en Chile," *Ensayo crítico del desarrollo económico-social de Chile* (Santiago: Editorial Universitaria, 1951), pp. 203–229. Printed by permission of the author.

trading-post of the large foreign consortia. Their penetration has not been violent; their methods include diplomacy, low-cost buying, the signing of loans, long-term concessions, monopolies, etc.—all of which have led to the handing over of the nation's resources. Diplomacy has played its role in Chile, just as violence and armed intervention have played theirs in Mexico, Nicaragua, Puerto Rico, and Panama.

Chile is a country that produces raw materials. A high percentage of its exports is unfinished goods. This creates negative factors that determine the standard of living of its population and also the domestic economy's strong dependence on foreign trade. Exports are the decisive factor; fluctuations in exports are responsible for the booms and depressions of the entire nation.

The dependence of the country on foreign trade is all the worse, inasmuch as its exports consist of only two products: saltpeter and copper. It is for this reason that exports are vulnerable to changes taking place in the overall world-trade situation, and to readjustments brought on by scientific findings, discoveries of new sources of supply, tariff increases, or other market variations, such as are generally beyond the control of an exporting country. Saltpeter is a good example: the development of synthetic products brought about a collapse in the nation's economy and a long period of disturbances.

It is a fact that the national economy is dependent on copper. Foreign consortia may, at any moment, reduce production if they feel that this would suit their private interests. This happened in 1946 when they decreased output by more than 100,000 tons, thereby causing grave disturbances in Chile. As a result of such phenomena, Chile maintains a series of relations that assure the country of a semi-colonial economic status. In spite of its being politically independent, Chile's economic ties with the industrialized nations are colonial in nature.

Imperialism has enjoyed the support of the nation's landowning class, because it strengthens the latter's domination, by assuring the survival of the large estates, whose low yield has had a secure market in places where mining is carried on. In addition, it has formed a financial bourgeoisie to look after its interests, which is united with the landowning oligarchy, and made up of new sectors: bureaucrats, managers, mercenary lawyers, venal congressmen, bribable magistrates, and elements of the upstart and money-hungry middle class. Lastly, imperialism leads to an oppressive parasitism—that is, to an increase in the number of those who live by means other than productive work. The large estates and imperialism in Chile explain why the working population constitutes hardly one-third of the total population. And, of that one-third, even fewer are real creators of wealth.

Education has been put into the hands of reactionaries or of an inert and fossilized bureaucracy; it has no truly democratic socioeconomic meaning. Professors have always been persecuted for their ideas about social reform, and have lived under harsh conditions and on meager salaries. The scarcity of classrooms is impressive. Among school officials, the attitude that has prevailed in their colonial minds toward the tasks of education has been one of downright scorn. Technical and professional education hardly exists. The misguided orientation of our state educational system can be seen in the following figures: in a mining country such as ours, the university granted, from 1898 to 1918, 1,700 law degrees, but only 22 mining-engineering degrees.

Our economic and social backwardness has brought on great moral decadence. Because of our permanent misery, national morality has greatly declined. The austerity, the sense of responsibility, and the sobriety that apparently existed in the nineteenth century—in short, the moral values that underlie the country's development—all have decayed and given way to an unbridled wave of corruption, mediocrity, and opportunism. A tragic demoralization has been manifest, since the time of parliamentary republican government. It would seem that the establishment of the saltpeter industry has indeed been a corrupting factor. The sharpening of class antagonism has helped to disintegrate the existing national consciousness. This event was expressed by the astonishing generosity with which mineral resources were handed over to foreign capital, in exchange for a ridiculously low tax (levied on foreign mining companies), which freed the rich class from paying taxes. This class shows incredible loyalty and devotion to foreign capitalists and is now leading us toward complete denationalization of the country's economy as well as to frightful poverty.

18

ANTONIO GARCÍA

⸻ ◦•◦ ⸻

Oligarchies and the
Agony of Bourgeois Democracy*

❋

In addition to the criticism of imperialism, one of the most recurrent themes in the Latin American left, both Marxist and non-Marxist, is the attack on those national groups that are accused of extending their support to foreign economic penetration. Antonio García, a distinguished Colombian writer and former professor at the National University in Bogota, tries to explain in this essay written in 1957 how the political strengthening of such minority groups paralyzes the democratic process and corrupts the entire social structure of the country.

When I speak of the "agony" of bourgeois democracy, I use the word as it might be used in political science: the disappearance of those forces that are the life-blood of institutions. What is meant, in other words, is a loss of "authenticity" on the part of those forms of government that have been identified with repre-

* Translated from Antonio García, "La agonía de la democracia burguesa," *La democracia en la teoría y en la práctica* (Bogota: Cooperativa Colombiana de Editores, 1957), pp. 126–130. Printed by permission of the author.

sentative democracy. Dead institutions can continue to stand simply as empty structures without necessarily having to be buried. Bourgeois parliamentary government, the principle of voting rights and that of free initiative, and the notion of the sovereignty of the people are still present, but they lack the authenticity that would breathe life into them. They subsist formally, without vitality and without any function, like those useless Greek columns that are slapped on to the stiff facade of an ugly building.

Bourgeois democracy has had to wither away slowly in order to prolong the life of capitalistic economy: its principles of freedom have not been compatible with the needs of an economy that is based on monopolies; its outdated humanistic philosophy has not fitted in with the domination of men by things, nor with the systematization of culture as a market; its machinery of popular representation has not been compatible with the dynastic empire of oligarchies.

In Latin America, the world war and the postwar period brought about a greater concentration of income in a small number of hands. Controls that had ostensibly been designed to ensure state intervention in the war and postwar economy did not fulfill their function as economic regulators because they had actually been set in motion in order to promote a black market based on corruption and privilege. All state controls became privileged sources of enrichment. Not only did what was known as the traditional order sink into political and economic decay in many Latin American countries, but its public morals, its way of life and the facade of honesty, which served to camouflage (and to limit) the use of fraud in politics, also collapsed. These ruins served as a foundation for the new psychology of the wealthy class. All traditional values were cast aside in this inflationary economy, which was the price Latin America paid for the war and for the peace as well.

It is in this environment that the psychology of arrogantly affirming the power of the wealthy class is being spread. The use of politics—that is, the use of the state, of parliament, of political parties, and of politicians—to defend the interests of wealth is no longer hidden. One of the results is, therefore, the *corporative organization of capitalism.* Whereas the people are scattered and unorganized, the rich class sets up huge, powerful corporations, ready to manipulate all segments of the political machinery.

These agglomerations of companies and corporations have political and social goals: the unification of the upper classes into a management class, into one merciless, solid bloc, and the establishment of an organization that is able to put political pressure on parties, the state, and public opinion.

This is the new social phenomenon in our countries —the organization of wealth on a corporate basis, in order to bring about a new oligarchical order. Political and economic control has not passed from one class to another, but rather from an open class to a closed group of that class; sociologically, oligarchy is nothing but an impenetrable circle imbedded within the class. An oligarchy not only wields economic control; it also uses all facets of political activity in its own interest. *The secret of its strategy and power* is thus its ability to distribute privileges. This is its political objective: to grab hold of all sources of privilege—which implies and leads to an annihilation of democratic government.

Politics logically adopted a new style. *One had to pass across the drawbridge of industrial corporations on the way to the Treasury Department,* and large private enterprises frequently took away from the state the officials who had been determining its labor, trade, and oil policies. Large stockholders, on the other hand, were able to serve as government advisers: in cabinet posts, national banks, development agencies, and economic planning commissions.

State organs also got in on this *dynastic insurrection.* What elements or groups in the nation were capable of resisting this insurrection of the privileged? The state was equipped to resist the insurrection of the underdogs, of the workers of all classes—in short, of all those who could have recourse to democratic machinery in order to obtain more democracy or, at least, an authentic democracy.

The unavoidable counterpart of this huge distortion of the parliamentary system is the absence of popular interest in parliament's activities and development. If the interests of the working classes are not expressed in congress, these classes no longer participate, psychologically speaking, in parliamentary life; they are just spectators.

In this regard, those factors that are most directly linked to public opinion should be included: newspapers, political parties, and labor unions. Newspapers thrive on the financial power of the upper classes and feed the people only propaganda. Political parties are bureaucratic hordes, which have never developed the people's political consciousness simply because they consider the people to be a mere electoral market, a vote but not a voice. Labor unions are the parties' electoral appendages and do not know how to play their great historical role, that of a political school for all working classes.

Political democracy has collapsed everywhere: above, in parliamentary or government circles within the state; below, in labor unions and political parties. If not even the unions or parties were democratic, they could hardly ask the same of or impose it on the government of a crippled country; nobody can give what he does not have, nor can he fight for a cause that he has helped to defeat.

19

CAIO PRADO, JR.

———•••———

Crisis on the March[*]

✳

Pointing up the extent and continuity of Marxist criticism eight years after Jobet described the problem in Chile, an eminent Brazilian historian, Caio Prado, Jr., analyzes the permanent and continuous deterioration of Brazil's economic situation as a result of the same basic cause: the penetration of imperialism. This selection is taken from one of the best known Marxist studies of the economic history of Brazil.

American imperialism is thus achieving the first (and perhaps the most important) part of its objectives in Brazil at the present time. The second aspect of its penetration (which coincides with the first one—control of our raw materials) is the monopolization of our major and most productive economic activities, thus placing them at the disposal of imperialism and reducing them to mere adjuncts of huge international trusts and monopolies. This is what is hap-

[*] Translated from Caio Prado, Jr., "La crisis en marcha," *Historia económica del Brasil* (Buenos Aires: Editorial Futuro, 1959), pp. 359–365. Printed by permission of the author.

pening in the fields of trade, finance, and industry, whose essential and most promising sectors are being progressively and ever increasingly penetrated and occupied (and many times absorbed) by the huge financial systems and blocs that dominate contemporary capitalism.

This process of penetration dates back to long before the last world war. But what characterizes it, in the phase in which we find ourselves today, is the intensity of its development, which is in turn reflected in the growing burden imposed on the country's finances. The intensive participation of foreign capital in Brazilian economic activities is the major cause of the chronic imbalance of our foreign finances, with all its grave consequences: financial instability, inflation, grave and uncontrollable disturbances that often repeat themselves, threatening to turn into endemic crises.

According to government calculations of our balance of payments, the mean annual outlay for the payment of foreign capital investments reached three billion cruzeiros in the years 1947–1953. We can better understand the significance of that figure if we bear in mind that it is surpassed only by coffee exports, and far outstrips that of the other commodities that are involved in our trade. Such a difficult situation, which tends to grow with the development of imperialist penetration, clearly surpasses our ability to pay. Our export receipts will never be enough to pay for imports, unless great sacrifices are made in regard to the latter, which is precisely what is now happening in Brazil. But even those sacrifices have not been enough, and we have been able to fulfill our obligations abroad only by running heavily into debt. This means an increase in our obligations and therefore an aggravation of the evil.

It is frequently argued that foreign investments can be determined or oriented in such a way that imports may be reduced. But it is, practically speaking, impossible to orient foreign investments, which naturally look for what is most lucrative for them and not what is most suitable for us. We must also bear in mind that virtually the only substantial saving in the field of imports would ordinarily be the cost of labor, as it is included in goods that were previously imported but would thenceforth be produced in Brazil.

Moreover, events in our economic history (particularly the most recent ones) show that the increase in foreign investments is accompanied by a growing imbalance in our foreign trade, which offers more and more reason for concern. The situation is now such that new investments cannot even balance the payments we are now making abroad as interest for those very investments. We conclude that foreign capital, in penetrating ever more deeply into our economy and taking over our economic activities for its own benefit (thus increasing our commitments abroad), is doing so at the expense of Brazil's resources.

The link between imperialism and our colonial system, which is based on the import of basic commodities, is very clear, inasmuch as the income coming from such exports is used by the imperialists to obtain the profits that are the raison d'être of the existence of imperialism.

20

SILVIO FRONDIZI

The Left and the Socialist Revolution in Argentina*

✳

In the following selection Silvio Frondizi, a professor at the University of Buenos Aires, disqualifies the old leadership that claims to direct the proletariat in its revolutionary struggle, at the same time that he radically posits the necessity of the socialist revolution. The raising of this issue by Frondizi, the founder of the Movimiento de Izquierda Revolucionaria or Revolutionary Left Movement (MIR) of Argentina, is symptomatic of the radical posture of the new Latin American left after World War II.

Although the word "left" does not have much scientific value, its use has conferred on it the meaning of a critical revolutionary position vis-à-vis the current capitalist society, aiming at its transformation into a

* Translated from Silvio Frondizi, *Las izquierdas en el proceso político argentino,* in news report edited by Carlos Strasser (Buenos Aires: Editorial Palestra, 1959), pp. 27–52. Printed by permission of the author.

future socialist society. All those who strive for the quickest and most clear-cut rise of the proletariat to power are, therefore, on the left.

Until the appearance of the Communist Party, the Socialist Party was the only political party with a scientific basis. The contradiction between its relatively revolutionary program and its reformist or evolutionist methods, however, led it gradually to a position that was out of phase with our actual historic conditions.

The Communist Party could have been a way out for the crisis of socialism, but once it abandoned the revolutionary path to act in furtherance of the national interests of the Stalinist bureaucracy, it lost its opportunity to win the political leadership of our proletariat. In this connection, let us not lose sight of the Party's attitude toward Anglo-Yankee imperialism during World War II, its alliance with the Unión Democrática and its seesawings vis-à-vis Peronism.

As for Trotskyism, we believe that, while it is the diametrical antithesis of Stalinism, it is not its vanquishing synthesis.

We consider Peronism to have been the most important attempt and the last accomplishment of the bourgeois-democratic revolution in Argentina, whose failure is due to the inability of the national bourgeoisie to accomplish this task.

The national bourgeoisie is incapable of bringing about the bourgeois-democratic revolution, because of its alliance with imperialism and with the oligarchy, and its profound hatred and fear of the working class. If we have to depend on it, not only will we not advance a single step, but we shall actually retrogress from whatever has been achieved and lapse into the worst forms of backwardness and dictatorship. Nor can the petty bourgeoisie serve as a guiding factor in the revolutionary process, because of its intermediate and fluctuating position, its heterogeneous make-up, and its disintegration. The task of the left is to help to redeem those elements and sectors of this class that are capable of backing up the proletariat's struggle.

The Movimiento de Izquierda Revolucionaria believes that the current crisis in Argentine society can be solved only by a socialist revolution. The transition to the new socialist society entails an important problem, for it is plain that not all aspects of the bourgeois-democratic revolution have been carried out in Argentina. Once this conclusion has been established and it is recognized that the bourgeoisie has become too feeble to be a force capable of bringing its own revolution into being, and that it is therefore upon the proletariat as a leading force that this mission must devolve, the problem is settled by thinking of it no longer as a question of accomplishing the bourgeois-democratic revolution as a self-contained stage, as a goal, but rather as one of performing bourgeois-democratic tasks during the course of the socialist revolution.

Included among these immediate tasks are: the struggle against imperialism, which can be waged only by a revolutionary Marxist party based on the masses. For us, therefore, the policy of Popular Fronts, of alliance between the left and the centrist petty bourgeois forces, may be one of the most dangerous forms of demagogy, with baneful consequences for the working class.

If the old leadership, which for decades had

marched apart from the Argentine proletariat, insists on choosing, not from among the movements of the left but from among the different factions of the bourgeoisie, whether these are called Unión Democrática, Peronism, or Frondizism, then their own masses will be the ones that will turn their backs on them, tired of circling about the well in a path that leads nowhere. The dilemma of the hour is very clear: either socialism or bourgeois dictatorship. Let each man choose his side in the struggle.

Part V

The Cuban Revolution and Its Aftermath

1959–1968

CHRONOLOGY
OF
IMPORTANT EVENTS

✳

1959　Revolutionary government is installed in Cuba.

1960　A split in Acción Democrática in Venezuela brings the Movimiento de Izquierda Revolucionaria (MIR) into being.

　　　A military coup takes place in Guatemala.

1961　Fidel Castro proclaims the Cuban Revolution as socialist.

　　　The Bay of Pigs expedition ends in victory for Castro.

　　　Molina Rafael Trujillo, dictator of the Dominican Republic for thirty-one years, is assassinated.

　　　João Goulart is inaugurated as president of Brazil (September).

1962　O.A.S. meets in Punta del Este: Cuba is expelled; the Alliance for Progress is born.

　　　The 13th of November Movement, commanded by Jon Sosa, initiates guerrilla warfare in Guatemala.

　　　In a *coup d'état* in Argentina, the government of Arturo Frondizi is overthrown.

　　　A military junta seizes power in Peru.

　　　The Cuban missile crisis takes place.

　　　Juan Bosch wins the presidential elections in the Dominican Republic.

1963　Belaúnde Terry, candidate of Acción Popular, is elected president of Peru.

Bosch is overthrown in a military coup in the Dominican Republic.

A military coup takes place in Honduras.

Elections are held in Venezuela: Raúl Leoni, the candidate of Acción Democrática, wins the presidency.

1964 Goulart is overthrown in a military coup in Brazil.

Eduardo Frei, the Christian Democratic candidate, is elected president of Chile.

A military coup in Bolivia topples Paz Estenssoro's government.

Chile and the U.S.S.R. re-establish diplomatic relations.

1965 A revolt erupts in the Dominican Republic: U.S. forces land on the island.

1966 The Tricontinental Conference is held in Havana; Castro criticizes China.

Joaquín Balaguer is elected president of the Dominican Republic.

A military coup takes place in Argentina.

The MIR and the Communist Party clash openly in Venezuela.

1967 Castro attacks the Venezuelan Communist Party.

Mounting guerrilla warfare in Bolivia.

Organization of Latin American Solidarity meets in Havana.

Ché Guevara is killed in Bolivia in a skirmish with the Bolivian Army.

1968 Castro names this year the year of "the heroic guerrilla fighter."

Aníbal Escalante and his followers are sentenced to fifteen years in prison in Cuba.

21

ERNESTO (CHÉ) GUEVARA

Cuba, Historical Exception or Vanguard in the Anti-Colonial Struggle?*

✳

The Argentine Ernesto (Ché) Guevara has been one of the few, if not the only one, among the participants in the Cuban Revolution who have tried to raise theoretical questions regarding the Cuban experience. In this article, the author of Guerrilla Warfare *presents the essence of a thesis that has been, and still is, the subject of widespread controversy among Marxists. The abrupt disappearance of Guevara in March 1965 gave rise to constant speculation. For many, the elimination of Ché, the authentic representative of the revolutionary left, represented the decline of the Cuban Revolution toward Soviet bureaucracy. In October 1967, perhaps a victim of his own legend, Ché was killed by the Bolivian Army after a guerrilla campaign that failed.*

Never in America has there been an event with such unusual characteristics, such profound roots and such

---

* Translated from Ché Guevara, "Cuba, excepción histórica o

far-reaching consequences for the destiny of the progressive movements in the hemisphere, as our revolutionary war. This has been the case to such an extent that some have characterized it as the cardinal event in our America, and the most important after the Russian Revolution, the victory over the military might of Hitler, and the triumph of the Chinese Revolution.

This movement, broadly heterodox in its form and manifestations, has nevertheless followed the general line of all of the great historical events of the century, which has been marked by the struggles against colonialism and the transition to socialism. Nevertheless, some factions have sought to find in it a series of extraordinary roots and features that have been artificially inflated to the point of labeling them "determinant." There is reference to the exceptional nature of the Cuban Revolution, whereby it is supposedly established that the form and course of the Cuban Revolution are unique products of that revolution, and that the historic transition of the peoples in other countries of America will be different.

We accept the fact that there have been exceptional factors that have given our revolution peculiar features, and it is an established fact that each revolution depends on such special factors. But it is no less established that all revolutions will follow laws that cannot be violated by society. Let us therefore analyze the factors of this so-called special case.

The first, and perhaps the most important, the most original, is that telluric force called Fidel Castro—a name that in just a few years has attained historic

vanguardia en la lucha anticolonialista," *Verde Olivo* (Havana, April 9, 1961), pp. 22–29.

significance and whose merits we consider worthy of comparison with those of the most outstanding figures in Latin American history. Fidel is a man of tremendous personal magnetism, destined to assume the role of leader in any movement in which he takes part. He has all the characteristics typical of a great leader: audacity, force, the desire to keep his ear attuned to the will of the people. But he has other important qualities: the capacity to absorb knowledge and experience, a grasp of the overall picture in a given situation, boundless faith in the future. . . . Fidel Castro did more than anyone else in Cuba to construct the now formidable apparatus of the revolution.

Nevertheless, no one can affirm that there were political and social conditions in Cuba that were totally different from those in any other country of the hemisphere, that it was precisely because of such difference that the revolution came about. Nor can it be charged that Fidel Castro made the revolution. Fidel directed the Cuban Revolution, interpreting the profound political unrest that was preparing the people for the great leap along the road to revolution. Certain conditions also existed that were not peculiar to Cuba but that could, with difficulty, be utilized again by other peoples, for the reason that imperialism—unlike some progressive groups—does learn from its mistakes.

The condition that we might describe as exceptional is that North American imperialism was confused and was thus never able to assess the true extent of the Cuban Revolution. By the time imperialism wanted to react, when it realized that the group of inexperienced young men who were parading the streets of Havana in triumph were clearly aware of their political responsibilities and had an iron resolve to carry them out, it was already too late.

We do not consider that there was anything exceptional in the fact that the bourgeoisie, or a large part of this sector, showed itself in favor of the revolutionary war, while at the same time it sought solutions that would make possible the replacement of the Batista government by elements that would be disposed to hold the revolution in check. Nor was there anything exceptional in the fact that some of the *latifundist* elements adopted a neutral attitude, or at least one of non-belligerency toward the insurrectionist forces. In this way, non-revolutionary forces in effect helped smooth the road to political power for the revolutionary forces.

By going one step further, we can point out another exceptional factor: in the majority of the localities in Cuba, the peasants had become proletarianized by the demands of the great capitalist, semi-mechanized farms and had attained greater class consciousness. But we must add that, throughout the original territory first dominated by the rebel army, there was a rural population of a different social and cultural origin than that which was to be found in the settlements around the large semi-mechanized farms in Cuba. In effect, the Sierra Maestra is a place where the peasants who go there to seek a new plot of land, which they wrest from the state or from some greedy landholder, find a refuge. The soldiers who constituted our first guerrilla army of peasants came from the latter group, a group that had already demonstrated in the most aggressive manner a love for the land and a desire to possess it, a group that displayed what might be termed "the spirit of the petty bourgeoisie." The peasant fights because he wants land, for himself, for his children, and wants to control it, to be able to sell it, and to improve his lot by working it.

Regardless of that spirit, the peasant quickly learns that he cannot satisfy his desire to possess the land without breaking up the *latifundia* system. Radical agrarian reform, which is the only way to give land to the peasant, runs counter to the interests of the imperialists, the large landholders, and the sugar and livestock magnates. The bourgeoisie is afraid to go against such interests; the proletariat is not afraid. Thus the progress of the revolution unites the workers and the peasants.

I do not believe that any other special factors can be cited. Let us now see what are the permanent bases for all social phenomena in America, or at least for those that bring about changes that can assume the magnitude of a revolution, such as that in Cuba.

First in chronological order, although not necessarily in order of importance, is the *latifundia* system. The large estate was the base of the economic power of the ruling class during the period following the revolution that was carried out in the last century in order to obtain independence from the colonial powers. But that class always lags behind the march of social progress, even though its more alert groups in certain places may change the form of their capital investment and at times make progress toward mechanized farming. In any case, the initial liberating revolution did not succeed in destroying the *latifundia* class, which continued to maintain a system of peonage on the land and invariably behaved in a reactionary manner.

The large landholder realized that he could not survive alone and entered into an alliance with the monopolies, the most vigorous and brutal oppressors of the American peoples. America was the battlefield in the internecine struggles of imperialism, and the wars between Costa Rica and Nicaragua, the separation of Panama, the struggle between Paraguay and Bolivia, etc., are merely facets of this titanic battle, a battle that was decided almost totally in favor of the American monopolies during the period following World War II.

What is underdevelopment? A dwarf with an enormous head is "underdeveloped," so long as his feeble legs do not support his body. That is what we are: countries with economies that have been distorted by the action of the imperialists, in subjugation to a single crop, a single product, a single market. This vicious circle produces what has become the common denominator of the people of America from the Rio Grande to the South Pole. That common denominator is the HUNGER OF THE PEOPLE, who are tired of being oppressed and exploited to the limit.

Thus, we see that there are these enormous and inescapable common denominators—the *latifundia* system, the underdevelopment, the hunger of the people —all which existed in that Cuba of before. . . . What did we do to free ourselves from them? We merely applied some formulas, which we have described on other occasions as our empirical remedy for the vast ills of our beloved Latin America.

The objective conditions for the struggle are provided by the people's hunger, their reaction to that hunger, etc. In America the subjective conditions are lacking; of these the most important is an awareness of the possibilities of achieving victory by following the road of violence against the imperialist powers and their allies within the country. These conditions are being created, however, by means of the armed conflict that begins to make the need for change more evident, by the defeat of the army by the people's army, and the subsequent annihilation of the former as an essential condition of any authentic revolution.

In pointing out the foregoing, we must repeat that the setting for this struggle must be the countryside, and that an army of peasants, working out of the countryside and seeking the noble objectives for which the rural population is fighting, will provide the great liberating army of the future, as it has already done in Cuba.

But there are also conditions that will make the struggle more difficult in other countries of America. Imperialism has learned its lesson and it will not let itself be taken by surprise in any corner of the hemisphere. The bourgeoisie of the various countries, despite their differences with imperialism, are in general incapable of maintaining a coherent position of opposition to imperialism: they fear the revolution more than they fear the despotic domination of the imperialists. The upper middle class is openly opposed to the revolution and does not hesitate to ally itself with imperialism and the feudal landowners in order to block the revolution's path.

Even when there exist great urban concentrations, it may be advisable to base the campaign outside the cities. The presence of a nucleus of guerrillas in the mountains maintains a continuing focus of rebellion. Something entirely different happens in the city; armed warfare against the repressive army can be carried to undreamed of ends, but only so long as there is a powerful force pitted against another force, not while there is only a small group. . . . There are no arms; they must be seized from the enemy. That is why the battle in the large cities must be initiated through a clandestine process designed to capture military groups or to continue to capture weapons, one by one, in a succession of surprise attacks. In the latter case, rapid progress can be made, and it cannot be denied that a popular rebellion, based on guerrilla tactics, would not be impossible within the city.

Dark days lie ahead for Latin America. Once the war against imperialism is launched, it is essential to be consistent, to strike hard where it hurts, without pause, never giving ground but moving constantly forward, constantly counterattacking, continually meeting any new aggression with ever stronger pressure from the masses of the people. This is the road to victory.

22

ALVARO MENDOZA DÍEZ

The Lessons of the Cuban Revolution*

Wary, like many other Latin American Marxists, in his analysis of the lessons to be derived from the internal process of the Cuban Revolution, which poses difficult questions regarding the participation of parties and social classes, in the following selection Alvaro Mendoza Díez dwells at length on the least problematical aspect and the one most agreeable to the Communists: the variation in the correlation of international forces in favor of socialism. This article is taken from a book written in 1960, when some still thought that Castro was not a Communist. Since then Mendoza Díez has modified his opinions on the Soviet Union, joining those who believe that the U.S.S.R. is now on the road to revisionism and capitalistic restoration.[1] *Currently teaching at the University of Trujillo in Peru, Mendoza has just completed a book on the sociology and metaphysics of man.*

---

* Translated from Alvaro Mendoza Díez, *La revolución de los profesionales e intelectuales en latinoamerica* (Mexico City: Instituto de Investigaciones Sociológicas U.N.A.M., 1962), pp. 160–169. Printed by permission of the author.

[1] Letter of May 3, 1967, from Mendoza Díez to Luis Aguilar.

In our opinion, the following are the principal lessons to be learned from the Cuban Revolution that is developing before our eyes:

1) The geographic "cradle of the revolution" has great importance for those countries of Latin America in which the land problem is the fundamental one. Apparently the revolution led by Fidel Castro serves to confirm the validity of the dictum that the mountainous regions constitute excellent locales from which to launch revolutions or to carry on prolonged resistance, with the possibility of eventual victory. Thus it was that in 1821, in the city of Lima, General San Martín proclaimed the independence of Peru although the Spaniards held out in the hills for more than three years until they were wiped out in 1824. Similarly, in the War of 1879 between Peru and Chile, the Chilean armies occupied the entire Peruvian coast, but that did not prevent Marshal Andrés Avelino Cáceres from continuing the resistance in the La Libertad Mountains in northern Peru. Although it was forced by persecution to retreat to the rural areas, the Chinese Communist Party took refuge there and incorporated the peasants into its shock troops. Finally, Fidel Castro launched his revolution from the Sierra Maestra.

It may therefore be concluded, first, that the mountainous rural areas constitute excellent strategic regions, which can be used for either revolutionary or reactionary resistance; and, second, that they also represent the social heartland for movements of an agrarian nature, since it is precisely in those areas that the land-hungry groups are to be found.

2) Therefore, economic and social victories are achieved over a shorter period. In this connection, it must be pointed out that, despite its greater age, the

Bolivian Revolution (which took place in 1952) has recorded less progress in the matter of agricultural cooperatives than, for example, the Cuban Revolution.

3) The triumph of the revolution is assured in the interior of the country, by providing the people with arms or maintaining the revolutionary army intact.

4) Imperialism and feudalism may both be attacked at the same time, when there is courage and daring on the part of the leaders and of the people's army. Moreover, all of the experience obtained from past revolutions that have taken place in other countries can be used—such as, for example, that of Guatemala, where the regime was overthrown at the very moment it had begun to affect the interests of American imperialism. From this point of view, it may well be said that the same phenomenon that appeared in Latin America during the revolutions for independence is again appearing in Latin America—for independence, that is, the first uprisings were put down, yet by that very act the ultimate victory that followed was prepared. In Peru, at least, this is what happened, just as it has happened before in the majority of the countries on this subcontinent.

The influence of the Cuban Revolution on other Latin American countries is another of its characteristics. Its spectacular victory, the courageous manner with which the leaders faced imperialism in all fields, even in the United Nations, the determination that has been noted in attaining the final results, etc., have not only won the support of public opinion, which is more or less apolitical, but are also encouraging revolutionary movements in other countries. The very presence of an Argentine in the revolutionary ranks—the famous Ché Guevara, who is also a doctor—is viewed with much sympathy and there is no lack of people who because of this mere fact say: the Cuban Revolution has an international character, since Guevara is holding an important position in the new regime.

6) The support given to the Castro revolution by the Soviet Union, as evidenced, among other things, by the promise to resort to the language of guided missiles if the United States attacked the Pearl of the Antilles. For us, this has singular importance, although what is called "impartiality" may be put to the test on this point. Opinions are divided with regard to the Soviet aid that Castro has not hesitated to accept openly. For many people, Castro has made a very serious error in entering into commitments with the Soviet Union. For us, it was undoubtedly a tactical measure on the part of the bearded revolutionary: it was the attitude of the shipwrecked man who grabs the first plank he finds, the attitude of the businessman who is threatened with bankruptcy and does not hesitate to accept the first loan that is offered to him, even though he may not like the lender, the attitude of the man who has been abandoned by all his friends (the Latin American nations) in the most difficult of situations.

There is no doubt that Castro is not a Communist; but there is also no doubt that it is not necessary to be a Communist in order to accept aid from communism, when it is on this acceptance that the survival of the ship of revolution depends. The charge of communism against the Castro regime is completely lacking in common sense and logic. Would the leader of the Cuban Revolution have accepted Soviet aid—not only economic aid but the promise of military aid as well —if all the Latin American nations, or the majority of

them, had supported his anti-imperialist movement
without reservations? Undoubtedly not. He accepted it
only when he realized that all or virtually all of them
were turning their backs on him, and not only that,
they had even gone so far as to drum up a meeting of
the countries to see what attitude would be taken
against the Cuban Revolution. If they did not go so far
as to adopt a position similar or analogous to that taken
in the case of Guatemala, it was because the circumstances had changed. At the time of the Guatemala of
Jacobo Arbenz, Russia had not yet launched the sput-
nik, nor had it perfected guided missiles; it was not,
in short, the leading military power on this planet, as
it now is.

Every nationalist revolution merely encourages other
countries to launch identical movements. But every
socialist revolution assures the future, guarantees the
triumph, of every nationalist revolution. When Egypt
nationalized the Suez Canal, for example, that act
stimulated a desire on the part of the people of Panama to make the Panama Canal their own. But this
event cannot be compared with all that is implied by
the promise of aid from the Soviet Union, when it thus
offers itself as the guarantor for the continued success
of nationalist revolutions that may occur in the future
in any part of the world, and not just in Latin America. To ignore this fact is to ignore the mechanics and
the dynamics of the great Cold War that is in progress
all over the world at this time, a contest that is not
between world imperialism and nationalism. This is
the first great contradiction that confronts the world
of today.

The petty bourgeoisie, whether it is labeled anarchist, nationalist, or "socialist" radical, etc., is sat-

isfied to believe that its anti-imperialist revolution is the most important of all; but that is an error. No anti-imperialism is more authentic than Communist anti-imperialism. This is an objective fact and not a subjective speculation.

The petty bourgeois spirit in political matters is causing serious harm in Latin America, especially if those who have it are intellectuals who enjoy prestige and guide public opinion, or if they are militant politicians who aspire to be leaders of the masses. Anti-imperialism of the petty bourgeois type may be enough in the first stages of agitation, but it becomes reactionary in the real revolutionary phases. The same sentiment may reverse itself even during the course of events.

23

JORGE ABELARDO RAMOS

—— • • • ——

Dangers of Empiricism
in Latin American Revolutions*

✳

*One of the sharpest critics of the Communist Party
of Argentina, Jorge Abelardo Ramos is a distinguished
Argentine member of the New Left who aspires to
a better and fuller application of Marxism in Latin
America. He rejects some aspects of Ché Guevara's
thesis, considering them dogmatic and not quite
Marxist. Arguments similar to those put forward by
Ramos have been employed, although in a less direct and less clear fashion, by various orthodox
Communists in their criticism of Ché's conclusions.[1]
It is significant that the book from which this selec-
tion is taken was written three years before Guevara
died trying to apply his Cuban formula to Bolivia.*

The Cuban Revolution has unleashed a wave of
indiscriminate admiration by Latin American leftists.

---

* Translated from Jorge Abelardo Ramos, "Los peligros del
empiricismo en la revolución latinoamericana," *La lucha por
un partido revolucionario* (Buenos Aires: Ediciones Pampa y
Cielo, 1964), pp. 93–109. Printed by permission of the author.

[1] A good example of orthodox criticism of Ché's thesis is G.

Substantially healthy in origin, this adulation threatens to paralyze the functioning of Marxist thought, and especially revolutionary action based on this ideology.

In reading Guevara's ideas on the Cuban experiment and its application to Latin America, it is sad to note that the treatment of the subject is inferior to the subject itself. Guevara does not seem to notice the unitary nature—historically and politically speaking —of our revolution. On the contrary, he dismisses the great strategic problem of the Latin-American revolution by adopting just one set of formulas. Although it is true that Guevara, in glossing over the existence of a nationalistic problem in Latin America, makes a serious error, his empirical solutions aggravate that tragic error even further. In view of the Balkanization of Latin America into twenty states, which in itself is the most obvious proof of imperialistic action, the application of the very same formulas to seize power in Panama, or Argentina, or Uruguay, or Venezuela, shows that Guevara's ideas are mistaken in regard to both strategy and tactics.

The domineering personality of Fidel Castro is, for Guevara, the first "exceptional" characteristic of the Cuban Revolution. Castro's personality is explained by Castro's virtues. Had Guevara not proclaimed himself a Marxist, this tautology would injure only Guevara. But, since he is at the same time a Marxist and an important leader in the Cuban Revolution, it is also Marxist ideas that turn out to be definitely jeopardized by this poor statement. If Guevara had told us that Fidel Castro personified his people, he

---

Luiz Araújo's excellent article "A revolução cubana e a teoria dos focos insurrecionais," *Revista civilização brisileira,* No. 14 (July 1967), pp. 85–108.

would have been telling the truth. No person can be explained intrinsically, except in terms of the idealistic view of history. To explain Fidel intrinsically and his personality by his intrinsic virtues is tantamount to removing him from the historical process, to overestimating the personal factor, and to transforming him into a sacred product.

It is surprising that Guevara uses the word "America" without any additions, thereby disregarding the existence of two different Americas. What is more astonishing is that when he mentions the separation of Panama from Colombia, he refers to it as the manifestation of the inter-imperialist struggle "between the great monopolistic consortia of the world." The transformation of the northern province of Colombia into the Republic of Panama in 1903 was not a manifestation of the inter-imperialist struggle, but rather of the fight between the Colombian Senate, which refused to relinquish a strip of Colombian soil, and Washington. This is called "Balkanization." Other examples were the creation of the Republic of Uruguay by Great Britain and the defeat and destruction of the Central American Republic created by Morazán.

Balkanization does not result from one-crop economies; but rather, one-crop economies are the result of Balkanization. Guevara rejects the monstrous manifestations of our economic subordination. But he does not seem to realize their political and historical origin.

The most dangerous aspects of Guevara's essay refer, however, to the role of "revolutionary adviser" that he spontaneously arrogates to himself with regard to the Latin American revolutionary movement. According to Guevara, the "objective conditions" for revolution "are given": colonialism, misery, degradation, etc. The subjective conditions, "of which one of the most important is consciousness of the possibility of victory through violence," have been missing. How could Guevara conceive the singular idea that the subjective conditions—that is, personal decision, boldness, faith in victory—have been lacking in Latin America? These are precisely the conditions that are over-abundant and have caused so much blood to be shed in Latin America. Was not Tupac Amaru a manifestation of these subjective conditions? And what about Sandino in Nicaragua? Or the uprising of workers and sailors in El Callao in 1948? The history of Latin America in the twentieth century is full of the boldest riots, uprisings, and struggles. What was missing were precisely the "objective conditions," which were present in Cuba, for example, when imperialism deceived itself by supporting the Sierra Maestra revolution, while Batista's mercenary army was wasting, as the result of its internal corruption.

Imperialism has thus far supported no Latin American revolution, and when it has done so (as in Bolivia), it has succeeded in paralyzing it. This revolutionary theory of "subjective conditions" is pure subjectivism, voluntarist nihilism, which has been given the status of theory by Guevara.

Guevara puts forth what he thinks is a new discovery; yet this can be found throughout Mexican and Bolivian history—namely, that in Latin America the key to revolution is the land problem. What he does not say is that land reform has been virtually completed in Mexico as well as in Bolivia; that in Chile there exists a capitalist agriculture, based on small landholdings; that in Uruguay, British imperialism created a capitalistic agrarian economy in order to facilitate the mass export of grain, meat, and wool; that the same thing occurred in Argentina; and that the "peasant" whom Guevara dreams of is the peasant of the *gringo* pampas of Argentina, who although land-hungry doesn't want to buy land at market prices, but prefers instead to buy cars and trucks and to lend out his capital at high interest rates.

Guevara reduces Latin America to one field—the servile or communal field; he reduces revolutionary strategy to an armed struggle (it is enough to gain a beachhead and to hold on to it); parliamentary rule is considered a chimera. And, as if to make sure that nothing is missing in this insurrectional intoxication, he mentions the possibility of a "guerrilla-type popular rebellion within the city." He is not afraid to give the same advice to basically capitalistic agricultural countries (such as Uruguay, Mexico, Chile, or Argentina, where the revolutionary movement is centered in the cities) as he does to countries where the basic problem lies not in the cities but in precapitalist rural areas (as in Peru, Colombia, or northeastern Brazil).

It seems that in Guevara's theory something is missing in the Latin American revolutionary movement—namely the working class. When it is mentioned at all, it is given secondary importance. The "peasant class of America" (a monstrous abstraction in itself) would make up a "liberating army." The working class appears as a mere specter; we find only a peasant army, which is to say an army of the petty bourgeoisie that directs itself according to Marx's ideas, obtained through divine intervention.

His ideas on guerrilla warfare in those Latin American countries with large cities are no less startling, and they are ambiguous. Guevara thus speaks of "guerrilla warfare in cities." As far back as the Second French Empire, Engels had already declared that the era of barricade fighting had technically come to an end. Neither barricade warfare nor guerrilla warfare is possible in modern cities under existing conditions. Santiago is part of Latin America. So are Buenos Aires, Montevideo, Asunción, and Rio de Janeiro. Is Guevara thinking of these capitals? If the Argentine peasant masses are one of the most solid mainstays of capitalist agriculture and the bastion of private property in Argentina, from where will that peasant army that Guevara plans draw its force?

The Latin American scene has other "exceptional cases" in store for us. The serious revolutionary should study their objective bases just as history describes them. Only the Latin American proletariat can become the guide and leader of the huge peasant masses or of the petty bourgeoisie in the struggle for economic independence, national unity, and socialism.

24

ORLANDO MILLAS

New Trends in Catholicism and the Policy of the Chilean Communists*

✳

One of the most provocative political themes of our time, to which Marxists and Catholics alike are devoting increasing attention, is the new spirit of struggle and reform that has swept through the Catholic Church in recent decades. The emergence of the Christian Democratic parties in Latin America and the influence of the new Catholic groups have led many Marxists to study this phenomenon. Here, Orlando Millas, one of the leaders of the Chilean Communist Party, judges the characteristics of the new currents. It is in Chile that Christian Democracy has exhibited its greatest strength by winning power six months after this article was written.

The upsurge of the national liberation movement in Latin America has had repercussions in Catholicism,

* Reprinted from Orlando Millas, "New Trends in Catholicism and the Policy of the Chilean Communists," *World Marxist Review*, VII, No. 3 (March 1964), 25–30.

which is quite influential on our continent. Traditionally, the Catholic hierarchy has always been an enemy of progress. From this standpoint the emergence of a new Catholic trend presenting the "Christian view" on revolution and revolutionary reform in Latin America is worthy of attention.

Take, for example, the Christian Democratic Party, whose activities vary from country to country. Whereas in Venezuela the Christian Democrats (COPEI) cooperate with Betancourt and share responsibility for his crimes, their counterparts in the Dominican Republic supported the military coup which overthrew President Bosch; in Peru the Christian Democratic Party acts as the right wing in the Belaúnde government, which is fairly progressive; in Bolivia it takes a rightist attitude vis-à-vis the nationalist revolutionary movement; in Argentina they resist the government's measures to nationalize the country's oil wealth; in Chile they join the Popular Action Front in opposing the reactionary policy of the Alessandri government with the obvious intention of being the alternative in the bid for power and engaging in a sort of contest with the more resolute anti-imperialist and anti-oligarchy forces. The position of the Christian Democratic parties differs in each Latin American country, but it is never genuinely left.

In an article headed "Religion and Development," published in *Mensaje* (October 1963), Mario Zañartu, a Jesuit lecturer at the Catholic University of Chile, admitted that "because many religions either actually or apparently adopt an obscurantist position of resistance to change, individuals, groups or ideologies most sensitive to the need for change take a critical attitude to such religions. The Catholic Church has been and still is accused of this crime." . . . What have the Jesuit theologians to offer in exchange for this concept?: "a new type of saintliness which would give us the model Christian, one whose dynamism would be placed in the service of his fellow men, whose life would be dedicated to revolutionary reform."

The Chilean Jesuits are by no means the vanguard of Latin American Catholicism. The Peruvian or Brazilian priests who have joined the liberation movements have proven more consistent and have gone further. As a matter of fact, the spirit of change emanates from the parish priests who live with their parishioners in the mining villages and working-class districts and among the peasants in the villages.

What is the real difference between the Marxist concept of revolution and the Catholic concept? . . . To begin with, the churchmen and their Christian Democratic political spokesmen stand for capitalism —but for a capitalism dressed in a different garb, a disguise which they call "partnership," the object of which is to give workers, office employees, and technicians an interest in the affairs of the enterprise, on condition, however, that the system of private ownership of the means of production remains unchanged. Their watchword is "involve the working man in the activity of the enterprise." Clearly these ideas are utterly alien to the working class.

As to the basic contradiction in Latin America— that between United States imperialism and the national interests of Latin American countries—representatives of the new trend in Catholicism are critical of the Alliance for Progress, not because they object to it in principle, but because it is being realized too slowly. On the whole they support the program. Their arguments are a model of hypocrisy. "Nationalization with compensation." "We cannot deprive our country of the opportunity to obtain the investments it needs." In a word, for the sake of "fair play" and "common sense" one should act as unfairly and senselessly as Frondizi or Betancourt.

Why is it that despite its opposition to the transition from capitalism to socialism and its resistance to the anti-imperialist impulse of the Latin American people, the Catholic ideology nevertheless appeals to broad sections and influences large numbers?

Apart from the advantage of its long-standing religious tradition and the immense resources at its disposal, the new Catholic trend is making headway because of its anti-oligarchic positions and its dynamic reformism.

One of the new features of this trend in our country is that it dissociates itself from *latifundism* and the landed aristocracy. It is precisely on the question of land reform that there is most disagreement between the conservative old Catholic Party, with its feudal ties, and the Christian Democratic Party, which is linked with the bourgeoisie. The Christian Democratic leaders are hesitant and generally speaking their policy prevents them from realizing the "rapid and drastic redistribution of land and water" they have proclaimed in the question of agrarian reform. Nevertheless the peasant movement is growing.

Another thing. Social-Christian reformism does not confine itself to general slogans, it also supports many of the demands advanced by different sections of the population, and participates, though not consistently, in mass actions for the more pressing demands and advocates progressive changes. They also have made serious studies to find a solution to the particular problems, albeit from the standpoint of Catholic reformism and with limited perspectives. And it must be said that the adherents of this trend are active in the trade union movement at all levels and in all other democratic organizations.

Clearly, a reformist movement of a new type is taking shape, a movement with a religious and theological tinge and designed to divert the Latin American revolution and frustrate it. In the sphere of ideological struggles the superiority of Marxism-Leninism is obvious. It is equally obvious that in the face of this adversary, the ideological struggle assumes first-rate importance.

25

VICTORIO CODOVILLA AND
RODNEY ARISMENDI

The Chinese Line and the
Latin American Communist Parties

✳

The veteran Argentine Communist leader Victorio Codovilla asserts that it is a fact that all the Communist parties of the continent have reaffirmed their loyalty to Russia in the ideological conflict with China. However, the picture is not quite so simple. Not only have there been expulsions and purges within the parties, but the Chinese arguments have penetrated many of the Marxist groups in Latin America. By means of a great theoretical display, Rodney Arismendi (see document 16) takes pains to identify the Chinese thesis with Trotskyism, Blanquism, adventurism, etc., thereby consciously providing a refutation that falls back on many positions of the New Left.

Marxism-Leninism in
Latin America*

. . . This struggle tempered the Communist parties ideologically; they were able, as a result, successfully

---

* Reprinted from Victorio Codovilla, "The Ideas of Marxism-

to combat Trotskyite deviation which draws on bourgeois nationalist and chauvinist ideas, a line which the leaders of the Communist Party of China are now assiduously following, resorting to methods inadmissible in the relations between fraternal Communist parties. They are doing this with the objective of foisting their anti-Marxist and anti-Leninist concepts on our parties, and failing in this, of splitting the parties as they have done in some countries.

The Communist parties of our continent realize that if the unity of their parties and of the world Communist movement is to be preserved, an uncompromising struggle must be waged against the line which the Chinese leaders are trying to impose on our movement. The fact that not a single one of the Latin American parties has supported the position of the Chinese leaders speaks of their ideological maturity. All of them have repudiated the disruptive policy of the Chinese Communist Party leaders and have united still more closely with the world Communist movement on the basis of Marxism-Leninism and recognition of the Communist Party of the Soviet Union as the vanguard party.

The Revolutionary Process*

From the standpoint of tactics, the phraseology of the Chinese leaders supports the old ideas and methods castigated by Marx, Engels, and Lenin—their derisive attacks against those who use parliaments for revolu-

Leninism in Latin America," *World Marxist Review*, VII, No. 8 (August 1964), 46–47.

* Reprinted from Rodney Arismendi, "Some Aspects of the Revolutionary Process in Latin America," *World Marxist Review*, VII, No. 10 (October 1964), 15–16.

tionary purposes (their attitude on this question amounts to a revival of the polemics between the "left" Communists and Lenin), or their disparagement of the struggle for immediate demands, in defense of democratic liberties and legal status for the revolutionary working-class movement. Today Chinese garb is being donned by petty bourgeois radicals who in the matter of methods of revolutionary struggle adhere to moth-eaten ideas about the "inspiring effect of direct action," ideas imported into the Rio de la Plata area half a century ago by anarchistic sects. Contrary to the Marxist orientation on mass action, these groups maintain that "direct action" carried out by a handful of bold men can rouse the people and hasten the social revolution. These concepts are akin to Blanquism or to the antiquated Socialist-Revolutionary and populist idea (borrowed today by the APRA youth and certain nationalistic petty bourgeois trends in Latin America) *that the leading role in our revolution belongs to the peasant and not to the proletarian masses.*[1] It is worth noting that of late (influenced by groups with Trotskyite leanings) its proponents have begun to indulge in thinly veiled criticism of Fidel Castro and other Cuban leaders, accusing them of having "capitulated to the Soviet Union."

From the standpoint of Party organization, the policy of the Chinese leaders is aimed at undermining unity (both on an international and on a national plane), at supporting all those who are bent on disrupting the Communist parties organizationally and ideologically.

[1] Italics mine [ed.].

26

JOSÉ MILLA

Problems of a United Democratic Front in Guatemala*

✻

*The guerrilla conflict has posed no end of problems
as to its necessity, methods, and objectives. In Guatemala, one of the countries where the struggle has
been most tenacious and prolonged, the Communist
Party has been accused, at one and the same time,
of being "pacifist" and wanting to control the direction of the guerrilla movement. In the present
article, José Millá, one of the principal Guatemalan
Communist leaders, maintains the classic posture of
"flexible unity" in the face of what he calls "provocations" of certain groups. The rupture of the Communist Party of Guatemala with Jon Sosa and the
13th of November Movement, which is merely
sketched here, became explicit and public in the
Tricontinental Congress (Havana, January 1966)
when Turcios Lima, then chief of the Fuerzas Armadas Rebeldes (FAR) was extolled as the legiti-*

* Reprinted from José Millá, "Problems of a United Democratic
Front in Guatemala," *World Marxist Review*, VII, No. 12
(December 1964), 46–48.

mate representative of the guerrilla struggle, while the 13th of November Movement was stigmatized as Trotskyist.[1]

In the struggle against the military dictatorship importance is attached to building a united front of all democratic forces.

An event of considerable significance was the establishment of the United Resistance Front (FRU) which comprises all the democratic political groupings, including our Party. The FRU, founded following the military coup of March 30, 1963, is a political alliance for the purpose of overthrowing the reactionary regime and forming a democratic government.

Another important event was the creation of the Rebel Armed Forces (FAR). The news of the formation of these forces had repercussions throughout the country. The FAR is a military-political alliance uniting all political groups and movements which support or help the armed struggle. Our Party is making an active contribution to its cause. The armed struggle in Guatemala is waged under a unified leadership.

True, beginning with last July, provocateurs who wormed their way into the "November 13" organization (one of the bodies belonging to the FAR) have been busy sapping the unity of the armed forces, trying to get their commander, Jon Sosa, to support their sectarian line, which completely ignores the real situation in Guatemala.

[1] In April 1966, the 13th of November Movement (MR-13) expelled Trotskyites from its ranks and broke with the Fourth International. The gesture does not, however, seem to have modified the Communists' attitude toward the 13th of November Movement.

This group launched vicious attacks on our Party in an attempt not only to seize the political and military leadership of the struggle but also to divide the revolutionary forces and isolate the Communists. Our Party is sparing no effort to uphold the unity of the FAR and the revolutionary forces generally, to resolve the differences, and it urges commander Jon Sosa and other representatives of the November 13 Movement to discuss with us the differences which are bound to arise in the course of the struggle.

Some of the parties belonging to the Front maintain that the overthrow of the military dictatorship necessitates a military coup. Other parties, ours included, believe that only through the armed struggle begun by the people in 1962 can the radical changes be effected. Hence it is unanimously held that things cannot be changed without the overthrow of the dictatorship, but there is no unanimity as to how to do this.

After the coup of March 1963, the functioning of all political parties was banned. The democratic parties, whose conditions had been unfavorable even before, were practically outlawed, not to mention our Party which for ten years has had to work underground. The ban disorganized the democratic parties, and hence reorganization of the Front is vital to the success of the revolutionary struggle. In view of the experience of the past ten years it is clear that the Front cannot be a political alliance of the type we find in other countries; it should have its own organizational structure from top to bottom, i.e. branches and leading committees in the towns and regions.

For a number of years now our Party has held that no one party or group is in a position to carry out a revolution in Guatemala, that this can be done only through an alliance of all the democratic forces. Therefore, we are patient even when we encounter difficulties. However, our members, especially at lower levels, have not yet fully grasped the significance of the task of building a united front.

Today, with the United Front mainly illegal in character, and its aim being the overthrow of the reactionary regime, concrete forms should be found which would "appeal" to all patriots and rally them in the spirit of unity; this should be done with great flexibility so as not to impose on people forms of activity which they do not like or for which they do not have the necessary qualities. What is needed is that each member of the United Front should feel that "at all times there is something that can and must be done," even when repression paralyzes the activities of the legal organizations. Those who are resolved to meet this danger should join the Front branches, around which more and more patriots can be rallied including those who, for one reason or another, can make but a limited contribution to the common cause.

27

JOSÉ MANUEL FORTUNY

Has the Revolution Become More Difficult in Latin America?*

*

The Marxist-Leninist challenge hurled at the continent from Cuba heightened the anti-Communist reaction in many Latin American sectors and toughened United States policy in Latin America. In dealing, in the light of this, with the paramount question of the possibilities of revolution, José Manuel Fortuny, a leader of the Communist Party of Guatemala, points out that in such circumstances revolution seems the only pathway open to reform, but he then immediately repeats the reiterated Communist warning on the multiplicity of situations and roads to revolution on the continent.

One of the many dialogues in the present discussion took place last year in New York between the Mexican writer Carlos Fuentes and the American sociolo-

* Reprinted from José Manuel Fortuny, "Has the Revolution Become More Difficult in Latin America?," *World Marxist Review*, VIII, No. 8 (August 1965), 38–45.

gist Irving L. Horowitz. Our attention was drawn mainly to the following idea expressed by Horowitz: "The price of revolutions in Latin America has sharply risen, and only in exceptional cases can a leader, a party, or a people speak of total revolution in Latin America. . . . Today the United States will without a moment's hesitation nip in the bud any hint of real independence."

It is evident that Horowitz tried to minimize the political significance of the victory of the Cuban Revolution, but we would remind him that by showing that it was possible to achieve complete victory over imperialism and to turn to building socialism in the Western hemisphere, Cuba was, for that reason alone not a "speck" but the bastion and banner of the revolution in Latin America. But it would be incorrect to deny the elements of foresight in Horowitz's conclusions. Take, for example, the brazen intervention of the United States in the Dominican Republic and the cynicism with which the Johnson administration tried to justify the landing of the Marines there. The "stick" is too big to doubt its existence.

It is very likely that before the Cuban Revolution the United States would not have acted with such brutality. The entire complex of reflexes which the Cuban Revolution aroused in the United States imperialist bore down on the small republic.

We share Carlos Fuentes' view that "paradoxically enough, after Cuba the revolution in Latin America is becoming more difficult and at the same time more imperative." As we see it, the Mexican writer wanted to stress that since the victory of the Cuban Revolution the situation in Latin America has acquired features which make it qualitatively different from the previous periods, that a revolutionary situation has arisen on the continent taken as an economic and political entity.

Nobody naturally maintains that a revolutionary situation exists in all Latin American countries (it is obvious that in a number of them such a situation has not yet matured). The existence of a revolutionary situation in one or another country does not necessarily mean that revolution will break out there and that the revolution will be triumphant. Nor does it mean that the revolution will be victorious in all countries, or that it will develop only along the tactical path followed by the Cuban Revolution.

Despite the lessons taught by the dialectics of historical development the tendency was after the victory of every revolution of world significance to universalize every detail of its experience as a general "guide to action." Lenin showed that such a tendency led to "schematism," to "revolutionary oversimplification." Unfortunately the full meaning of this counsel, like other precepts and warnings of Lenin of those years, was not properly heeded. A similar phenomenon, the belief that copying the experience of the victorious revolutions could bring victory to all countries, was to be observed after the Chinese Revolution, and after the revolution in Cuba among the revolutionaries of Latin America (and not only among them).

As the facts show, one of the most important aspects of the Latin American scene is the resistance of the ruling oligarchy, of most of the governments, to any democratic, let alone revolutionary, changes. This resistance goes hand in hand with Washington's aggressive course, with its policy of supporting or creating dictatorships, and even of direct military intervention.

The fear that the upsurge of the revolutionary movement might develop into a new Cuba is engendering an explosive situation. This situation leaves most of the Latin American countries only one realistic way of furthering the revolution today: the armed struggle against the violence of reaction and U.S. imperialism.

With few exceptions (the most obvious—Chile) there is no possibility at the present stage of a peaceful revolution in Latin America. The U.S. intervention in the Dominican Republic marked the culmination of the reactionary policy theoretically substantiated in the Mann Doctrine—a doctrine aimed at setting up "strong" governments in all countries of the continent. Most of the coups in Latin America since the Cuban Revolution were to overthrow regimes which, in the opinion of the Pentagon and the local military, were unable, because of their general weakness (or as a result of mass pressure) to suppress the discontent and the growing revolutionary struggle of the people. The most glaring instance of this was the military coup against the democratic and nationalist Goulart government in Brazil, the full implications of which still have to be properly assessed.

Another important aspect of reality, which we cannot evade and which calls for a profound analysis, is that the subjective conditions for revolution are maturing all too slowly in Latin America. This is particularly apparent in the "lagging behind" of its vanguard: the revolutionary parties of the working class, of the leftist forces. We believe that this is due not only to the fact that in the sixties the problems of the revolution or its "mechanics" have become more complicated but also to other circumstances dating back many decades.

And it is also true that a number of objective factors today hamper the growth of our influence among the basic mass of the working people. These include the absence of democratic liberties, constant repressions against the Communists, the appearance of "ultra-revolutionary" adventurist groups who have been hurting the prestige of the Communists in the eyes of the people (the case of the Mexican Trotskyites who got into the Guatemalan revolutionary movement), and the anti-Communist propaganda carried on by the imperialists, their agents, and the clergy.

But to say that the aggressiveness of the U.S. imperialists is costing the revolutionaries great effort, that it is hampering the carrying out of the revolution, is to see only one side of the matter. The other side is that the militant spirit of the masses is growing as is also the scope of their struggle, that the Communists and other leftist forces are becoming more experienced and that this is making the revolution more "imperative," to quote Fuentes. Cuba has given us— in the broadest outlines—the Latin American model of the way to socialism, has proved that Latin America too is a continent of socialism.

28

LUIS F. DE LA PUENTE UCEDA

The Peruvian Revolution*

✳

Representative of the new radical left, which believes as did Guevara in the possibility of creating subjective conditions through direct action of the insurrectional process, Luis F. de la Puente Uceda, ex-member of Alianza Popular Revolucionaria Americana (APRA), rebel, and founder of the Movimiento de Izquierda Revolucionaria or Revolutionary Left Movement (MIR), explains the reasons for his struggle and points out how the division and lack of ability among many leaders of the left have prevented the creation of a broad revolutionary movement in Peru. Puente Uceda died while fighting in the mountains of his homeland in December 1965, in the midst of an effective anti-guerrilla campaign conducted by the army.[1] His analysis of the Peruvian situation is basically valid for the radical left in all Indian countries of Latin America.

Peru is one of the countries with deepest roots in the history of America, due to the high levels of culture

* From Luis F. de la Puente Uceda, "The Peruvian Revolution," *Monthly Review*, XVII, No. 6 (November 1965), 12–28. Reprinted by permission of the publisher.

[1] For an official version of the campaign against the guerrillas,

attained by the pre-Hispanic civilizations; to its having been the center of Spanish colonial power in South America; and to the undeniable survival of structures, systems, traditions, and habits belonging to the stages of autochthonous and colonial development.

Feudalism was transplanted here through the Conquest in the sixteenth century, and pure forms of slavery through the importation of Negroes during the eighteenth century. The feudal regime grew even stronger after independence, in the first decades of the nineteenth century. By the second half of that century an incipient capitalism began to develop, and the imperialist penetration started from the first decades of this century.

Thus we find, in today's Peru, hybrid systems that could fall into the generic denomination of a feudal-bourgeois-imperialist regime. In addition, there are national minorities still submerged in stages of savagery or barbarism in the Peruvian Amazonia.

This country, perhaps the most contradictory in all Latin America, has entered upon an insurrectional process, the special features of which deserve to be known and analyzed. For this purpose, it is indispensable to outline some essential aspects of national reality.

It must be noted that during the last few decades a process of interbreeding (*mestización*) and, so to speak, of Peruvianization of the cities has been under way. Thousands of peasants are fleeing from landlord oppression in the Sierra, from misery and backwardness, and emigrating to the coastal cities looking for a better life. The coastal cities are growing rapidly

see *Las guerrillas en el Perú y su represión* (Lima: Ministerio de guerra, 1966).

because of these peasant migrations. The Indians who could not reconquer the land in their native territories are now conquering the sandy grounds surrounding the cities; and their "marginal" or "clandestine" neighborhoods shoot up like mushrooms. Miserable huts made of reeds, matting, cardboard, tin cans, and paper house these thousands of migrants, who vegetate in unemployment or underemployment and exert pressure upon the wages of the employed workers. They constitute real "belts of misery and resentment" surrounding the coastal cities of Peru. To appreciate the importance of this phenomenon, let us remember that Lima, with a population of a million and a half, has 160 "marginal neighborhoods" inhabited by 600,000 people. Proportions vary between 20 and 50 per cent in other cities of the coast, such as Arequipa, Chimbote, Trujillo, Chiclayo, and Piura. The oligarchy is becoming alarmed, living in permanent fear of an invasion of their residential areas by the dispossessed. It has been proposed that some sort of a passport system be set up for highland peasants who try to settle in the cities, or that the migratory stream be diverted toward the Selva, in order to provide manpower to the *latifundists* or concessionaires who monopolize the land, and to ward off the danger feared by the oligarchy.

We must complete this sketch of Peruvian reality by stating that there are over six million peasants in the country, and nearly half a million workers, including farm and mining laborers. Given our condition as an oppressed and dependent country, the petty bourgeoisie is numerous and impoverished, and constitutes an important social sector. For the same reasons, the national bourgeoisie is small and weak. The big bourgeoisie and the landlords compose the national oligarchy and control the land, capital, import-export trade, and certain branches of domestic trade. Imperialism relies upon and uses them to penetrate our country and gain control over its economy, mainly in the extractive sectors but also in commerce, manufacturing, banking, and services.

Wages are miserable. They vary from 20 to 40 soles a day in the coast and the mines ($0.80 to $1.60). In large parts of the Sierra there prevails a system of servile labor based on sharecropping. Incomes there are as low as one sol a day. The feudal regime is the source of cheap manpower; the big mining companies own latifundios in the Sierra in order to satisfy their need for a cheap captive labor force.

The parties of the bourgeoisie and latifundists— APRA, Acción Popular and Unión Nacional Odriista —exert control over the masses, especially on the coast. The left is represented by the Communist Party (now divided into two factions); the Frente de Liberación Nacional (divided into three factions); the Trotskyites (comprising three small groups); and the Movimiento de Izquierda Revolucionaria.

It must be remembered that because of illiteracy most of the national adult population remains outside the electoral process.

A background of defeat and skepticism impregnates the collective consciousness. The phrase "No one can save Peru" expresses a general conviction. The betrayals committed against our people by parties like the APRA and demagogues like Belaúnde Terry, to mention only the most recent ones, and the failures due to the lack of a wise revolutionary leadership, have resulted in generalized skepticism and fear.

This reality poses the problem of reform or revolution. American imperialism, some sectors of the national bourgeoisie and latifundists, afraid of revolution, are trying hard to offer Latin America some sort of reform or peaceful revolution that may serve to safeguard their fundamental interests.

In a short time, we have seen Kennedyism buried together with its creator, and American policy is more and more evidently dictated from the Pentagon, that is, toward more irreconcilable positions regarding the defense of their interests and our country's submission, and toward an indiscriminate selection of puppets, accepting or fostering whatever military coups may suit the self-interest of the United States. Guatemala, El Salvador, Honduras, Ecuador, Brazil, and Bolivia all provide examples of this. Moreover, under Johnson this policy has gone as far as outright military intervention in the Dominican Republic to check a merely reformist movement, in spite of its unquestionably popular and democratic character.

The looting of our countries by American imperialism and its allies and the growing impoverishment of the great majority of our peoples nullify whatever reforms are instituted within the ever-narrowing frame established by those interests, forcing our peoples to follow the only other way, the revolutionary way.

But when choosing the way of revolution it is essential to determine which class or classes are to lead it.

On February 7 last year, speaking to a meeting of the Peruvian left at Plaza San Martín, in Lima, we said:

> In other stages of world history, the bourgeoisie performed a revolutionary task when it destroyed the feudal regime. The bourgeoisie, as a class, fulfilled its historical mission through the liberal revolution. But

in the present stage of world history, given the conditions prevailing in countries like ours, the bourgeoisie is incapable of leading the struggle against exploiters from within and without. . . . To the bourgeoisie, the masses represent a greater danger than the oligarchy or imperialism. In the presence of this danger, the bourgeoisie prefers to give up and adapt itself. It manipulates the people through electoral demagogy in order to seize power and later betrays the people, leaning on the oligarchy and imperialism to stay in power. The bourgeoisie can but betray in order to survive. . . .

Yet agreeing with all this, which has been fully confirmed by the Belaúnde Terry government, there are some people who, though calling themselves members of leftist, revolutionary, and Marxist parties, maintain that the objective and subjective conditions for starting an insurrection are not present in Peru. These people therefore look for ways to compromise with the bourgeoisie, embrace reformist schemes, and brand all those who disagree with their views as provocateurs and adventurers.

It is unnecessary to speak about the objective conditions because they are not only ripe now but have always been. I think there is not a country in America where infra- and superstructural conditions are so unjust, so rotten, so archaic as in ours.

As to the subjective conditions, we start from the idea that they are not fully ripe, but that the beginning of the insurrectional process will be the triggering factor leading to their development in ways which no one can now foresee. Moreover, it must be stressed that if such subjective conditions have not attained their necessary ripeness, this is partly due to the inability of the leftist parties and groups to foster and cultivate the ground.

The MIR's insurrectional scheme is based on the following principles:

1) The objective and subjective conditions are present, and the latter, even if they are not fully ripe, will mature in the process of struggle.

2) The exploited masses must immediately propose the seizure of power through armed struggle.

3) The strategy and tactics must in the first stage be those of guerrilla war, and later those of maneuver, or even positional warfare.

4) Given our condition as a mainly peasant country, and our geographic features, insurrection must start in the Sierra or in the eastern Andean escarpments.

5) Given the size of our country and its lack of geographical integration and transportation systems, its multiplicity of languages, races, and cultures, it is advisable to organize several guerrilla centers to initiate and develop the struggle.

6) The impact of guerrilla actions will serve to build and develop the party and to start mobilizing the masses, stimulating their consciousness, and incorporating them in the struggle, both in the countryside and in the city.

7) Due to our condition as an underdeveloped country suffering from the combined oppression of latifundists, big bourgeoisie, and imperialists, it is essential to unite the exploited sectors: peasants, workers, petty bourgeoisie, and progressive sectors of the national bourgeoisie, within a united front led by the worker-peasant alliance repre-

sented by the revolutionary Marxist-Leninist party.

8) The Peruvian revolution is part of the continental and world process, which demands progressive forms of integration in every aspect and stage, in order to defeat the oligarchic and imperialist forces which are working together all over the continent.

We think that American imperialism will desperately call on its huge resources in order to choke the continental war of emancipation. We feel sure that American armed intervention in our country will come more quickly than in other nations, because the Pentagon is perfectly aware of the importance of a triumphant or developing insurrection in the very heart of Latin America. In any case, we hope that the national liberation war in our country will be a positive factor in mobilizing and stiffening popular consciousness against the foreign exploiter and interventionist.

American imperialists are already fostering a so-called Inter-American Defense Force directed against our people's liberation movements; but just the same it must be understood that our national revolutionary struggle will become, sooner or later, a continental revolutionary struggle, because all our peoples feel the same eagerness for liberation, and the process in one country will help to radicalize the others and make them join the struggle through methods and forms suited to their own realities.

The insurrectional process started by the Revolutionary Left Movement is that of a national and popular, anti-oligarchic and anti-imperialist revolution destined to establish a democratic government and the foundations for the building of socialism in our country.

We rely on our glorious people and have faith in the revolution. This nourishes our decision to continue, regardless of whatever sacrifice, along the road we have chosen, and to be worthy representatives of the revolutionary vanguard of the Peruvian people.

29

FIDEL CASTRO

————•—•—•————

The Duty
of Marxist-Leninists and the
Revolutionary Line

*

Fidel Castro has never been noted for his theoretical vocation or his conceptual analyses; his Marxism-Leninism, usually reduced to occasional passages in his oratory, has at times been limited to anti-theoretical postures (first selection) or to vehement defenses of revolutionary action (second selection) that place him definitely closer to the New Left than to the official Communist line. It may yet prove significant that the first selection, brimming over with scorn for "theoreticians" who cannot solve practical problems, is taken from a speech given by Castro one month after the sudden disappearance of Ché Guevara, ex-Minister of Industry of Cuba.[1]

[1] One of the supposed differences between Castro and Guevara was the latter's insistence on the moral and ideological incentives that ought to be brought to bear on the workers, over and above material advantages. To reaffirm once more how difficult it is to outline conclusions on the Cuban process, suffice it to point out that while for some Marxists, as we said earlier, Guevara was the representative of the genuine left in Cuba, for others his errors are due to his "petty bourgeois," radical ideal-

*The Duty of Marxist-Leninists**

Marxism-Leninism is an explanation of historical events. Marxism-Leninism is a guide for action. Marxism-Leninism is the ideology of the proletariat, which should guide and make its action felt to overthrow the exploiters, to create a classless society.

But when in a country the workers and peasants have taken power, they have to face a series of practical problems. They have to face, as we did, international problems; they have to face the forms of international dominance of the exploiter classes of the most developed and powerful capitalist countries.

And they have the task of solving the practical problems of the people, of satisfying the needs of the people: they have the task of creating the necessary goods to satisfy the hunger of the people.

And it is our duty, the duty of the revolutionary leaders, not to limit ourselves to theorizing philosophically; it is the duty of Marxist-Leninists to develop technology, to develop science, to develop the practical roads to feed the people with the abundance that is required by the people.

There are some who tend to forget all this. There are some who tend to believe that Marxism-Leninism is a pure philosophical category, a philosophical en-

ism. See, for example, Sol Arguedas, "Dónde está Ché Guevara?," *Cuadernos Americanos,* No. 3 (Mexico City, May–June 1966). On the other hand, if the situation is judged through the speeches given in the Twelfth Confederación de Trabajadores de Cuba (CTC) Revolutionary Congress, held in Havana on August 26, 1966, it seems as if the policy of "moral incentives" for the workers is still considered most important by the labor spokesmen of the Cuban regime and by Castro himself.

* Translated from *El Mundo* (Havana, April 20, 1965), p. 6.

telechy that has nothing to do with daily practical tasks.

And we should ask those who call themselves Marxist-Leninists: . . . Are you capable of guiding me in the fight against the exploiters and against imperialism? . . . Are you truly capable of guiding me to assault revolutionary power? . . . But are you truly capable of telling me how to solve the practical problems of revolutionary power? . . . Are you truly capable of showing me how to feed the people? . . . Are you truly capable of teaching me how to overcome the hunger and the misery of the people?

Let us beware of those Marxist-Leninists who are only and exclusively worried about philosophical questions, for socialism has many practical and serious problems to solve. And it is the duty of Marxist-Leninists to solve them, a duty which becomes more essential when we realize that it is precisely revolutionary power that offers the greatest possibilities of solving them.

The Genuine Revolutionary Road[*]

. . . the fact that a number of guerrilla efforts have failed and that the triumph of none of these guerrilla movements has yet occurred—that is to say, the conquest of revolutionary power—serves as material for the enemies of the revolutionary struggle to predict the failure of the revolutionary road that the bulk of the peoples of Latin America may take today!

Defeatist elements always crop up, and when they suffer a defeat say, "Now you see, we were right—

---

[*] Translated from *El Mundo* (Havana, July 27, 1966), pp. 4–6.

this road was a failure." And the imperialists say: "Now you see, we were right, too, those revolutionaries have failed." And there occurs this strange coincidence between what imperialism and the oligarchies predict, and what a number of gentlemen and organizations who call themselves revolutionaries predict.

It is not that we claim that the same conditions that exist in Cuba exist in all countries, even on this continent; there are some exceptions, but very very few exceptions, where conditions are different, where the possibilities are more difficult.

But one thing we are convinced of is that, in the vast majority of the countries in Latin America, better conditions exist for making the revolution than those that existed in Cuba, and that if revolutions do not occur in these countries it is because conviction is lacking in many of those who call themselves revolutionaries.

It is customary to speak, and it is always customary to speak of something, and it is usual to employ a number of clichés and the clichés sometimes do more damage than imperialism itself, because imperialism excites and stimulates the peoples' struggle with its reprisals and crimes, and the dogmas, the clichés, kill the spirit in the revolutionaries, and lull them to sleep.

And one of the very well known and oft repeated phrases is the one that refers to objective and subjective conditions.[1] Speaking the language the masses

---

[1] It might be worthwhile to point out the similarity between the position of Castro and that of Stalin in his report to the Seventeenth Congress of the C.P.S.U. (1934): "There can be no justification for references to so-called objective conditions. Now that the correctness of the Party's political line has been

understand, this question of objective and subjective conditions refers, first, to the social and material conditions of the masses, that is to say, the feudal system of working the land, the inhuman exploitation of the workers, misery, hunger, etc.; and the subjective factors are the ones that have to do with the degree of awareness of the people. There are those who refer to the level of development of the peoples' organizations. And they say: There are many objective factors, but the subjective conditions are not yet given. . . . If this schema had been applied to this country, the revolution would never have taken place here, never.

The objective conditions were bad, naturally, but they are even much worse among most of the peoples of Latin America. And the subjective conditions . . . well, possibly there were no more than twenty, at the outset no more than ten, people who believed in the possibility of a revolution here. In other words, these so-called subjective conditions of awareness in the people were non-existent. We would have been in a real pickle, if, in order to make a socialist revolution, we had had to spend all our time catechizing everybody in socialism and Marxism and only then undertake the revolution. . . . This business of thinking that the awareness must come first and the struggle afterward is an error! The struggle has to come first, and after the struggle the revolutionary awareness will inevitably come, and with increasing impetus!

confirmed . . . the part played by so-called objective conditions has been reduced to a minimum. It means that from now on nine tenths of the responsibility for the failure and defects in our work rests, not only on 'objective' conditions but on ourselves, and on ourselves alone." Robert V. Daniels, *A Documentary History of Communism* (New York: Random House, 1960), p. 38 [ed.].

If I were asked who are the most important allies of imperialism in Latin America, I wouldn't say that they are the professional armies, nor the Yankee Marines, nor the oligarchies, I would say that they are the pseudo-revolutionaries . . . and there are lots of pseudo-revolutionaries, lots of charlatans, lots of fakes, swindlers of all kinds.

Revolutionaries of conviction, who feel a cause deeply, who have a theory and are capable of interpreting that theory in accordance with the facts are, unfortunately, very few. But if and when there are men with such convictions, even though they be only a handful, then where the objective conditions for revolution exist, there will be revolution. For history makes the objective conditions, but man creates the subjective conditions.

30

ALFREDO FERNÁNDEZ
AND ÓSCAR ZANETTI

———·•••·———

Dilemma of Leadership:
The Guerrilla*

✱

One of the most debated topics among Latin American Marxists today is that of revolutionary leadership. The Communist parties, with their power largely based in urban areas, generally defend the traditional line of the urban proletariat as the vanguard of the revolutionary struggle; the New Left usually proclaims the peasantry as the real force for national liberation. Below the theoretical polemic lies a more fundamental question: Should the Communist parties guide the political and the armed struggle or should the guerrilla fighters be able to command all revolutionary forces? The Cuban answer, as measured in the following article (written in 1966 by two young Cuban students at Havana University) is definite and clear: the guerrilla fighters are the real and only vanguard of a true revolution. This article originally appeared in November 1966 in El Caimán Barbudo, *the literary supplement of* Juventud Rebelde.

* Reprinted from "América Latina: política y guerra de gue-

The sacrifices which a civil war involves are only justified when it is designed to bring about a radical change in the existing situation. For this reason, the only goal those proposing armed struggle can propose is revolution. However, hesitant leaders, ill convinced of the potentialities of revolutionary warfare, develop very different goals. For them, military action should be carried out until it has produced a situation that will strike fear in the hearts of government leaders, obliging them to reestablish the old "democratic" conditions in the country which will permit the free play of the traditional political methods again.

In this case, warfare ceases to be a tool of the revolution and becomes merely one more political measure, simply a mechanism of political pressure. . . .

Warfare conceived as a means of pressure tends to become a double-edged sword for those who use it thus. If the war is pursued successfully, it will be impossible to make those who have fought, who are fully aware of what they are capable of doing, see that the war must stop completely, and this division in policy will create schism. If, on the other hand, the political organization involved is not capable of pursuing the war successfully, its weakness will become evident and the dominant classes, not in the least frightened, will not be ready to make any concessions. Even when in the best of cases such war achieves its goals, the results will never be stable, because everyone knows that the sole guarantee of the final elimination of reactionary violence is the seizure of power. . . .

The development of guerrilla warfare calls for a

rrillas," *Translation on Cuba*, No. 567 (Washington: U.S. Department of Commerce, March 20, 1967), pp. 11–13.

radical change in regard to the location of the command forces or the leadership of the revolution. Everyone knows that in Latin America the rural sector and its population are the proper framework for the development of this struggle. . . . In almost all parts of this continent, the beginning of armed struggle with the establishment of a guerrilla force in the rural sectors represents the highest point the class struggle can reach, since it is at this time that the break with the form of struggle pursued previously occurs. . . .

The entire political and military command should be placed in the hands of the guerrillas, the true effective vanguard of the revolution. In the long run, the guerrilla leaders themselves, who are in some cases members of the political leadership of parties or organizations based in the cities, will become the agents of the unity of a double political and military nature which the war requires. . . .

It is guerrilla warfare as a new form of struggle that has fully brought about the worker-peasant alliance, which has to date been a matter of constantly repeated slogan rather than fact (particularly since in Latin America the peasantry represents the majority class). It is guerrilla warfare that is doing away in deed and not in words with the lack of confidence on the part of those who live under the worst conditions; the peasants who regard those who come from the cities as symbols of wealth. . . .

31

JOINT DECLARATION
OF THE COMMUNIST PARTIES
OF COLOMBIA AND VENEZUELA

Dilemma of Leadership:
The Communist Party*

✳

*The radical and aggressive policy officially adopted
by Castro's government (document 29) has thus far
not effected any substantial change in the attitudes
of the majority of Latin American Communist
parties. They all praise the "glorious Cuban Revolution" but at the same time most reject Castro's
formula as the only road to victory. The following
excerpts, taken from a joint declaration by the
Communist parties of Colombia and Venezuela and
published one month after the July 1967 meeting
of the OLAS (Latin American Organization of Solidarity) in Havana, are typical expressions of this
common attitude. It is significant that both parties
speak of coordinating "revolutionary" and "democratic" movements and of building a "united front"*

* Translated from "Comunicado de las delegaciones de los
Partidos Comunistas de Colombia y Venezuela," *Documentos
Políticos,* No. 68 (Bogota, July and August 1967), pp. 93–99.

against imperialism. The ratification of the position of the Communist party as the vanguard of the revolutionary movement, the assertion of the right of each national movement to decide its own tactics, and the insistence on "mutual respect" are clearly answers, even if indirectly, to Castroite arguments and attacks.

In order to face a situation that seriously menaces the development of the national liberation movement a better cohesion of revolutionary and democratic movements in our countries is essential. Since the initiative for that coordination belongs primarily to the workers' parties, finding a way to bring these elements together has been the foremost concern of the participants in this meeting.

Because of their class structure, their ideology, and their vast experience, the position of vanguard in the revolutionary struggle undoubtedly belongs to the Communist parties and to the workers' parties, which should attain that position through practical combat against the enemies of the people. History has shown the vigor of the proletarian parties and the role they should play in the common struggle. The defense of this position, against erroneous concepts which tend to grow in force because of peculiar developments in a given situation, must be a constant objective in the ideological struggle of both parties. The representatives of the Colombian and Venezuelan Communist parties reaffirm their intention of intensifying their efforts to perform properly the role of leaders of the revolutionary and democratic activities of their people.

Both parties are firmly convinced that the elaboration of the political line to be followed in the framework of each national reality belongs to each national movement. This should be achieved through the adequate combination and proper use of diverse methods of struggle, giving special attention to that form of struggle which best suits the particular national reality according to the principles of Marxism-Leninism and to the experiences derived from revolutionary actions. It is not possible to forge a single political line, a single tactic and method of struggle to be applied in every country. The Colombian and Venezuelan Communist parties, faithful to their revolutionary duties, believe that, working within the framework of the particular conditions existing in their respective countries, they should guide the struggle of their peoples against their enemies—imperialism and oligarchy. Mutual respect and noninterference in the internal affairs of other parties are considered by the participants in this meeting as rules which should be strictly followed. Any action or attitude which violates these norms weakens the necessary cohesion and unity of the parties and the integration of a united front against Yankee imperialism and its national agents.

32

LUIS SANCHEZ

Dilemma of Leadership, To Whom Does the Vanguard Belong?*

✳

The arguments of the New Left against the Communist parties many times went beyond the theoretical question of who should guide the revolutionary struggle. The Communist parties were and are accused of being too passive, too conservative, too willing to seek solutions through political compromises, in other words, of having forfeited their role as "revolutionary vanguard." The Communists usually dismiss the attacks by calling their critics "petty-bourgeois revolutionaries," "adventurists," "ultra-radicals," and so forth. But the excerpts below show that they are not totally immune to that kind of criticism. This is one of the rare occasions when a Communist leader admits and discusses the validity of the charge. Typically, the concession appeared in an article dealing with a minor Communist party, that of Nicaragua. The reader should also take note of the date of the publication. In 1968, the "guerrilla theory," even if declining, was still an important topic in the Marxist camp. Since 1968, the Sandino National Liberation Front, mentioned in this article, has become a revolutionary movement capable of challenging Anastasio Somoza's dictatorship in Nicaragua.

For a long time this disturbing question was reduced in Party documents to the formula, widely current on the continent, that since we are the party of the working class, the vanguard role automatically belongs to us alone. But other forces, too, lay claim to this role, for example, the revolutionary petty-bourgeois, whose most politically articulate spokesman in our country is the Sandino National Liberation Front.[1]

Reality obliged us to reject this convenient and pretentious phraseology, which concealed political inactivity. We realized that the vanguard role is something that has to be proved and won. We saw the justice of Lenin's words: "For it is not enough to call ourselves the 'vanguard.' The first thing is *to act*, to head the masses in their revolutionary struggle. Only in this way, and not by monotonously repeating pseudo-theoretical formulas, can this or that political organization affirm its vanguard role. "Vanguard of the revolutionary movement" is not a juridical status based on some document. It is a concrete attitude toward revolutionary action, a clear and effective political line and flexible tactic. How much effort was needed, however, before the Party realized that simple

*From "Nicaraguan Communists in Van of the Liberation Movement," *World Marxist Review*, XI No. 2 (February 1968), 34–35.

[1] A revolutionary organization named in honor of Augusto Cesar Sandino, a guerrilla leader who fought the American Marines in Nicaragua from 1928 to 1933. He was assassinated in 1934, allegedly by orders of General Anastasio Somoza. Somoza's son is the present ruler of Nicaragua.

truth! How many mistakes did we make because of our complacent and dogmatic attitude! For whereas in words we did not accept that anybody could so much as dispute our vanguard role, in practice we calmly relinquished it to other forces, even including the parties of the bourgeosie!

Part VI

From the Peruvian "Military" Revolution to Cuban Intervention in Angola

1968-1977

CHRONOLOGY
OF
IMPORTANT EVENTS

*

1968   A military coup in Peru, headed by General Juan
Velasco Alvarado, deposes President Belaúnde
Therry and proclaims a "revolutionary" program.
Fidel Castro publicly supports Soviet invasion of
Czechoslovakia.

1969   The Brazilian armed forces kill urban guerrilla leader
Carlos Marighella.
Navy training center and garrison are occupied by
Tupamaros in Uruguay.
Castro announces a "revolutionary" mobilization in
Cuba to produce ten million tons of sugar.

1970   Marxist Salvador Allende is elected president in
Chile.
The Uruguayan Communist party succeeds in organizing the Broad Front, a political coalition, to
fight for the presidency of Uruguay.
Castro admits the failure of the ten million tons of
sugar effort.
Leftist general Juan José Torres becomes president
of Bolivia.

1971   Chile establishes diplomatic relations with China.
General Juan José Torres is forced to abandon Bolivia.
Tupamaros release kidnapped Brazilian Ambassador Aloysio Dias Gomide after receiving $250,000.

Castro visits Chile. Five thousand women march in the streets of Santiago protesting high price of food.

Lefist coalition (Broad Front) receives only 19 percent of the votes in Uruguay.

1972 Uruguayan army mounts a successful operation against the Tupamaros.

Juan Domingo Peron returns to Argentina after seventeen years in exile, and announces his candidacy for president.

Chile expropriates all foreign-owned copper companies. Truck owners strike. Allende names a new cabinet which includes three high-ranking military officers.

1973 Peron is elected president of Argentina. The Communist party becomes legal.

Allende is killed during a successful military coup in Chile.

General Ernesto Geisel is elected president of Brazil.

1974 Brezhnev visits Cuba and Castro endorses Soviet détente policy. Many Latin American countries re-establish diplomatic relations with Cuba.

Peron dies in Argentina. A wave of terrorism follows his death.

1975 Representatives of twenty-four Latin American and Caribbean Communist parties meet in Havana.

OAS lifts its sanction against Cuba.

General Velasco Alvarado is deposed in Peru. The new government announces a policy of moderation.

1976 Cuban troops intervene in Angola.

1977 U.S. and Cuba establish "limited" diplomatic relations.

The new Panama Canal Treaty with the U.S. becomes a Latin American issue.

33

FIDEL CASTRO

Cuba's Support
of Soviet Action against
Czechoslovakia *

*

In August 1968, the Russian army invaded Czechoslovakia and crushed what was considered a trend toward liberalizing a Communist regime. To the surprise of many, Fidel Castro approved the Russian action. Several observers considered this speech as another proof of the continuing "sovietization" of the Cuban Revolution. The speech, nevertheless, deserves closer attention. Even in these excerpts, one can see that Castro's words had many different implications.

Some of the things that we are going to state here will be, in some cases, in contradiction with the emotions of many; in other cases, in contradiction with our own interests; and, in others, they will constitute serious risks for our country.

However, this is a moment of great importance for the revolutionary movement throughout the

---

*From *Appearance of Major Fidel Castro Analyzing the Events in Czechoslovakia* (Habana Instituto del Libro, 1968), pp. 5, 8, 9, 13, 14, 20, 26, 28, 31, and 32.

world. And it is our duty to analyze the facts objectively and express the opinion of our political leadership, the opinion that represents the judgment of the members of our Central Committee, of the leaders of our mass organizations, of the members of our Government, and that we are sure is profoundly compatible with the tradition and sentiments of our people.

A whole series of changes began taking place in Czechoslovakia at approximately the beginning of this year. A process of what was termed democratization began. The imperialist press invented another word, the word "liberalization," and began to differentiate between progressives and conservatives—calling progressives those who supported a whole series of political reforms, and conservatives the supporters of the former leadership.

Even some European Communist Parties, facing their own problems and contradictions, began to express their sympathy for the liberalization movement. It was a situation that everyone was trying to use to his own advantage, to resolve related problems stemming from incorrect methods of government, bureaucratic policy, separation from the masses and, in short, a whole series of problems for which the former leadership was held responsible. There was also talk about the need to create their own forms for the development of the socialist revolution and the socialist system in Czechoslovakia.

Thus, these tendencies were developing simultaneously, some of which justified the change and others of which turned that change toward an openly reactionary policy and this divided opinion.

We, on the other hand, were convinced—and this is

very important—that the Czechoslovak regime was dangerously inclined toward a substantial change in the system. In short, we were convinced that the Czechoslovak regime was heading toward capitalism and was inexorably heading toward imperialism. Of that we did not have the slightest doubt.

We must begin by saying this because we also want to say certain things about matters related to the situation there. As to this matter, there are some people in the world who do not share these opinions. Many considered that this danger did not exist. Many tendencies favored certain freedom of artistic expression and some of those things. Because, naturally, there are many people in the world who are sensitive to these problems. Many mistakes, many blunders, have been made in this area. And, naturally, certain concepts exist in relation to how to approach this problem. The intellectuals are also concerned over other problems. They have been very concerned over the problem of Vietnam and all those questions, although it must also be said that part of the progressive intellectuals of the world, facing its own problems, the problems of Europe in general, the problems of the developed world, the problems of the developed societies, are more worried with all these questions, questions which are of less concern to the greater part of the world, the world which lives under imperialist oppression, under neocolonialism and under the exploitation of capitalism in the underdeveloped regions of the world.

Provisionally, we reached this conclusion: we had no doubt that the political situation in Czechoslovakia was deteriorating and going downhill on its way back to capitalism and that it was inexorably going to fall into the arms of imperialism. . . . We must analyze the causes and ask what factors made this possible and created the necessity for such a dramatic, drastic, and painful measure.

Because what cannot be denied here is that the sovereignty of the Czechoslovak State was violated. This would be a fiction, an untruth. And the violation was, in fact, of a flagrant nature.

An analysis of the factors involved must be undertaken. And it behooves the communist movement as an unavoidable duty to undertake a profound study of the causes that have given rise to such a situation. Obviously, this is not the time to make or pretend to make that profound analysis, but we can cite some facts and ideas: bureaucratic methods in the leadership of the country, lack of contact with the masses— contact which is essential in every true revolutionary movement—neglect of communist ideals. And what do we mean by neglect of communist ideals? We mean forgetting that men in a class society, the exploited in a class society, the enslaved, struggle for a whole series of ideals, and when they speak of socialism and communism they are not only speaking of a society where exploitation does actually disappear, and the poverty resulting from that exploitation disappears, and the underdevelopment resulting from that exploitation disappears, but they are speaking also of all those beautiful aspirations that constitute the communist ideal of a classless society, a society free from selfishness, a society in which man is no longer a miserable slave to money, in which society no longer works for personal gain, and all of society begins to work for the satisfaction of all needs and for the establishment among men of the rule of justice, fraternity, equality and all those ideals of human society and of the peoples who have always aspired to achieving those objectives. And these objectives are possible, as we have explained on other occasions, as we explained amply last July 26.

In future stages it will be necessary for our revolutionary people to go deeply into the concepts of what they understand by a Communist society. The ideal of the Communist society cannot be the ideal of the industrialized bourgeois society; it cannot, under any circumstances, be the ideal of a bourgeois-capitalist consumers' society.

We must learn to analyze these truths and to determine when one interest must give way before other interests in order not to fall into romantic or idealistic positions that are out of touch with reality.

We are against all those bourgeois liberal reforms within Czechoslovakia. But we are also against the liberal economic reforms that were taking place in Czechoslovakia and that have been taking place in other countries of the socialist camp as well.

It is understandable that the countries of the Warsaw Pact sent their armies to destroy the imperialist conspiracy and the progress of counterrevolution in Czechoslovakia. However, we have disagreed with, been displeased at, and protested against the fact that these same countries have been drawing closer economically, culturally and politically to the oligarchic governments of Latin America, which are not merely reactionary governments and exploiters of their peoples but also shameless accomplices in the imperialist aggressions against Cuba and shameless accomplices in the economic blockade of Cuba. And these countries have been encouraged and emboldened by the fact that our friends, our natural allies, have ignored the vile and treacherous role enacted by those governments against a socialist country, the policy of blockade practiced by those countries against a Socialist country.

And we wonder whether possibly in the future the relations with Communist Parties will be based on principled positions or whether they will continue to be guided by their degree of willingness to maintain a spineless attitude, to be satellites, lackeys—a situation in which only those that maintain a spineless attitude, say "yes" to everything and never assume an independent position on anything, would be considered friendly.

We acknowledge the bitter necessity that called for the sending of those forces into Czechoslovakia; we do not condemn the socialist countries that made that decision. But we, as revolutionaries, and proceeding from positions of principle, do have the right to demand that they adopt a consistent position with regard to all the other questions that affect the world revolutionary movement.

And if the day should ever come when this Revolution had to buy its security and its survival at the price of some concession to the Yankee imperialists, we would prefer—as our Central Committee unanimously would prefer and as our people would prefer—this people to disappear with the Revolution rather than survive at such a price!

34

JOÃO QUARTIM

Leninism or Militarism?
The Dilemma
of the Urban Guerrilla *

✳

By 1970, under the impact of several disastrous defeats, the "peasant guerrilla" formula had almost completely lost its strength and prestige. The left, mainly the New Left, concentrated its hopes for revolutionary victory on the feats of the "urban guerrilla." The Tupamaros in Uruguay and the VPR (Revolutionary Popular Vanguard) in Brazil had achieved considerable success and seemed to be (especially the Tupamaros) even unbeatable. But the urban guerrillas were also confronting a multiplicity of problems. Externally, the authoritarian regimes were studying and beginning to apply new counterinsurgency methods; internally, and perhaps as a consequence of their success, the guerrillas were beginning to be divided by different strategic concepts. Here an ex-member of the VPR examines one of the dilemmas facing the Brazilian guerrilla and defends a Leninist position.

*From João Quartim, "Leninism or Militarism?" in James Kohl and John Litt, *Urban Guerrilla Warfare in Latin America* (Cambridge, Mass.: M.I.T. Press, 1974) pp. 149–160.

*In 1972-1973, the military offensive against the urban
guerrillas almost totally annihilated them in Uruguay
and Brazil.**

We can summarize the limitations of urban guerrilla:
it is cut off from the masses by its clandestinity. The
mobile strategic detachment in the country can retreat in space to progress in time, since rural guerrilla
warfare is a war of attrition in which mobility gives
the guerrilleros choice of terrain on which to fight.
The urban guerrilla fighter on the other hand, can
only repeat indefinitely the same operation. Starting
from a clandestine base of support, he attacks some
objective only to return immediately to the point of
departure. The role of time as a factor in the build-up
of strength, which enables the rural guerrilla movement to shift the balance of forces bit by bit, and to
become a peoples' army through the constant recruit-
ment of sections of the peasant masses (a process
which signals the transition from strategic defence to
strategic equilibrium), has not the same effect in the
case of the urban guerrilla. For as long as there is
no permanent contact between the armed vanguard
and the masses, there will be no progressive transformation of the vanguard detachment into a peoples'
army. This is what is meant by saying that urban
guerrilla action is not a mass struggle. The urban vanguard is thus in no way an 'insurrectional foco', that
is, a political-military organization of revolutionary
cadres that develops into an insurrection via protracted war. Proselytism in the urban guerrilla movement is individual proselytism: the urban guerrilla
movement recruits new cadres; it does not recruit
sections of the masses.

The revolutionary organizations' use of terror as a tactic was a new feature of political struggle in Brazil, since apart from isolated cases, this form of violent action was previously unknown in our country. The first terrorist attacks (bombing of the U.S. Consulate-General in São Paulo, of the oligarchy's newspaper O Estado de São Paulo, and of the headquarters of the Second Army in the same city) were accompanied by the first bank raids, and coincided with the upsurge of the mass movement (March-June 1968)....
The armed organizations of the revolutionary left have nevertheless overestimated the "mobilizing" value of terrorist attacks. Their rejection of the methods of the "traditional left" often became, especially for those militants and groups that lacked a minimal Marxist-Leninist training, a sort of cult of action for action's sake, in which the most blind "activism" was passed off as political "theory." ... Actions of this kind no doubt demoralize the regime, particularly since it has committed itself so openly to the "crushing of subversion." However, they pose the problem which arises in debate on tactics: should one's main goal be to crush the enemy or to win the masses?

The political error made by the partisans of unlimited terror does not arise from a tactical choice which presents "armed propaganda" as a specific form of struggle, but from believing dogmatically that any action directed "against the system" produces a propaganda effect, and from failing to understand that a struggle isolated from the broad masses is always a limited form of struggle. The danger does not lie in the armed propaganda as such. On the contrary, this can be an important moment in the process of formation of the peoples' armed vanguard. The danger lies rather in the tendency to make armed propaganda a substitute for the mass struggle.

For the armed organizations in the cities, the slogan that "action builds organization" revealed its one-sidedness in practice. The opposition to this tactic started toward the end of 1968, lasted for a whole year, and ended in the absolute hegemony of what we have called the "militarist" tendency, characterized by the following positions:

1. rejection of systematic work in the mass movement;
2. rejection of the "traditional" forms of agitation and propaganda;
3. tendency toward reducing organizational structure to armed groups alone;
4. adoption of the foco theory as presented in "Revolution in the Revolution?"[1]

The Leninist tendency held quite opposed positions, and was accused of seeking to return to the "theory of the party"—a completely justified charge, if by "party" one understands the fighting vanguard of the popular masses. This accusation really touched the root of the problem of the nature and tasks of the revolutionary vanguard in Brazil: whether or not the generalization of guerrilla warfare presupposes the existence of a national organization able to coordinate the popular struggle as a whole. The militarists replied in the negative and the Leninists in the affirmative. The former believed that guerrilla warfare could be indefinitely extended by the action of urban and rural "small motors" alone; the latter insisted on the dialectical interdependence of the political and the mili-

[1] A book by Regis Debray, previously mentioned in this volume.

tary tasks of the revolution. This internal struggle was interrupted for a time by the police and military offensive that followed Institutional Act V of December 1968[2] and by the "Fourth Infantry Regiment action" in January 1969. The latter episode deserves a close analysis. Besides providing a concrete example of partisan warfare in São Paulo, it spotlights the practical implications of the political and tactical debate within the armed organizations, and particularly the VPR.[3]

By the time of the Fifth Act, the VPR was no longer a small, isolated grouping. It had made links with important sections of the popular movement, sought to take a public position on all major national problems and took on responsibilities that went far beyond the limited perspectives of a small urban armed nucleus. Institutional Act V signalled both a deepening political crisis within the ruling classes and the regime's decision to move to the counteroffensive. It was obvious to all that this final liquidation of the facade of "redemocratization" would only pay off for the ruling classes if they succeeded in "crushing subversion." In these circumstances, the correct response for the armed organizations would have been tactical withdrawal until the wave of repression had subsided. This tactic would not have been imcompatible with carrying out a few rapid and effective armed actions in order to discredit the repressive apparatus and to show the urban masses that "subversion" could not be abolished by decree. The application of such a tactic

[2]An emergency law of the Brazilian government, aimed at curbing terrorism.

[3]Vanquardia Popular Revolucionaria (Popular Revolutionary Vanguard).

would have shown a correct understanding of the balance of forces between revolution and counterrevolution, and would have been a practical development of the strategy of protracted war. . . . But the VPR did exactly the reverse. While mass prison camps were being improvised in almost every city in the country, while all those vaguely suspected of "communism" were being arrested, and torture was being used for the first time as the principal means of extracting information from the detainees, the VPR decided to attack the Fourth Infantry Regiment, stationed in the suburbs of São Paulo, near the workers' district of Osasco. The very fact that such a decision could have been taken in this conjuncture shows that the militarists had already prevailed within the organization. In fact, following a stormy conference, the urban military sector seized control of the central VPR command and prepared for the attack on the Fourth Infantry Regiment. The aim of this operation was purely logistic: to secure a few hundred FAL automatic rifles, submachine guns, flame-throwers, etc. The existence of a VPR cell within the regiment seemed to justify the operation, all the more so as the VPR leadership at this time had an unfortunate tendency to confuse the military possibility of an action with its political correctness. This cell was organized by Captain Lamarca. . . .

The attack on the Fourth Infantry Regiment was prepared in an almost suicidal fashion. Despite the vigorous protests of the Leninists, powerless since the internal crisis of December 1968, the VPR mobilized militants from all sectors of its organization, and particularly principal field of struggle. Prepared in such an irresponsible way, the project was bound to fail.

In fact, it was never even carried out. The militants of one cell were discovered painting a truck in army colors, and the whole of the dictatorship's repressive apparatus was put on the alert. The cell in the Fourth Infantry Regiment had just enough time to take flight, in a truck loaded with automatic weapons—which proves that the operation could have been carried out without committing to it almost the entire VPR strategic potential. The cost of this action was too heavy. The four militants arrested on the eve of the operation were savagely tortured and ended by disclosing everything. (One of them even went beyond the limit that separates weakness in the face of pain—which is always understandable—from collaboration with the enemy.) The vicious circle of capture-torture-confession-further captures, etc. rapidly endangered the very survival of the VPR, which found itself on the edge of disintegration. The manhunt raged for two months, and enabled the regime to penetrate deeply into the organization's clandestine structure. By March the police could boast of having arrested around thirty VPR militants. However, in April the VPR was already reborn from its ashes, if no longer quite the same. Without understanding the profound reasons for the disaster that they themselves had prepared, the militarists took the occasion to purge the most prominent militants among the Leninists, while managing, thanks to their undeniable courage and tenacity, to reconstruct the organization's urban infrastructure. The VPR came out alive from the ordeal of January-March 1969, but it had squandered its strategic resources in operations of a purely tactical significance. It emerged decimated, but "homogeneous." However, the problems brushed under the carpet with the purge of the Leninists were to reappear some months later.

35

ISMAEL FRIAS

Should the Left Support the Peruvian "Revolution"? An Independent Marxist Explains Why It Should *

*

On October 3, 1968, the Peruvian armed forces deposed the government of President Fernando Belaúnde Terry and took control of the government. Considering that this was another reactionary military coup, almost all the leftist organizations of the nation condemned the action. But very soon the military government, headed by General Velasco Alvarado, began to take measures—nationalization of American companies, Agrarian Reform, and the like— which the left had been clamoring for in their programs. That policy posed a vital dilemma. Should the left support a military government—their traditional enemy—which was trying in a "revolutionary" fashion to shatter the old structure of the nation; or should they avoid falling into the trap of backing a regime which was only "apparently revolutionary"? In this excerpt, a distinguished Marxist of Troskyite tendencies, leader of the Socialist Revolutionary

*League, explains what he considered the duty of the
left to be.*

The degree of imperialist domination in Peru was so
profound that not even the word "neo-colonialism"
could define it. Everything that was nominally Peruvian actually belonged to the United States. The
fish industry, the copper mines, iron, lead, coal . . .
nothing, not even the banking system, escaped the
penetration of American capitalism. What was Peru
truly—we demanded in anguish—a nation or a
Yankee viceroyalty?

We all knew that only a revolution of national and
social liberation could save Peru by destroying our
external dependence on imperialism and our internal
dependence on the oligarchy. But no one seemed
capable of doing it. APRA,[1] which was born with that
goal, had been transformed into an instrument of the
oligarchic-bourgeois system. Acción Popular, which
appeared in 1965 precisely to fulfill the betrayed
promises of APRA, was deeply divided between those
who, following Belaúnde, had yielded to the system
and those who remained loyal to an anti-imperialist,
anti-oligarchy stand. The small Christian Democratic
party had failed to acquire enough political strength.

The situation of the Marxist left was as dishearten-
ing. The heroic guerrilla fighters of the MIR and the

---

[*] From Ismael Frias, *La Revolución Peruana y la Vía Socialista*
(Lima: Editorial Horizonte, 1970), pp. 16–20, 46, 47.

[1] APRA (Alianza Popular Revolucionaria Americana), American Popular Revolutionary Alliance, was founded by Victor Raúl
Haya de la Torre in 1924. With the years it lost some of its initial radicalism.

ELN[2] had been annihilated. The rest of the Peruvian Marxists were deeply divided and reduced to impotence.

In those moments of national prostration and extreme danger, the armed forces intervened, assumed power, and expelled Belaúnde and the APRA, puppets of foreign interests.

We interpret Peru's present course as national revolution capable of being transformed into a social revolution . . . but what exactly is a "national revolution"? What are its differences from a "democratic-bourgeois revolution" and from a "socialist revolution"? Are we facing a revolution or only a process of modernizing a traditional society?

Let's examine certain essential points. A national revolution aims at obtaining the real and political independence of a nation, which means independence from the neo-colonial dominance of imperialism. While the bourgeois-democratic revolution fights against all forms of feudalism (a system which never existed in Peru, for we were under colonial capitalism), the enemies of the national revolution are imperialist capitalism and its native bourgeois agents. Evidently, the only chance for success of a national revolution is to become a socialist revolution. As long as capitalism remains, the domination of underdeveloped countries by developed nations is inevitable.

We cannot judge a priori if the Peruvian process is one of revolution or one of modernization: both alternatives are possible. But as independent Marxists

---

[2]MIR (Movimiento de Izquierda Revolucionaria), Movement of the Revolutionary Left, and ELN (Ejército de Liberación Nacional), Army of National Liberation, were revolutionary groups who waged an unsuccessful guerrilla campaign in 1965.

and socialist revolutionaries we are, naturally, in favor of the revolution, which implies the duty of participating in the process. The socialist left cannot exist outside of or in opposition to the national revolution. Its destiny is, precisely, to become the socialist left of this revolution, remaining independent and free to criticize, but always from within the process, supporting the process.

We are far from harboring the illusion that this regime will inevitably, by the will of our military leaders, move toward socialism. As Marxists we reject all forms of historical fatalism. This revolution could go forward in a non-capitalistic way (and eventually toward socialism) or backward toward a new form of dependency. We must fight for the first alternative. The strategy to follow is to help in transforming the present national revolution into a socialist revolution (as the agrarian reform is already accomplishing). The tactic is to support the revolutionary government of the armed forces against imperialism and the oligarchy, while simultaneously encouraging new and more radical structural changes. The program should follow a model of socialist development, democratic and humanist.

We have already warned the leaders of the armed forces that the only way forward is along the non-capitalist path, and that to hesitate is to fail. For those who try half-way revolutions are only digging their own graves.

36

ANÍBAL QUIJANO

Should the Left Support
the Peruvian "Revolution"?
An Independent Marxist,
Gives An Implicit Negative*

✳

*It is very difficult, or at least it is for me, to define
the ideological position of Aníbal Quijano. I remember when he jokingly qualified himself as a "nihilist-
Marxist-Leninist of the Anarchist-Left." At any rate,
Aníbal Quijano is a lucid writer who has been involved with the problems of his native country, Peru,
since he was very young. When many leftists were
enchanted with and defending the Peruvian revolution of the military, Quijano refused to follow the
trend. For him what was happening in Peru was the
creation of state-capitalism. Here are some excerpts
from his very impressive arguments, published much
before the Peruvian regime's alleged "turn to the
right" in 1975.*

*From Aníbal Quijano, *Nationalism and Capitalism in Perú: A
Study in Neo-Imperialism* (New York: Monthly Review Press,
1971).

There has been a great deal of confusion, both inside and outside Peru, about the nature of the new regime which came to power as the result of the coup d'état of October 3, 1968. Conservatives and even some leftists have seen Peru as a new Cuba. Others, again including leftists, have variously described the new regime as pro-oligarchy and pro-imperialist, bourgeois reformist, military populist, and so on. This confusion has arisen not only from what spokesmen for the regime have said about its nature and intentions but also because the measures it has actually adopted have often been, or seemed to be, inconsistent and contradictory.

If we are to avoid becoming victims of this confusion, we must put the problem in its proper Latin American and world perspective.

On the one hand, there is in all Latin American countries an internal crisis of the existing social order, involving its economic, political, and social dimensions. On the other hand, there is an equally profound crisis in the traditional forms of domination which have served to keep Latin America subordinate to and dependent on the imperialist powers and especially on the United States. This latter crisis in turn has been brought on by changes in the methods and organization of capitalist production processes in the leading countries and by shifts in the power relations among them.

The present stage of imperialist domination in Latin America is characterized by two overlapping, tension-filled, and contradictory implicit models. The first is what may be called "traditional" imperialism, with the United States as the hegemonic power operating in the economic field largely through "enclaves," i.e., enterprises totally controlled by imperialist capital and with relatively few ties to the rest of the economies of the host countries. The second pattern is of more recent origin, dating from approximately the Second World War and consisting of a progressive shift in the axis of domination from agroextractive sectors to the urban-industrial sector. Simultaneous with this shift there have taken place (1) a relative decline in U.S. hegemony and a concomitant rise in the weight of the other imperialist powers, especially Germany and Japan, and (2) a tendency for old forms of financial domination to be replaced by now monopolistic conglomerates on the one hand and "cosmopolitan" or "supranational" nuclei within the imperialist bourgeoisie on the other. All these changes have gone along with and partly resulted from the so-called scientific-industrial revolution, which of course has affected the different imperialist powers and different branches of industry unevenly.

From the political point of view, the decline in U.S. power and the repeated failure of its counter-revolutionary efforts in Indo-China have brought about an irreversible loss of prestige. Unlike what happened after the First World War and in the early years after the Second, when the United States presented to the world an image of an authority capable of restoring the international order and re-establishing the legitimacy and respectability of the bourgeois social system, this image is at persent rapidly turning into its exact opposite, not only on the battlefield but also, and no less importantly, in the political realm.

Under these conditions two things have happened: (1) The other imperialist powers have had fair warning that they can and must widen their margin of autonomy, both economically and politically. And (2) the dependent bourgeoisies and the national-dependent states they control are beginning to understand that they have considerably greater freedom to maneuver on the inter-imperialist battlefield, with the result that they are pressing for new advantages, for more flexible economic ties, and for new political alliances.

In certain countries the deepening of the political crisis under the changed conditions in the structure of inter-imperialist power, the inability of the major sectors of the dependent bourgeoisie to assert full control over state power and in this way to re-legitimize the rule of the bourgeoisie, the precariousness of the popular revolutionary movements—all these factors created a sort of growing fragmentation of power out of which arose the most interesting political phenomenon of recent Latin American history, one which has not been studied in sufficient detail: *the relative autonomization of the sectors of intermediary authority, the armed forces and the technocratic bureaucracy,* two groups and two types of bureaucracy which were the only ones in a position of intermediary authority and the only ones with the potential ability to control this fragmentation of power. Of the two, the armed forces was the only sector which was really organized and the only one, moreover with decisive instruments of power in its hands. That is the essential background to understand the Peruvian military coup of 1968.

Judged as a whole, the measures the Military Junta has put into effect with regard to imperialism justify the conclusion that while it is trying to eliminate imperialist control of the production of agricultural exports, as well as the traditional form of "enclaves" in mining and petroleum, it is at the same time tending to strengthen the role of foreign capital both in the mining sector and in the urban-industrial sector of the economy. The implicit logic of the economic policy of the regime is not only leading to the final elimination of the traditional pattern of imperialism but is also enhancing the possibilities for a new model.

Several years ago, in La Prensa, the most reactionary Lima newspaper, Federico Costa Laurent coined an ironic but true phrase concerning the relations between Peru and the United States: "What happens," he said, "is that when the United States says to us 'sit down,' we lie down."

The measures the Military Junta has carried out, as well as its expressed intentions, represent a situation that is obviously of quite a different nature from that which obtained previously. That is to say, for the first time in this century, Peru has a government capable of quietly sitting down face to face with the principal dominator of the country, and even of remaining on its feet in the face of the latter's threats. But the facts also make it plain that this government is not carrying matters to such a point that Peru will leave the house whose principal owner is Uncle Sam, slamming the door behind it.

Dependency is not going to be eradicated. But if it is to continue it must undergo substantial modifications. What has been done to date in Peru may be summed up without too much hesitation as an attempt to negotiate the terms of the redefinition of dependence. What happens from now on, however, may go beyond this framework.

The Immediate Prospects

This highly condensed and tentative examination of the economic policy thus far pursued by the military junta justifies our drawing at least two important conclusions:

(1) The Peruvian military regime is guided by an ideology of limited nationalism within the imperialist order.

(2) On the other hand, it is also guided by an ideology of class reconciliation, to be brought about by integrating the interests of the workers with those of capitalist enterprise.

Both these central features of the regime reveal the role played by the current wielders of political power as social intermediaries. But the regime's ability to carry out its plans also shows the great margin of relative autonomy it has managed to obtain in the face of the fundamental social classes of the society. This autonomy has come about as a result, first, of the feebleness of the dependent bourgeoisie within the domestic framework, which in turn has been aggravated by the crisis of political hegemony; second, of the weak political development of the workers; and third, of the difficulties that the imperialist bourgeoisie and the present principal imperialist state have encountered in their efforts to find a coherent repressive line of conduct.

37

JORGE DEL PRADO

Should the Left Support the Peruvian "Revolution"? The Communist Party Answers in the Affirmative*

✳

The author is the secretary general of the Peruvian Communist Party.

More than two years ago we had a new military coup. It was new not in the sense of one more, but because it was different from the previous putsches. In other words, it was a military coup of a new type.

This was not quite obvious at first. On the face of it, the coup differed from the traditional pronunciamientos, so profuse in Peru's history, only in form, for it was not a caudillo, a Sanchez Cerro, Benavides or Odria, who had seized power, but the army as a political institution.

The "gorilla" regimes in Argentina, Brazil and Honduras are also "institutional", which does not alter the

---

*From "Is There a Revolution in Perú?" *World Marxist Review*, XIV, No. 1 (January 1971), 17–27.

fact, however, that they are mercenary and pro-fascist, a militarist variety of Yankee neocolonialism and a materialization of Pentagon strategy devised by U.S. state-monopoly capitalism and the military-industrial complex.

That the coup might be reactionary was suggested by the fact that the Fifth Conference of American Army Representatives presided over by General West-moreland, former commander of U.S. armed forces in Vietnam, had closed just a few days before in Rio de Janeiro; the Peruvian army representative at the con-ference, General Ernesto Montagne, was appointed Prime Minister of the Revolutionary Government two days after returning home. Admittedly, no one knew then what he had said at the conference.

Soon the facts showed that this was no "gorilla" putsch. We were witnesses to a situation unprece-dented in Peru's history giving a start to substantial changes.

To begin with, the new regime differs from the "gorilla" governments for objective reasons, that is, the methods of administration. Apart from the vio-lence involved in overthrowing President Belaúnde's government and the arrest and banishment of some of his most corrupt followers, the new regime has so far taken no repressive action of a political nature.

There is scarcely any doubt that the changes in Peru are oriented against imperialism and the oli-garchy, although in the teeth of the facts some be-nighted people prattle about their being "neo-coloni-alist," "subversive," even "pro-imperialist." It is as much of a mistake, however, to describe the changes, and the government itself, as merely "progressive" or, worse still, merely "reformist."

By virtue of our Marxist-Leninist analysis, we Peruvian Communists hold that the changes now in process affect the socio-economic structure, that is, possess revolutionary content.

Socially, the agrarian reform law eliminates the landowner class and establishes new rural relations of production. Medium-sized farms and cooperatives predominate. The last of Indian communities, appropriated by the big estate holders, has been returned. The main principle is: "The land must belong to its tillers."

Economically, apart from eliminating large estates and encouraging middle-sized peasant farms, the agrarian reform law has encouraged the growth of a strong cooperative sector. The state sector has grown much stronger, and tends to become predominant in our economy. This is due to the nationalization of oil fields and refineries, state control over processing and export of minerals, production and export of fish meal and cod liver oil, nationalization of the telephone service, consolidation of the National Bank, and monetary controls.

Politically, the oligarchy and the venal bourgeoisie have been ousted from government. Though replaced by the armed forces, rather than the working class, allied with the peasants and other strata, the political role of the proletariat, peasants and urban strata is growing, whereas the pro-imperialist and pro-oligarchic political parties and forces are losing ground and falling to pieces.

Would it be right to call the process a bourgeois-democratic revolution? If we regarded the agrarian reform as the only radical government measure, we would answer in the affirmative. As it is, however, the development in Peru, more than those of Bolivia in 1952 and Guatemala in 1953, show that in our time it is impossible to have a bourgeois-democratic revolution in its pure, classical form, i.e., as an exclusively anti-feudal agrarian revolution.

Until recently, Peru was principally a country of farmers and workers. To this day, the larger part of the population is rural. Despite this, dependence on imperialism, and to a lesser extent the low level of capitalist development, acts as a brake on the country's path. It is easily seen, too, that even the agrarian reform affects the interests mostly of the big American and West German companies, and it will be recalled that the U.S. imperalists reacted to it by threatening to invoke the so-called Holland Amendment, in cutting Peru's sugar quota in the U.S. market. Despite this, the government went ahead with the agrarian reform, beginning with the U.S. sugar enterprises, and in so doing acted with as much firmness as it did when expelling U.S. military missions.

It will be recalled that Marx and Engels spoke of a certain advance of forces, produced at a time of profound political crisis, when the prestige of the ruling classes declines and revolutionary governments grow. It is at this juncture that the army, one of the most potent weapons of power, can stand above the classes it formerly served, and at times even act contrary to their interests.

As we see it, the government's present class positions express the interests of the radical petty bourgeoisie. Its political creed is to build a society somewhere half-way between capitalism and socialism. But since this conception (let us call it "petty-bourgeois" or "semi-socialist") is unrealistic, the course of events compels it to gravitate closer and closer to the proletariat and the masses in the countryside. In the circumstances, the petty bourgeoisie is gradually ceasing to be its main socio-political support.

Would it be right to say that the masses had no hand in the developments? Or that the working class and the Communist Party played no role at all, that the further unfolding of the revolution depends solely on the armed forces?

The 1960's saw a numerical growth of the proletariat; it grew more solid organizationally and politically, and was able to step up its struggle; the revolutionary consciousness of the people grew in town and countryside. The General Confederation of Labor is coming up its forces, and the peasants' fight for land is expanding.

Our Party is firmly opposed to reactionary regimes and the cruel repressions of the pro-imperialist and pro-oligarchic forces. It keeps the ranks pure, getting rid of all splitters and opportunities. It is renewing its organizational structure and hammering out a new political course. All this is part of a drive to build up strength, reflected in the founding of the Oil Defense Front, the National Liberation Front and the election success of the United Left.

At present, with the Revolutionary Government of the armed forces at the country's helm, the Party line is clear, firm, and conclusive, and backed by the masses. Not only have we worked out and elucidated our political standpoint; we are also carrying forward our line in practice. We have promoted conscious and active involvement of the organized working class in defending and advancing progressive, anti-imperialist, and anti-oligarchic reconstruction.

And we are doing our best to secure organized and constant participation of the students, farmers and non-proletariat urban strata of the whole nation.

The Communists see the way ahead clearly. We support a government, which launched the anti-imperialist and anti-oligarchic revolution that we have worked for so unremittingly. But we do not forget the role of our Party and the hegemony of the proletariat. The revolution is still in its first stage. We remember our historic mission and are doing our best to accomplish it.

38

JAIME FIGUEROA

And Later Qualifies Its Support*

✻

On August 29, 1975, the head of the Peruvian "revolutionary" regime, General Juan Velasco Alvarado, who had been confronting increasing economic and political difficulties (riot in Lima in February resulted in one hundred dead), was peacefully removed from office. General Francisco Morales Bermudez became the new president. Soon it became evident that something more than a change of names had occurred. Some "radicals" were dismissed from high positions, private enterprise received new assurances, and a moderate tone prevailed in the government. Those who backed this "reorientation" proclaimed that the Peruvian "revolution" had entered into a "second phase"; to others, Morales Bermudez was trying to save Peru from economic chaos; many welcomed the government's openness to political dialogue and elections. As usual, even though to a lesser degree than in 1968, the left was divided. While some, like Ismael Frias (see document 35), continued to support the military government, many condemned

*From Jaime Figueroa, "Que queda en la fuerza armada," *Unidad* (Communist Party newspaper; Lima), March 31, 1977, p. 7; and *ibid.*, April 14, 1977, p. 3.

this "turn to the right" and even called for a mass revo-
lution against the regime.[1] Following the strategy
asserted at the Conference of Communist Parties of
Latin America and the Caribbean (see document 44),
the Peruvian Communist Party, while deploring the
"revolutionary setbacks," continued to support the
military government.

The Road to Follow

What is left in the armed forces? Many would like to
answer this question with a radical and negative subjectivism. But what has happened in the Peruvian
armed forces and in our country in the last eight years
is important enough to make us avoid that mistake.
The study of what has been called the Peruvian military phenomenon is a fundamental question for every
revolutionary .

In terms of military intervention, what has occurred in Peru is qualitatively superior to what happened in Brazil (1932–1962), or in Venezuela in the
decades of the fifties. While in those countries the
revolutionary action of some radicalized military sectors was and remained isolated, in our country the
revolutionary action was institutional and comprised
of military and civilian elements. It is quite important
to clarify the content and the projections of that first
phase of the revolution, that is, the meaning of "Plan
Inca."[2]

[1]See, for example, the article of Trotskyite Jorge Villaran, published in *Equis-X* (Lima), No. 54 (April 7, 1977), calling for
the beginning of revolutionary struggle against the "bourgeois-
imperialist counterrevolution."

[2]Plan Inca was the basic plan formulated by the government
of Velasco Alvarado explaining the objectives of the "revolution."

We Communists have always characterized that plan as revolutionary, in the first place because it was anti-oligarchic and anti-imperialist, and in the second because it incorporated many aspects of the working-class program and moved our revolution closer to socialism. Many people misinterpreted our position and thought that we were substituting the historical program of the working class for Plan Inca. That was totally false. We were supporting one step forward in the road toward socialism.

But like any institution whose members come from different social classes, the armed forces are also subjected to changes and transformations. The nationalistic revolutionary trend within the armed forces has many historical roots. It is part of a general process of increasing social conscience which has affected many sectors of our society, including the Church. The problem is that this nationalistic phenomenon is not a single, one-way road. It can adopt different modalities according to the different groups and social classes which support it. It could go from a radical leftism to an open support of rightist or even fascist positions. And that is what is happening inside the armed forces.

The key to the problem of our present situation is to know if the nationalistic revolutionary spirit of the first phase has penetrated deeply enough and has left roots in the armed forces. Our party has said that the new Plan Tupac Amaru[3] "reflects the government's

[3]The plan Tupac Amaru, proclaimed by the Peruvian government in February 1977, explains the process of the "second phase" of the revolution. The government announced the liberalization of state control on many enterprises, reduced the role of workers and peasants in the political structure, and promised a new democratic constitution and democratic election for 1980.

turn to the right." Does that mean that the displaced revolutionary forces have come to the end of the road? No, of course not. As long as there are sectors with revolutionary ideologies, inside or outside the armed forces, the process could be frustrated but not destroyed. And there are still enough revolutionary forces mobilized during the radical period eventually to retake political positions and continue the process into the future.

The simple fact that the armed forces are still defending the basic achievements of the revolution is a hopeful sign. In spite of the reactionary pressures inside the armed forces, it is very difficult to think that they could turn back and again become a reactionary instrument. Even if they cannot or do not want to recognize it, by defending national independence, by refusing to return to the past, the armed forces are still holding leftist positions.

That perspective is what has made us Communists create a slogan which represents our present position: "Let us mobilize the masses to defend the gains of the revolution and to stop the advance of the reactionary forces!"[4]

[4]For a detailed explanation of the Peruvian Communist Party attitude, see Pedro Mayta Zapata, *Ofensiva Reaccionaria* (Lima: Ediciones del P.C., 1977). On July 31, 1977, all the issues of the weekly publication of the Communist Party, *Unidad,* were confiscated by the government.

39

PABLO GONZALEZ CASANOVA

Proletarian Conscience
and Marxist Rhetoric*

*

*For more than four decades the Mexican govern-
ment's official party, the PRI (Institutional Political
Party) has exercised virtually complete control over
Mexico's political affairs. Not even the presence of
numerous, occasionally strident, Marxist groups seems
able to dent the party's system of political control.
A noted Mexican sociologist and professor offers an
interesting diagnosis of this phenomenon. Written in
1972, and applicable to a general malaise of the
Latin American Left,[1] his words ring valid today and
for the forseeable future.*

The Mexican proletariat is reformist and even con-
formist. It continues to support the government's poli-

---

*From Pablo Gonzalez Casanova, "Enajenacion y Conciencia de
Clases en Mexico," in *Las Clases Sociales en Mexico* (Mexico:
Editorial Nuestro Tiempo, 1974), pp. 192–197.

[1]In addition to many examples already given in this book, denouncing the tendency to excessive verbalism in the left, see
Carlos Guzman-Bockler, "Internal and External Colonialism in
Today's Guatemala," in *Guatemala: una interpretación historico-
social* (Mexico: Siglo XXI, 1972), pp. 165–190, where he sum-
marizes the individualistic tendencies of all leftist groups in their
tenacity to proclaim: "I, and only I am the Left!"

cies, and there are no signs that organized masses of a revolutionary character are appearing.

Workers with some sort of class conscience are to be found only in certain groups in the public sector and, exceptionally, in some industries in the private sector. But those groups enjoy a position which in relation to the proletariat places them at the same level as the middle class. Even though at times they use a Marxist rhetoric, they accept labor unions and, after some concessions, they become reformists. To this group we could add small groups of intellectuals, students, and leaders with almost no influence among the workers. Those who show that kind of class conscience are generally members of the "petty-bourgeoisie," or of the upper level of the proletariat, the "affluent workers." They all display what Ousgane has called "a socialism of luxury" (*un socialismo de lujo*), with "spontaneous" or "anarchist" attitudes, usually accompanied by a *verbal radicalism*, which have no impact on the masses.

There are, naturally, workers' groups which do have the characteristics of a radical class conscience which they proclaim Marxist. Those organizations have true popular bases, mainly among well-developed sectors of the peasantry. The leaders of these groups usually belong to the Communist Party or to the Socialist Popular Party. But in many cases this leadership makes alliances with politicians of the ruling class or with governmental leaders who call themselves "Marxists." As a result, the political struggles have to be carried out according to the conditions and rules set by the ruling-class groups.

Until recently there were four Marxist-Leninist parties in Mexico. Today they are only two: the Communist Party[2] and the Socialist Popular Party. The Communist Party has such a reduced membership (approximately 5,000 members) that to be able to participate in the electoral struggle it is constantly trying to form some kind of political coalition with other radical groups. The Popular Socialist Party was until recently guided by Vincente Lombardo Toledano,[3] who was part of the government from 1929 to 1948. The party seems to work as a "leftist" party in close contact with the government. With a not too impressive popular base, it uses Marxist symbols to help it participate in the political contest, but usually gives its support to government candidates.

All other groups and leaders of the left are linked in some way with members of the ruling class; by the same token, each important member of the ruling class has leftist partisans. The effectiveness with which a "man of the left" can act in politics is measured by

[2]For the history of the party, M. Marguez Fuentes and O. Rodriguez Araujo, *El Partido Communista Mexicano* (Mexico: Ediciones El Caballito, 1973).

[3]Vicente Lombardo Toledano (1894–1968), a leading and influential figure in Mexico's political struggles, proclaimed himself a Marxist, but had many polemics and clashes with other leftist individuals and groups, especially the Communist Party. In 1961 he declared: "The three groups of Marxist-Leninists which exist in Mexico have been unable to unite because the Communist Party says that Marxism-Leninism belongs exclusively to it and warns the other two that they cannot use that philosophy without its consent." See Vicente Lombardo Toledano, *Teoria y Practica del Movimiento Sindical Mexicano* (Mexico: Editorial Magisterio, 1961), p. 146. For a typical Communist attack on Lombardo Toledano, see Gerardo Unzueta, *Lombardo Toledano y el Marxismo-Leninismo* (Mexico: Fondo de Cultura Popular, 1966). An evaluation of his ideas can be found in Robert Paul Millon, *Mexican Marxist: Vicente Lombardo Toledano* (Chapel Hill: University of North Carolina Press, 1966).

his contacts with this or that political group of the ruling class. All the organized Marxist-Leninist factions defend the necessity of developing capitalism and bourgeois democracy, and tend to postpone indefinitely the socialist revolution.

Among the many different groups and individuals of the left exists a sort of obsessive tendency toward mutual discrediting. This proclivity is based on: (a) the tendency of contemporary Marxism to give more importance to ideological analysis than to structural analysis; (b) the use and abuse of Marxist rhetoric to call each other "opportunist," "sectarian," or "adventurist" without any attempt to give a comprehensive explanation: (c) the lack of mass workers' support of those groups, who have instead the support of different factions of the ruling class or government figures; (d) the divisions among the leftist groups as usually a reflection of the divisions among the sectors of the ruling class on which each of them basically depends.

It is then not surprising to find many similarities between the economic and political programs of the Marxist-Leninist groups and those offered by official labor unions or the party of the government. Upon analysis, it is easy to discover points of coincidence on what should be done *to develop capitalism* (according to the terminology of the left) or *to develop the country* (according to the terminology of official organizations).

This similarity becomes more evident in the speeches and proclamations of both groups. In the popular meetings of the government party one can listen to a language which in any other country would express an ultra-radical position. But in the Mexican political context that language is only the expression of the special form in which our capitalism was born. For the essential fact is that in the ethic of Mexican capitalism, Marxism was one of the formative elements. This is why in the biographies of many members of the ruling class, or of our politicians, we can find a Marxist youth. And in the future of many young Marxist students or intellectuals we can visualize a politician of the establishment or an entrepreneur. Even today—in spite of many anti-Communist campaigns—the education of a young bourgeois frequently includes some Marxist learning, and even a period of Marxist activity. This cultural phenomenon keeps growing, explaining the above-mentioned similarities in programs and proclamations and making it impossible to ascribe Marxist ideology and rhetoric to the working class.

How can we explain this phenomenon? Is it a case of controlling the forces of the proletariat? . . . In Mexico there are obvious aspects of ideological and political manipulation aimed at controlling the working class and the radical groups (in Marxist terminology a case of "alienation of the working class"), and there are also cases of police repression and pressure groups in the labor unions. But to reduce the explanation to these phenomena, as many writers and opponents of the government system do, is to accept very superficial arguments. The most effective propaganda cannot alienate anyone without a certain acquiescence on the part of the alienated person. And repression as a system requires a large repressive apparatus, which Mexico, whose military budget is proportionally the lowest in Latin America, evidently does not have.[4]

We believe that the most valid hypothesis is that the workers' movement is part of the type of government established in Mexico through an internal and external "sui generis" characteristic of an underdeveloped country in the process of developing. This means that even if Mexico is in the stage of "original accumulation" and "take off," actually her actions are different from those of classical capitalism and her political culture is also different. In economic terms, Mexico's capitalism is very similar to European capitalism during its original period, but in the political area our capitalism has the knowledge and the political culture of contemporary capitalism. Therefore, Mexican capitalism can use and apply the ideological and structural answer that contemporary capitalism discovered in order to face the development of a class-divided society. The explanation for the situation of the Mexican proletariat must then be found in structural factors and not, as many Marxists tend to do, in pure ideological factors, arguments about psychological alienation, or political causes like manipulation and repression.

[4]An interesting study of political control in Mexico today is Octavio Rodriguez Araujo, "1976: Las elecciones en México y el control político," in *El Estado y La Economia* (Mexico: Ediciones El Caballito, 1977), pp. 137–160.

40

SALVADOR ALLENDE

Chile:
A Perilous Way to Socialism*

✳

On September 4, 1970, after an electoral process that attracted world attention, Salvador Allende, candidate of leftist coalition known as Unidad Popular (Popular Unity)¹ won the presidential race. The new president, who had been a candidate on three previous occasions, was a Marxist and a leader of the Socialist Party. The electoral victory of a Marxist stunned the right in Chile, divided the Christian Democrats, and was hailed by the Communists as a proof of the soundness of their political strategy: mass struggle instead of minority violence. An era of expectations followed. Could Chile traverse what her president proclaimed as "the peaceful road to Socialism"? In a few months it was evident that the problems and the obstacles were formidable. Loyal to his principles, Allende defended to the end the viability

*All excerpts have been taken from Juventudes Políticas Argentinas, *Allende: su Pensamiento Político* (Buenos Aires: Gránica Editor, 1973), pp. 19–26.

¹Popular Unity was formed by the Radical Party, the Socialist Party, the Communist Party, MAPU (Movement for United Popular Action), the Social Democratic party, and API (Independent Popular Action). MAPU had been formed by former Christian Democrats; the last two were minor parties.

of his course. On September 11, 1973, a military coup ended the "Chilean experiment." Allende was killed, or committed suicide, as the army attacked the "Casa de la Moneda" (the presidential palace).

These excerpts, taken from three different speeches, give the reader an idea of Allende's tragic road: from an initial optimism to an almost desperate attempt to convince his own comrades to avoid violent methods. I have tried to select those passages which deal more with ideological aspects than with factual problems.

Our Glorious Way
(November 5, 1970)

Without precedents anywhere in the world, Chile has just given an extraordinary demonstration of political development. By the free will of our citizens exercising their rights, an anti-capitalist movement has reached power. We have assumed power in order to give the country toward a new and more humane society. Our goals are the rationalization of economic activity, the progressive socialization of productive means, and the superseding of class division.

As socialists, we fully know which are the forces and the agents of historical change. Personally, I know that, as Engels wrote, "The peaceful transition from an old to a new society can be conceived in countries where the popular forces hold all power, where it is possible to do everything one wants in agreement with the Constitution once one has behind one the majority of the nation." . . . This is our Chile. Here, at last, Engels' version has been fulfilled. And let all of us remember that the theoretician of Marxism has never proclaimd, nor has history shown, that a single party is a necessity in the process of transition toward socialism.

After a series of dramatic events, our most prominent national characteristic has prevailed: the capacity to maintain in the political framework the most opposing views. Chile begins her march toward socialism without suffering the tragic experience of a fratricidal war. The greatness of that gesture will guide this government in its task of transforming the nation.

Our road is the road of Freedom.

The Chilean way is the way of Equality.

We are going to create a society where men can satisfy their spiritual and material needs, but without exploiting other men.

To those of you who have come from other countries, I made a request. Take back to your countries the image of what Chile is and this positive hope of what Chile is going to be.

Proclaim that here history is experiencing a turning point, that here a whole people managed to hold in their hands the direction of their destiny to move, through democratic means, toward socialism.

This Chile which is beginning to transform itself, this Chile in springtime and celebration, feels, as one of its most radical aspirations, the desire that in this world each man see in us his brothers.

Less than one year later, by November 1971, Allende's tone had become much more somber. International, economic, and political pressure, inflation, mounting opposition and radicalism from the left and the right was transforming the "Chilean way to Socialism" into a very dangerous road.

We have had serious difficulties—earthquakes, snow, volcanic eruptions—but the people have kept marching forward. Economic difficulties were provoked by the decline in the price of copper. During the previous government the price was 84 cents per pound; this year the average price won't reach 50 cents. World inflation is forcing us to pay more for what we import. True, we found 400 million dollars in the national reserve, but we also inherited a public debt of 2,560 million. We are the most indebted country in the world. Only Israel, a country at war, has a per capita debt (in relation with the national debt) higher than that of Chile.

We have had to face serious obstacles in the international field. We have disturbed powerful interests . . . and we can already hear threats of reprisals. There are rumors that many international economic organizations are going to deny any credit to Chile. . . . And we have been attacked by the international press.

But don't let those facts and publications impress you. The campaign against us is enormous, nothing positive in our actions is recognized, every mistake is magnified, but your answer is spontaneous, total condemnation of those actions and attitudes.

And that is why we are sorry to watch the political divisions among our forces. We would like to see the Radical Party reunited and back among us. We have invited the Christian Left (which broke with the Christian Democrats) to join Popular Unity. We must make stronger ties among Marxists, lay persons, Christians, and all those who feel the desire, the revolutionary fervor of the Chilean people.

We want to point out how the "ultras," the pseudofascists, who never said a word about the foreign control of our resources, are talking now with a dema-gogic nationalism that the people reject. They are the reactionaries who, to defend the privileges of a mi-nority, now display an anti-Communist stand. The people will stop them! Fascism will not triumph in our country.

We have also told many "extremists" (of the left) that we are not afraid of dialogue, of explaining our ideological situation, but that they should begin by reading the little book of Lenin, *Extremism: The Infantile Disease of Communism.* For it is very easy to be part of a revolutionary process without taking any sort of responsibility in the process; it is easy to criticize without any real base for criticism.[2]

The basic strength of the revolution is the iron-bound unity of the popular masses. Anyone who is trying to break that union is endangering the present and the future of the revolution. To reach power, the workers must conscientiously win over the majority. And that cannot be achieved by creating a climate of insecurity, violence, and eventually chaos.

By 1972, the political situation in Chile was visibly deteriorating. Inflation, strikes, violence, rumors of an impending civil war, had shattered the dream of a "peaceful way." Criticized from almost every side, besieged by misunderstanding and virulent attacks, Allende was even forced to speak to his socialist "compañeros" and to use Marxist arguments to reject some violent aspects of the Political Report of his own party.

[2]Allende here refers to the MIR (Movement of the Revolu-tionary Left), which had refused to participate in the govern-ment but not in the revolutionary process.

Our party has assumed governmental responsibility, which demands new efforts at examining all problems from a different perspective from when the party was in the opposition. We cannot keep on making general statements; we have an obligation to be precise and concrete in our proposals and plans.

Obviously, a party with the responsibility of sharing the direction of the government cannot simply assert: "The fundamental step for destroying the bourgeois state is control of political power by the proleteriat." That is too well known. The party must propose the methods which the organized action of the workers can and should follow—a task that the party will not be able to fulfill without a serious understanding of what the Chilean state is and represents in our present historical moment. And we have found in the Political Report of the Party profound contradictions, theoretical contradictions which can produce interpretations of how the party should act, . . . and those interpretations could be in open conflict with the program of the government, with the political line of the government, and, still more dangerous, with the historical reality of our country.

The report cannot begin by defining the present government as "a tool of bourgeois power" and later admit that "the bourgeoisie cannot tolerate that forces which are his enemies administer bourgeois laws. All the state institutions exist to ensure the dominion of the bourgeoisie, . . . but when they are administered by his class enemies they become a menace to bourgeois stability."

The Political Report cannot limit itself to arguing: "The State is organized and conceived to allow the minority class of exploiters to exercise a dictatorship over the exploited. This dictatorship is based on two pillars: the bureaucracy and the repressive apparatus." That assertion, valid when applied to capitalistic states, is too simplistic when applied to present-day Chile. It could produce a confusion capable of perturbing the entire political effort of the government, because today the bureaucracy and the repressive apparatus of the state respond to the popular government, the government of the workers, and not to the bourgeoisie.

How can anyone maintain that the structure of Public Administration should be destroyed—which assumes violence—when today that Public Administration is an instrument to act, transform, and create for the benefit of the workers?

It is theoretically incorrect to attribute an absolute value to norms and institutions. Beyond their form there is the social position of those who apply or use those norms and institutions. An institution in the hands of the monopolists will produce quite different results from what is produced when that same institution is in the hands of the workers. To insist on the abstract character of such instruments is incompatible with any Marxist analysis. The Political Report appears to have forgotten the fundamental principles of Marxist dialectic.

The creation of a socio-economic regime entails the development of social and economic factors which are essentially opposed to that regime. Those factors, engines of revolutionary change, are not the laws or the institutional apparatus of the state; they are inherent in the economic structure, in the new relations of production which we are promoting, in the conscience of the workers, in the new labor organizations which are changing the infrastructure. It is a rudiment of materialistic scientific analysis that the accumulation of quantitative changes produces qualitative changes. No one can have illusions of changing from day to night a socio-economic regime. The institutional form of a state can be transformed rapidly, but not its economic structure.

No one can dismiss the possibility of the bourgeoisie's escalating its attacks on the government and trying to create the conditions for a violent rupture. The organized workers should be conscious of the danger and ready to assume their role. But that does not mean denying the evidence that the present regime is transforming the system of production, breaking the power of imperialist capitalism, and strengthening the power of the workers.

Neither the Program of Popular Unity nor the government are looking forward to the risks of a jump into a vacuum. The militants of the Socialist Party should realize that, contrary to what the Political Report maintains, the shortest way to achieve qualitative transformations of the present political system is not that of breaking and destroying the constitutionality of the regime. That is a profound mistake. The institutional regime is based on the expressed free will of the Chilean citizens. Sixteen months ago, the will of the Chilean people allowed the organized workers to take power. The imperative today, the task of the popular forces, is to convince the majority of the people through revolutionary action, example, and efficiency to fight with us for our objective and our revolutionary goals.

41

GERRY FOLEY

———

The Extreme Left, the Communists, and Reformists inside the Chilean Government[*]

✳

This is how a Trotskyite viewed the Chilean situation in September 1972, one year before the military coup.

The regime's shift to the right has forced it to attack the revolutionary left. And it is on this front that the decisive battle seems to be developing that will determine the future of the popular front government.

At present most of the reformists' fire seems to be centered on the MIR, which has increased its influence in the past two years. Like most of the revolutionary groups that have developed in Latin America under the impact of the Cuban Revolution, the MIR was founded on the premise that guerrilla warfare was the only effective way of fighting for national liberation against increasingly repressive forms of rule by imperialism and the native capitalists. As a corol-

---

[*]From Les Evans, ed., *Disaster in Chile: Allende's Strategy and Why it Failed* (New York: Pathfinder Press, 1974), pp. 113–115, 117–118, 141–142.

lary, the group tended to de-emphasize the importance of specific political and economic demands,
stressing broad anti-imperialist slogans.

In keeping with this approach, the MIR favored
voting for Allende's popular front ticket while at the
same time expressing a very pessimistic view about
the possibilities of his being either elected or inaugurated. When Allende did win and was allowed
to take office, the MIR was confronted with a problem. Should it support the government or continue
preparing for guerrilla war? . . .

At first the MIR seemed to want to do both, and it
provided Allende's bodyguard, among other things.
Recently, however, the MIR has been raising sharp
criticisms of the reformism of Allende and the CP
and trying to offer an alternative line. Thus a very
acute confrontation has been developing.

This split came into the open dramatically on May
12, two days after CP legislator Volodia Teitelboim
gave a speech in the Senate blaming the "ultraleft"
equally with the right for the increasing violence in
the country. "There is an extreme right that traffics in
arms and is aiming for a civil war. But there are also
'ultra' groups that call themselves 'left' who are following the same course, playing the role of partner in
a mad waltz with their political opposites. They feed
on each other. . . .

But the Communists "are against any form of violence that might unleash a fratricidal struggle in this
country. However, it takes two to make a fight and
likewise you need at least two to prevent a quarrel.
And in this respect we think that this is the responsibility not only of the Unidad Popular but also of the
Christian Democratic Party and of all those who

think deeply about the dilemma of Chile and believe that just men can save this country from being plunged into a catastrophe."

Allende followed up the attacks of the CP, launching a violent denunciation of the People's Assembly in a statement issued July 31. He seemed to have borrowed his style of argument from his allies:

The people of Chile are facing a powerful enemy who uses modern techniques against them. And every member of the Unidad Popular, as well as every sympathizer of the national cause not active in the parties of the UP, must realize this. The enemy studies our weakness and exploits them. He is able, for example, to give indirect financial aid to any adventure, or exercise a psychological influence on any person who, impelled by impatience that comes from a low ideological level, splits away from the collective struggle to carry out individual actions.

"For the second time in three months in the province of Concepción a divisionist phenomenon has developed, disrupting the unity of the Unidad Popular movement. I do not hesitate to characterize it as a deformed process that is aiding the enemies of the revolutionary cause.

"The enemy has sought and insists on creating an artificial confrontation dividing the country in struggles whose ramifications the participants themselves cannot foresee. Nothing would suit him better for this purpose than an artificial confrontation within the Unidad Popular.

"I have said that there is no clash between the branches of the Chilean government, and that the executive branch is facing a political conflict created by those persons who from the positions they hold in the other branches of government are exceeding their powers and violating the constitution in order to block our historic mission. . . .

"To overcome the roots of this problem I have set the main objective as winning the 1973 general elections for parliament. . . .

"People's power will not come from a divisionist maneuver by people who are using political romanticism to create a lyrical mirage, which, out of touch with all reality, they call the People's Assembly."

The most consistent supporters of the People's Assembly seemed to be the MIR. They proposed not only to use the assembly as a means for mobilizing the masses to resist rightist intimidation and pressures; they also presented a concrete program around which the assembly could organize the people to smash the power of the bourgeoisie and the imperialists and begin fighting immediately against the reactionary sabotage of the country's economic life.

Despite the CP's timid centrism and the repeated success of the bourgeois opposition in rendering the government more and more impotent, the mobilization of the workers during the recent crisis shows that the margins for maneuver in the Chilean situation are getting dangerously tight, for both the reformists and the bourgeois moderates. The capitalists' minds are on arms.

The MIR and the left wing of the Socialist Party have raised sharp revolutionary criticisms of the Allende regime. The existence of substantial far-left forces is a factor that has not been present in other reformist governments such as the Goulart government in Brazil; it has clearly had an effect in pushing forward forms of revolutionary mobilization and workers' power.

But it is still unclear whether any of these forces is developing the capacity for leading the workers in a decisive confrontation with the bourgeoisie. Neither the Pliego de los Trabajadores nor the Pliego del Pueblo, for example, calls specifically for arming the workers, although this demand would seem to follow logically from creating vigilance groups to guard the factories against sabotage by well-armed rightist commandos. The MIR has said that it favors an alliance with soldiers, not just generals. It seems a safe assumption, however, that the generals in the cabinet will not extend "patriotic cooperation" to the point of permitting soldiers to participate in the processes of direct democracy developing in the country. The next few months will show how effectively the revolutionists can surmount this obstacle. In any case, if there were a mass workers' militia, it is likely that soldiers and police taking the side of the people would be attracted to it.

The MIR's concept of organizing the people to take power seems a little static. "In the factories, in the mines, on the ranches, in the villages, and in the schools. First there, then in the townships, the towns, and the cities, and finally the battle for all power." This is the way the November 6 *El Rebelde* described it. But if the delicate balance in Chile should suddenly be tipped toward a decisive confrontation, which seems a real possibility after October, it is not likely that people's power will grow regularly from the "grass roots" to the centers. The battle for power in Chile could be decided in a few rapid operations.

The bourgeoisie is capable of coordinated national

maneuvers, since most of the machinery of society remains in its hands. The reformists are paralyzed by their own ambiguities. What is yet to be seen is whether a Chilean revolutionary vanguard is developing that can weld the nuclei of popular power that emerged in October into a coherent force and direct it according to a precise strategy.

Significant advances were won in October in raising the consciousness and level of organization of the workers. These cannot be obscured by the miserable capitulation of the UP parties. But more decisive tests may develop in the near future.

42

CARLOS ALTAMIRANO

The Socialists against Reformism in the Government *

✳

As social and political conflicts sharpened in Chile, the parties which formed the Popular Unity Government began to be riddled by old and new antagonisms. At the beginning it was only the MIR who opposed the conciliatory attitude of the Communist Party toward the opposition and especially the Christian Democrats—an attitude that they considered bordering on treason—but soon radical elements of the Socialist Party also joined the protest against the Communist policy of "consolidating the Socialist gains." Here one of the leaders of the "radical" Socialists attacks "reformism" and obliquely defends the MIR. The leftist wing of the Socialist Party increased its radicalization during the last months of Allende's government.[1]

As we have pointed out many times before, we must be aware of the many dangers of all kinds which

---

*From Carlos Altamirano, *Decision Revolucionaria* (Chile: Edicion Homenaje al 40 aniversario del Partido Socialista, 1973), pp. 56, 64, 80, 82.

[1]For Altamirano's explanation of the fall of Allende and the role of the Socialists, see his *Dialéctica de una derrota* (Mexico: Siglo XXI, 1977).

today menace the Chilean process. Those dangers exist outside and inside our frontiers. . . . Outside we have imperialism and its long tentacles. . . . Inside, the right and fascism.

But inside our own ranks there are also dangers— dangers which are the result of conscious and unconscious mistakes and weaknesses.

And this happens because there are those who were ready only for revolutionary theory, but who are not ready for revolutionary action! They expected a drop-by-drop revolution! And they misunderstood or were frightened by the historical force which this process is gaining. They became disoriented when faced with the extraordinary force of the people.

Quite contrary to that position our party is fighting at all levels to stop certain conciliatory tendencies from taking root in the revolutionary process. We cannot accept that—for example—leaders and workers of the Industrial Belts[2] could contemptuously be called "ultras" or "hot-heads" or "extremists." The Socialist Party looks at the revolutionary process as an uninterrupted march, without pauses or premature consolidations within the capitalist system, a march aimed at the conquest of power, total power, by the workers. . . . From this point of view, the process is from the very beginning a socialist process. Any effort to seek an understanding with bourgeois political groups, as the Christian Democracy, to solve through traditional political means the conflicts produced by class struggle, will harm the ascendant course of the revolutionary process.

[2]Zones around Santiago (the capital) with a heavy concentration of industries. They became the centers of action and propaganda of the MIR and other radical groups.

We warned the Communist Party that the economic policy offered by the minister of economy, "compañero" Orlando Millas, would provoke splits in the popular front and would be resisted by the workers, forcing them to oppose the Popular Unity Government. Recent events have shown that we were right.

Our Position toward MIR

In a letter addressed to MIR, by the secretary general of the Communist Party, it is said that some of the "suicidal proposals" of that party had been echoed favorably in certain sectors of Popular Unity. We must clarify our position. We do not agree with many of MIR's ideas. . . . But we think that that organization is a revolutionary force which, even if it rejects the programs and policy of the UP government, is essentially fighting to defend and expand the Chilean revolutionary process.

The program is not to fall into academic discussions but to clarify how we interpret correctly the ideas of the working class. All our problems are rooted in one vital issue: the conquest of power.

To gain that objective it is essential to develop the revolutionary process, which means that, under the guidance of Marxist-Leninist principles, the workers must reaffirm their role as vanguard of the revolution. Otherwise, we'll remain in a "reformist" position which will leave the bases of capitalism untouched.

To try to "consolidate the process," stopping all advance, will inevitably strengthen the enemy and produce ideological disarray among the ranks of the people. Victory can be achieved only by reinforcing the revolutionary conscience of the masses, who had already created their own valid slogan: "avanzar sin tranzar," "to advance without compromise."

43

VELODIA TETOBLIAN

The Failure in Chile and the Future of a Strategy *

＊

During the entire history of the Allende regime, the Communist Party, the best organized of all the parties which formed the Popular Unity government, maintained a position of moderation. Basing its tactics on the essence of the Popular Front strategy, the party maintained that it was necessary to gain the support of the majority of the Chilean people before accelerating social change and that it was very dangerous to alarm the middle class with violent methods. Their motto was "to consolidate before advancing."

As the reader might guess, after Allende's political collapse, and with their usual discipline, the party ratified its doctrinal position and continued to blame the "extremists" for Allende's failure. These excerpts are taken from an article surprisingly called "Chile: Prelude to Future Victories." Its author is a historian and a member of the Political Commission of the Chilean Communist Party.

Chile is still very much in the news, mostly in connection with the unparalleled atrocities of the mili-

*From *Political Affairs* (New York), August 1974, pp. 40–48.

tary junta, the heroic resistance of the people, and the massive international protest and solidarity campaign. However, the Chilean events raise many problems that go far beyond our country and have evoked unabating interest throughout the world.

I need hardly say that the Communist Party of Chile is making a critical and self-critical analysis. And not only to understand the experiences of the past, but also to draw lessons for our present struggle so that, sooner or later, our country can be freed of the fascist yoke. Analysis of Chile's problems is not the monopoly of the Chileans. It is the right of all revolutionary parties, of everyone who is not indifferent to the fate of other nations, and everyone is free to pass judgment. We do not intend to hide behind a wall of so-called ideological nationalism, maintaining that we alone are entitled to speak of our mistakes. Of course, since we are responsible for them, we are especially anxious to get down to their root causes; that is the first prerequisite for avoiding more mistakes.

False pride and belief in one's infallability are alien to true Communists. Friendly, benevolent criticism by fraternal parties only helps us.

After September 11 many have been asking: Can a people come to power without recourse to arms? Everyone is entitled to his own answer. Our Party's is: that path is not closed despite the overthrow of the popular government.

Marxism-Leninism envisages both the armed and nonarmed path to power. The latter has a very definite meaning for us: all the components of socialist revolution as a process of aggravated class struggle, but without civil war. The Chilean events confirm rather than refute Marxist-Leninist theory.

The Chilean experience has clearly demonstrated the possibility of forming a people's government following on an election victory of a Left bloc led by the workers' parties and subscribing to Marxist-Leninist ideology. Life has debunked the bourgeois contention that revolution and democracy are "incompatible" and has vindicated the idea that the struggle for democracy is an inalienable part of the struggle for socialism.

What our people has gone through suggests this conclusion: the choice of path is determined by the imperative need daily to infuse new strength into the struggle for the people's cause.

In the conditions of today as in the past, the Chilean Communists choose the forms of struggle most likely to unite all the democratic forces. At each given moment we must gauge the level of consciousness of the masses and the real alignment of forces, in order that every step we take shall be in the interests of the people.

A statement by our Party urges avoiding dogmatic imposition on the popular movement of forms of struggle against the putschists. Some comrades of the Left are already suggesting that civil war is inevitable. It is too early to discuss that.

On the other hand, the Communists warn against the danger of individual terror or coup attempts. The junta would like nothing better—it would use them to justify the terror upon which its rests. In the past extremism and provocation were of no mean help to the enemies of the people. Today, too, rash adventurism would play into the hands of the fascists Leigh and Arellano Stark, enabling them to impose their own "rules of the game."

We Chilean Communists say that under all circumstances a revolutionary must reckon with the realities of the mass struggle and be prepared for changes in the situation, and not invent artificial schemas. Most important, he must continue his day-to-day painstaking work among the thousands of working people. That is the key to success in the fight against the dictatorship.

What are the reasons, we are asked, for the temporary defeat of Chile's revolutionary forces? In our view there was a complex of objective and subjective factors. We have repeatedly stressed that when Popular Unity won a part of the political power in 1970, it inherited a multitude of problems. They could not be solved in three years, especially in view of opposition by the reactionary forces, who still wielded considerable power in the economic and political fields, in the legislature, judiciary and armed forces, and controlled the press.

The Popular Unity government's stay in power was a veritable kaleidoscope of subversion by the imperialist monopolies and local oligarchic groups bent on instituting fascism and crushing the revolution, which the people wanted to carry out by relying on their democratic freedoms. The terror methods used by the putschists bear foreign trademarks. The tragedy of the Chilean people rests on the conscience of those who hampered the popular government, did everything to torpedo its program of revolutionary change, inflated the difficulties, spread chaos and supported the putschists.

In discussing the reasons for the temporary defeat, we must take into account also this negative factor: the existence of two opposite trends within the Popular Unity bloc and government, the absence of a united and consistent strategy and tactics and of a clearcut plan for the winning of full power.

The Communist Party consistently maintained that the popular movement must win over the overwhelming majority of the population so as to resolve the issue of power once and for all in favor of the people. Guided by Leninist theory, we acted in accordance with the objective laws of social development, faithfully adhering to the Popular Unity program, which envisaged uniting the people around the working class, the mainstay of the revolution.

Representatives of the other trend, unfortunately, took a sectarian attitude and constantly hampered our work by undermining the Popular Unity bloc from within and without. Its activity was paralyzed; there were endless futile discussions. As a result, the initiative in the battle for the masses was lost to the counter-revolutionaries, and they mounted an offensive. The working class was isolated from its allies.

44

Conference
of Communist Parties
# of Latin America
and the Caribbean [*]

*

This meeting of Communist parties, held in Havana in June 1975, was the largest ever held in the hemisphere. There were twenty-four delegations. The discussions and the resulting declaration confirmed the rigid pro-Soviet position of all the parties, including the Cuban. The essence of the strategy, applied from Argentina to Mexico, is to support any government or any action which is anti-imperialistic, that is, anti-American. Beyond the usual generalizations and Marxist formulas, there is a pragmatic insistence on a basic point: anything that weakens American imperialism could be an "objective" revolutionary step toward socialism.

We communists consider that socialism is the only system capable of truly guaranteeing the development of Latin America at the accelerated pace which our

[*]From *Gramma* (Havana), June 22, 1975.

countries demand. Cuba has proved to the brother peoples that in our time, it is possible to undertake the building of socialism under existing conditions in the American continent and is able to show its victorious accomplishments. Socialism is our unforsakeable objective. Nevertheless, we communists understand that socialism will become an immediate program for all the countries of Latin America only through a period of intense struggles and radical transformations, of direct experiences of the workers, and of consistent and tenacious ideological struggle of all those who aspire to socialism, in order to overcome the oligarchies in sectors of the Latin-American people's forces through their control over the mass media and education.

At the same time, it is evident that the Latin-American peoples will not be able to achieve true progress without the political overthrow of the representatives of the classes and sectors allied to imperialism; nor will it be possible for them to introduce substantial socioeconomic changes in our countries— much less pass on to the achievement of socialism— without defeating the oppression of U.S. imperialism over each one of our countries, without eliminating the control of the transnational corporations.

The battle for democracy for the masses, the struggle for urgent structural changes and for the transition to socialism, are indissolubly linked to the struggle against monopolies and imperialism which, aside from maintaining control over our riches, uphold and support the oligarchies and their governments.

Since U.S. imperialism is the main, common enemy, the strategy and the tactics of the revolution in Latin

America, for those of us who conceive it as a revolution whose final aim is socialism, go through anti-imperialism. Therefore, we communists judge the political positions of the other Latin-American forces fundamentally by their attitude toward that enemy. Without diminishing the importance of the struggle for democratic rights and for the achievement of new structures within our countries, we communists are willing to support and push forward those positions of Latin-American governments which may constitute a defense of our natural resources or the efforts to put an end to the pretensions of transnational corporations to maintain and increasingly extend the control over our economies.

It is true that the measures of defense of the domestic economy are not always accompanied by a genuine anti-imperialist policy. In some cases, it is strictly bourgeois nationalism which does not result in aspirations of transformation of the domestic economy, nor places the government that puts them into practice in progressive positions in view of the principal problems debated today. Nationalism can be transformed into anti-imperialist and revolutionary positions to the extent that the people's forces decisively participate in the struggle, to the extent to which the contradictions between nationalistic governments and imperialism sharpen.

There are countries in which the defense of the national resources and the determination to recover the economy from the hands of the transnational enterprises are effectively united to programs of social transformation. Where governments go beyond the nationalization of the riches controlled by imperialism and carry out a people's program for the development of the domestic economy like in Peru, the communists—as the ones in that country do—can grant their most loyal and resolute support of these measures. The fact that communists have a conception of social development different from the one that guides those programs will not weaken their support to the positions of the government, nor will it be an obstacle to jointly face the problems of the future.

The anti-imperialist struggle that will lead Latin America to final independence allows and demands the participation of the broadest social sectors, and the leading role in that struggle corresponds to the working class. The working peasants are their natural allies. These are the social classes that aspire to the most profound transformations.

Although under the domination and dependency of imperialism, the capitalist development of Latin America has generated important modifications in the social composition of the different countries.

The growth of the urban and rural working class stands out. The number of wage-earners today surpasses fifty million and represents more than sixty percent of the economically active population of the continent. Approximately one-half of the wage-earners is made up by agricultural workers. The structure of the working class has also changed and its concentration in the big factories has grown. All these phenomena are reflected in the heightening of the role of the proletariat as the principal productive and sociopolitical force.

At the same time, the working class betters its organization and projects itself as the social force capable of determining the political panorama in the different countries of Latin America. The proletariat also tends to become the principal factor for the unification of the other democratic and anti-imperialist social sectors.

The struggle for achieving full national liberation and economic independence is interrelated with an intense class struggle against capitalist exploitation, fundamentally against foreign and local monopolies and latifundia. Under the yoke of capital, the degree of exploitation of the working class grows. Sheer hunger wages prevail in many places of Latin America. The part of the National Income received by the working class diminishes progressively and the real wage decreases due to inflation and the ever higher cost of living.

The experience of the revolutionary movement in Latin America, rich in heroic and combative actions of the working class, clearly shows that this class also represents the most firm principles of solidarity with the struggle of other peoples against imperialism, for the triumph of the national liberation revolution, for democracy and socialism.

The example of the governments which in Latin America today resist imperialism and attempt to implement programs of true national recovery, shows that the struggle for Latin-American and anti-imperialist liberation can count on other social forces and elements which constitute, due to their contradictions with imperialism, allies to which the progressive forces cannot but grant attention.

The economic process of the countries of Latin America created a situation in which the highest levels of their local bourgeoisies became so greatly linked to and dependent on imperialism for its own growth and invigoration that in fact they have become part of the mechanism of imperialist domination in their own countries. That is the way it happened in Cuba with the sugar and importing bourgeoisie; that is the way it happens today with a great part of the bourgeoisies which in Mexico, Argentina, Columbia, and Brazil share monopolistic positions linked to the domination of these economies by imperialist corporations. Those denationalized bourgeoisies defend the dependence and oppose the anti-imperialist process. Even in the cases where differences or clashes come up between those monopoly bourgeoisies and their imperialist partners, the class interest of the former will lead them to try to solve them through a conciliatory way. At the same time, they oppose the attempts made by governments which try to break the ties of foreign domination which suffocate their countries. Some of these bourgeois sectors join the big landowners to whom they are related economically in order to constitute a pro-imperialist local oligarchy opposed to the interests of the working class, of the peasants and middle classes and of other bourgeois sectors interested in the development of an internal market and in national progress.

The historic reality does not mean that there are not sectors of the Latin-American bourgeoisie which, in view of the contradiction of their interests with those of imperialism, adopt positions that coincide with those of the proletariat, the peasants, and other noncapitalist strata of the population in their anti-imperialist struggle and for the conquest of economic independence and full national sovereignty. These bourgeois sectors, consequently, can take part in the democratic and anti-imperialist united action together with the people's forces. The communist parties and all other fighters against imperialism and for social progress in Latin America give great importance to that possibility, taking into account that it represents an element found with varying degrees of strength and importance in the different countries, which nevertheless constitutes an indispensable ingredient in that complex, multifarious, and difficult struggle.

At the same time, it would be erroneous to ignore the limitations and hesitations of those sectors of the bourgeoisie in regard to its participation in the anti-imperialist process. In Latin America, the bourgeoisie lost a long time ago the possibility of playing the leading role which belongs to the proletariat. It cannot carry on the new battle for independence to the end. The incorporation of forces and organizations representative of such sectors of the bourgeoisie to the wide front of anti-imperialist and anti-oligarchic struggle is highly important; but it will never take place at the expense of the essential alliance of workers, peasants, and the middle strata, nor of the class independence of the proletariat for the benefit of junctural compromises.

The revolutionary struggle of Latin America is characterized as a difficult and complex battle in which all forces that oppose U.S. imperialism have their place, and in which the most varied forms and methods of struggle should be used by the Latin-American revolutionary movement, adequately adapting its location and moment of use to the diversity of conditions in each country. The utilization of all legal possibilities is an indispensable obligation of the anti-imperalist forces, and the defense of the right of the peoples to decide, through democratic means, the transformations they demand, is a constant principle of our struggle.

Revolutionaries are not the first to resort to violence. But, it is the right and duty of all people's and revolutionary forces to be ready to open the way, through various means, to the peoples' actions, including armed struggle to the sovereign decision of majorities.

Communist parties which deepen their roots in the cardinal interests of the working class, play a decisive historical role and have an exceptional responsibility in the struggle. As political forces that are guided by the Marxist-Leninist doctrine, the only one capable of setting a possibility of playing that role within the alliance of the revolutionary forces. But that role is not guaranteed only by virtue of the social forces they represent and the exact theory that guides them. They will fulfill it to the extent that they become the most firm combatants for national and social liberation, taking authentic vanguard positions in the struggle, through practice, showing the peoples their programs of action, their strategic and tactical positions directed to unite all anti-imperalist forces and to orient the processes for ultimate revolutionary transformations.

We communists have the right to expect from those who act jointly with us in the national struggles of each of our countries, in spite of the immediate programmatic differences and the varied final aspirations, reciprocal respect for our political stands and our ideology.

The leaders of the various movements who, from within governments of Latin America or from without, have today as their purpose the liberty of their peoples, have every right to categorically define their socioeconomic aims as noncommunist. History will decide who has been right in the selection of the options for Latin-American development. We communists have no doubt about that verdict.

There is a difference between being noncommunist and being anti-communist. To be anti-communist means a historical blindness that places those who suffer from it on the road of identifying themselves with the worst, backward forces and inevitably leads them to failure. Anti-communism is a reactionary position and the center of the counterrevolutionary ideologies of our epoch. We can respect those who are not Communists, but we can never silence our criticism of those who, by mistake, define themselves, as anti-communists, nor can we avoid the combat to death against those who consciously take on anti-communist positions.

If anti-imperialist unity is indispensable, the unity of the forces of the left within it is even more essential.

The influence of socialist ideas in the world, resulting from the irreversible victories of the Soviet Union and the other socialist countries of Europe and Asia, and from the example of an unbreakable confidence in Cuba's economic, political and social progress, the advance of Marxist-Leninist theory as the only one capable of giving a solution to the problems contemporary society faces, and the active presence of the communist parties permit in Latin America today—outside the framework of these parties and of the old socialist organizations—the existence of a left of various shades, some of whose organizations call themselves Marxist-Leninist and proclaim socialism as their objective of struggle.

The communist parties when pointing out what they disagree with in regard to the strategic conceptions or tactical approaches of those forces, will take into account that some of these movements are guided by the purpose of defeating imperialist oppression and advancing toward genuine socialist positions.

The communist parties do not silence their discrepancies with these trends, but they distinguish between erroneous positions and the adventurist attitudes they condemn. The anti-communist or anti-Soviet left is inconceivable and with this criterion the communists endeavour to isolate those who adopt such attitudes.

Controversy between the forces of the left must always start from positions of unity and serve unity on the basis of shared principles and purpose, and tactics appropriate to the circumstances and conditions in which the common struggle is waged.

At different moments of the development of anti-imperialist struggle, various social sectors might fall into attitudes or be influenced by conciliating reformist conceptions or narrowly sectarian ones. The permanent struggle against both noxious influences will allow the consolidation of unity of action on a truly solid basis, affirming more and more the independent and class role of the revolutionary proletariat.

On this occasion of reckoning, the communist parties of Latin America pay homage with our banners to the thousands of communist combatants who have fallen during the last decades in every corner of Latin America for the cause of the independence of their countries and for the achievement of socialism. We greet all communist militants who are imprisoned, who are being tortured and persecuted, among whom we specially recall comrades Luis Corvalán, Antonio Maidana, Jamie Pérez, whose freedom we demand. We greet the revolutionaries and patriots—nomembers of our parties—who suffer imprisonment and torture and we renew our homage to those who have fallen in the common struggle for national liberation.

The fierce repression unleashed against the patriots and progressive forces, and very especially against the Brazilian Communist Party and its leadership, due to its firm opposition to the fascist regime, and against all progressive forces, affirms the need to continue and broaden the solidarity of Latin America with the democratic and anti-imperialist struggle of the Brazilian people.

We likewise express our solidarity with the vigorous resistance of the workers and the people of Bolivia against the affliction suffered under Banzer's dictatorship; with the patriots who suffer persecution and imprisonment in Paraguay; with the people of Haiti, oppressed by a terrible dictatorship; with the progressive forces of Argentina, subjected to barbarous provocations by the groups of facist murderers organized into the so-called "Triple A"; with those who suffer from the fascist persecution of Bordaberry in Uruguay; with the Puerto Rican patriots, persecuted and imprisoned by the colonial regime, and with all those who suffer imprisonment and tortures at the hands of dictatorial and anti-democratic governments in other places of our America. We ratify our support to the people of Guatemala and the Guatemalan Labor Party, stressing the courage and the decision with which they wage battles for national and social emancipation in

Guatemala in the face of an usurping and bloody regime; with the revolutionaries and democrats of Nicaragua who suffer from all types of persecution on the part of the Somoza dynasty, which together with the reactionary government of Guatemala, perpetrates an abusive interference in the internal affairs of the area.

We express our special solidarity with Lolita Lebrón, Puerto Rican patriot who is the oldest political prisoner of the continent and who is a symbol of all those who suffer imprisonment because of their ideas.

In proclaiming close unity and solidarity for the common struggle against imperialism, which has working class internationalism as its firm basis, we communists of Latin America reaffirm that each of our parties, following the principles of Marxism-Leninism and taking into consideration concrete national conditions, elaborates its own policy.

45

The Communist Party
of Ecuador Supports
the Military Junta[*]

*

*On January 11, 1976, after the resignation of Briga-
dier General Guillermo Rodriguez Lara, a military
junta, headed by Vice-Admiral Alfredo Pereda Bur-
bano, assumed power in Ecuador. The new government proclaimed a plan for the legal reorganization
of the nation and promised elections before January
1978. While many political groups expressed their
skepticism, the Communist Party, following its traditional tactic, officially recognized in the conference
held in Havana in 1975 (see document 44), publicly
announced its support. By May 1977 there were signs
that, to gain strength, the Communist Party was encouraging the formation of a political coalition with
center and leftist parties.*

The Central Committee of the Communist Party of
Ecuador, meeting in plenary session, examined the
Plan for Legal Reorganization of the State, submitted
by the Government of the Armed Forces and consis-

[*]From "Translations on Latin America," *U.S. Joint Publications
Research Service* (Washington: D.C.: No. 1515, July 9, 1976,
pp. 55–57.

tent with political position of the party, arrived at the following conclusions:

1. To express its agreement with the above-mentioned Plan for Legal Reorganization of the State.

2. Proper implementation of the Plan for Legal Reorganization of the State entails stimulating with determination the achievement of those basic revolutionary changes that will ensure the country and the people of a better life, social progress, sovereignty and independence. These changes are the basic requirements of the present time and must be carried out immediately, during the application of the plan.

3. The following are those revolutionary changes:

   a. Achievement of a real, democratic agrarian reform that will turn the land over to those who work it, that will destroy large landholdings, that will give the real farm-workers technical, credit, marketing and other assistance required and that will be supported, for this change, by rural organizations, whether they be unions, cooperatives, committees, and so on. Vigorous, [immediate implementation of article 25 of the agrarian reform law].

   b. Total nationalization of the oil industry in all its aspects: extraction, transportation, marketing, industrialization. Not one single concession of any kind to oil monopolies. Greater speed in setting up the state refinery and state petrochemical industries. Expansion of FLOPEC (Ecuadorean Oil Tanker Fleet). Continuation of Ecuador's membership in OPEC.

   c. Maintenance of a firm defense of our sovereignty

over 200 miles of territorial sea. Establishment of a state fishing industry and of a state fishing fleet. Assistance to the private fishing sector. Collaboration with socialist countries in all these aspects.

d. Democratization of the nation's activity by giving participation to the workers and their organizations and to people's organizations with a democratic position in decision-making bodies.

e. Development of state industry. Incentive to large jobs for electrifying the country. Complete nationalization of the electrical industry in the country. Complete nationalization of the cement and sugar industries. Establishment of a strong state flour industry. Support and expansion of TRANSNAVE (ECUADOREAN SHIPPING TRANSPORTATION). Renovation of the national railroad system.

f. Improvement of the people's living standard:

(1) Raising of wages and salaries. Expansion of the determination of minimum wages by labor branch.

(2) Revocation of antilabor decrees as requested by labor union federations.

(3) Proper solution of labor conflicts.

(4) State control of the distribution of some basic products: gas, sugar, rice, fats, wheat.

(5) Distribution of essential commodities by state agencies (ENAC and ENPROVIT [National Enterprise for Vital Products]) through commissary stores in enterprises, directly to the consumer, through labor unions, enterprise committees, people's

committees and, in a controlled manner, through small businessmen.

(6) Price control on industrial items and popular consumer goods.

(7) Rent reduction.

g. Attention to education and the people's health. Drive against illiteracy. Expansion of technical education. Construction of sufficient local schools. Complete state takeover of welfare services. Environmental improvement and preventive medicine drive.

h. Attention to the requirements of the provinces and various sections of the country.

i. Investment of public funds in these objectives. Elimination of the system of subsidies to private enterprises. Change of the policy of the Finance Corporation, devoting the funds preferentially to state industry.

j. Maintenance of an independent, sovereign, peace policy. Consolidation of the steps taken in this connection. Relations with [Cuba, Democratic Republic of Vietnam, People's Democratic Republic of Korea, People's Republic of Angola].

These conquests are indispensable steps on the way to the social and national liberation of the people of Ecuador and they were included, to a considerable extent, in the 1945 Constitution and in the Philosophy and Plan of Action of the Nationalist, Revolutionary Government, for whose fulfillment the armed forces have a commitment with the people.

4. The Communist Party of Ecuador will continue its inescapable struggle for this program, which must be included and consolidated in the legal instruc-

tions resulting from the application of the Plan for Reorganization.

5. In order to make a democratic orientation of the Plan for Reorganization possible, the commissions contemplated by it must be made up of persons with a tried and tested democratic, anti-imperialist stand, civilians and military, including representatives of the organized sectors of workers and complete exclusion of persons with a fascist position or a position of subservience to imperialism.

6. The work of these commissions, likewise, must not become secret, but, rather, their discussions and conclusions must be reported to the people periodically and systematically for their knowledge and deliberation.

The Central Committee of the Communist Party of Ecuador calls on all anti-imperialist, democratic, patriotic forces, civilian and military, to unite our forces in a great patriotic front that will fight for the revolutionary changes that have been pointed out and that will prevent the Plan for Reorganization from being utilized by the oligarchies and imperialism to revert to an ignominious past condemned by the people and by history, as they attempted in their Plan for Return to the Constitution.

Guayaquil, 6 June 1976

Central Committee of the Communist Party of Ecuador

46

FIDEL CASTRO

The International Dimension of the Cuban Revolution: Africa,…China,…U.S.A.*

✱

After the "successful" intervention of Cuban troops in Angola, Castro returned to one of his favorite subjects: the role and "mission" of the Cuban revolution in the Third World.

I don't want to talk about our military cooperation. I can't say that we Cuban revolutionaries helped the Angolan revolutionaries and patriots: we simply did our internationalist duty.

Following the war, the difficult period of national reconstruction began. But the imperialists weren't about to let the people of Angola work in peace, and they demanded that Cuba withdraw its military cooperation from Angola. What did they want? To renew their acts of agression against the people of Angola. To attack Cabinda, to attack from the north and the

---

*From *Gramma* (Havana), April 10, 1977, and May 22, 1977 (English edition).

south again. What was our duty? For one thing, to maintain our military cooperation with the Republic of Angola while the Angolan FAPLA was organized, trained and equipped.

The day will come when you won't need our military cooperation; the day will come when the Angolan people have enough military units, tanks, cannon, planes and soldiers to hold off any and all imperialist attacks.

Following the war, the number of Cuban fighters in Angola was progressively reduced and the number of civilian workers—that is, technicians for the reconstruction of the country—increased daily. Above all, there is a very important question of international policy. As you know, our country, a small country on the other side of the Atlantic, is constantly being threatened by the imperialists. The imperialists established an economic blockade against Cuba that has already lasted more than 17 years. The Yankee imperialists demanded that Cuba withdraw its military cooperation from Angola, saying that, if Cuba didn't do so, the blockade and the hostility toward our country would be continued.

This is why I would like to take advantage of this opportunity to define Cuba's positions. Our military and civilian cooperation with the Government of Angola is based on the agreements between the Governments of Angola and Cuba. We will never submit this cooperation to negotiation with the imperialists. Do what they will, say what they like, we will never submit this point to negotiation with the imperialists. They have no right to say how the sister peoples of Angola and Cuba should work and cooperate.

There are agreements between Angola and Cuba

on what arms and how many Cuban fighters will be in Angola for how long. The Governments of Angola and Cuba decided on this, and we don't have to discuss it with the Yankee imperialists.

Logically, once the war was over, the number of Cuban fighters in Angola decreased, and the number of civilian workers for the country's reconstruction is increasing. But the reactionaries and imperialists shouldn't misunderstand this. The forces of FAPLA are growing, and, together with FAPLA, the number of Cuban arms and fighters is sufficient to crush any attack launched against Cabinda or the rest of Angola —in the north, south, east or west, by land, air, or sea.

So this point should be perfectly clear. The imperialist Government of the United States egged on the attacks against Angola. Everybody knows that the FNLA was financed right from the start by the CIA and the Yankee imperialists. Everybody knows that UNITA was financed by the Portuguese colonialists and then by the South African racists. It was the imperialist Government of the United States that egged the neocolonialist, reactionary Government of Zaire on to send troops into Angola, and it was the imperialist Government of the United States that egged the South African racists on to invade Angola.

What I have seen all over Angola, wherever our delegation has been, has been encouraging. We have talked with doctors, health technicians, construction workers, with Cubans who are cooperating with Angolans on many work fronts; and I have observed their real enthusiasm, spirit of sacrifice, fraternity and— above all—immense affection for the Angolans and the Angolan Revolution. I have observed the same interest in work and struggle in our compatriots as they would have in their own homeland. But I should say something else. It is your duty to work harder in Angola than you would if you were in Cuba.

The imperialists don't understand this, and they ask themselves why the Cuban are helping the Angolans. They don't understand what revolutionary feelings are or what internationalism is. They don't understand our disinterestedness. For Marxist-Leninists, all peoples are brothers, and all workers should unite to struggle against the exploitation of man by man, against imperialism, against injustice, to struggle for the brotherhood of all mankind. And every victorious revolution is a victory for all the peoples of the world, every success of a people a success for the other peoples. Only in unity, only by cooperating with one another, will we manage to defeat imperialism.

Angolan brothers and sisters, we are pleased and it makes us happy to see the fruits of our lofty brotherhood and cooperation. The colonialists thought that Angola couldn't move forward without them; the colonialists thought that the industries couldn't go back into operation once they decided to leave because they didn't accept the Revolution or because they didn't resign themselves to Angola's independence. They thought that Angola would go down in ruins, yet here it is just a year after the victory and many factories are already back in production, many schools and hospitals are functioning and agriculture is getting more and more attention. We know that, in the field of construction alone, more than 100 factories are in operation. And every industry, sugar mill, cement plant, construction materials factory and every machine that is gotten running is a victory for the Angolan Revolution. . . .

On China:

For a long time I thought that the Chinese leadership was making great mistakes, though I didn't think it was consciously and deliberately betraying the cause of internationalism and Marxism-Leninism. That seemed unbelievable. I couldn't understand how a country that had carried out the socialist revolution, led by workers and peasants, could adopt such an absurd international policy, that was so similar to that of capitalism and imperialism. Now I'm absolutely convinced that it isn't a matter of mistakes but is rather a conscious policy of betrayal of internationalism and of an alliance with imperialism. There isn't a single aspect of the international situation on which the Chinese leaders' policy doesn't coincide with that of imperialism. There are numerous examples of this. In Chile, they associated themselves with Pinochet and fascism. In the Latin-American countries, they associated themselves with the most reactionary and antinational elements. In Africa—and this was evident in Angola—they supported the groups associated with the CIA and neocolonialism. It is a shameful thing that they went so far as to become the allies of the fascists, especially those of South Africa, in the aggression against Angola and the MPLA. Now they are deeply committed to the Government of Zaire, one of Africa's most reactionary, neocolonialist and repressive regimes. They are completely in accord with Morocco's and French and U.S. imperialism's intervention in the internal affairs of Zaire, and they are sending a large number of light and heavy-caliber weapons to the regime in Zaire. As a general rule, China's foreign policy goes hand in hand with neocolonialism in

Africa and with the Arab reaction in the Middle East. In Europe, the Chinese leaders associated themselves with the policy of NATO and U.S. imperialism and with the most reactionary parties, such as the Christian-Democrat Party in Federal Germany and the British Conservative Party, whose most notorious leaders are invited to visit China and are paid all kinds of honors. In Europe, fascist groups and so-called extremist groups that are infiltrated by the CIA are receiving subsidies and other support from China. China also supports the FRG's position on the unification of Germany, as opposed to the policy and the interests of the GDR, and supports the existence of NATO and the presence of U.S. troops in Europe. China encourages chauvinism and splits within the socialist camp. Acting in an adventurous and irresponsible fashion, the Chinese leadership is trying to cause a war between the Soviet Union and the United States, trying to intensify the arms race and opposing all peace policies. The Chinese leadership insanely fails to realize that a world war with nuclear and other weapons of mass destruction would be suicidal for mankind. They believe that their country would emerge as the only survivor of such a war.

With its treason, the Chinese Government has created a deep split among the world's revolutionary forces, just when they were about to achieve a balance of forces that would have been decisive for the victory of socialism in the world.

The Chinese leadership is waging a disgusting slander campaign against the Soviet Union. Without the victory of the October Revolution and the struggle waged by the Soviet Union against fascism—at the cost of 20 million lives—it would have been impossible to eliminate the colonial system and to increase and support the world socialist and progressive movement. Without the existence of the Soviet Union, imperialism would not have hesitated—in this time of the energy crisis and of a growing lack of natural resources—to begin a new division of the world. In fact, the Chinese Revolution would never have taken place.

This same Chinese policy can be seen in Asia, where the Japanese imperialists' demands for territory are being backed by Peking, in opposition to the Soviet Union. This policy supports all the reactionary policies in that part of the world. It is a coarse, opportunistic, demagogical and cynical policy.

As far as Cuba is concerned, the Chinese policy is infamous, to say the least. China is waging a campaign of revolting lies to combat our Party's solidarity with the liberation movements—something which goes hand in hand with U.S. Imperialists' attacks against our country. China is opposed to the lifting of the U.S. economic blockade of Cuba and to the return of the territory of the Guantánamo base, occupied by the United States. We have been informed by reliable sources that the Chinese secret services are working in close collaboration with those of France, the United States, West Germany and NATO. Even though this may seem incredible, we have to say it, because it is absolutely true.

A number of political events took place in the People's Republic of China only recently that led to the elimination of what has been called "the band of four." Now, everybody knows that, for ten years, this band laid down the country's policy and was responsible for all the things I've just mentioned. I ask myself how it was possible, when Mao Tse-tung was alive, for his wife and a handful of ambitious men to have so much power.

Either Mao was completely senile in the last period of his life or else he wasn't the genius, the god of the revolution, that the Chinese leaders are trying to present him as having been. I sincerely believe that all this stems from the cult of the personality and from the deification of the leaders—neither of which is tolerated by a true Communist.

We can see that, thus far, neither a real policy of principles nor a return to a truly revolutionary policy is being discussed in China. So far, there is just a disgusting power struggle.

However, I believe that China's present policy is objectively absurd and that there's no future for the Chinese people in this alliance with imperialism and world reaction. We believe in the Chinese people. We know full well that they are an exceptionally self-sacrificing, heroic and revolutionary people. And, though you may be able to fool a people like that for some time, you can't do so forever.

On the U.S.A.:

President Carter is the first president in more than 16 years who hasn't committed himself to a policy of hostility against Cuba. Kennedy inherited Eisenhower's policy of premeditated aggression, and, when Kennedy was killed, Johnson, who was involved in the Vietnam war, maintained that same policy. As for Nixon—who was vice-president in Eisenhower's administration—his complicity in the preparation for the 1961 attack on Cuba and his close ties with the counterrevolutionaries and severaly wealthy Cuban-born families in the United States made him a prisoner of the same policy of hostility. As far as the Ford-Kissinger administration is concerned, it should be pointed out that the latter felt very irritated with and hostile toward Cuba, especially when Cuba assumed her internationalist duty of giving concrete support to the Angolan people in their struggle against the racists and imperialist aggressors. Thus, the U.S. economic blockade of Cuba has been maintained, unchanged, for 16 years.

President Carter hasn't committed himself to this policy, but we might add that he has taken a number of steps, namely:

1. his public declarations in favor of discussions with Cuba,

2. the declarations made by U.S. Secretary of State Cyrus Vance to the effect that the United States was ready to hold talks with Cuba without setting any previous conditions, and

3. the authorization granted U.S. citizens to visit Cuba (the prohibition of such visits had been constantly renewed and maintained throughout the last few years).

I might add two more things here: we have noted that, since Carter's inaugurations as president, there have been no more flights by U.S. spy planes over our territory, and we have also discussed the setting of fishing rights within the 200-mile limit.

We haven't returned the agreement on aircraft hijacking with the United States, because, after the sabotaging of the Cuban plane, we said that we were willing to discuss the matter with the United States only on the basis of its completely abandoning its policy of hostility against Cuba—and its economic blockade of Cuba is a very serious act of hostility. A number of U.S. senators have proposed that the blockade on food and pharmaceutical products be lifted, but that doesn't solve the problem. Partial lifting isn't enough. The United States has trade with China, with the USSR and with other socialist countries. Why, then, all this arbitrary discrimination against us? Now then, I repeat, fishing rights are the only things being discussed between us.

Prior to his election, Carter took some positions that we might mention here—such as, for example, his statements criticizing what happened in Chile and Nixon's policy with regard to Allende's Popular Unity Government. There's also his statement to the effect that he's ready to try to find a solution for the Panama Canal problem. He's also taken a stand on southern Africa that differs from that of his predecessors in some respects. Now we must see how Carter's policies are put into practice. We'll have to see how all this turns out, but I would like to say that Carter took positions that were a far cry from Ford's—a little more critical with regard to certain international problems—prior to the election. We'll have to wait and see what he does now. . . . For Cuba, the key issue is the economic blockade. It isn't a question of a partial lifting. In order to create a climate favorable to an improvement in relations with the United States, it is absolutely necessary that this so discredited and untenable economic blockade be lifted completely.

How could it be possible to overlook the 1961 invasion; the terrorist attacks; the subversive activities by the CIA; the plans to assassinate Cuban revolutionary leaders; the germ warfare—that caused epidemics that killed off half of the hogs in our country and spread diseases among our chickens? What can be said about the CIA's acts of sabotage and terrorism carried out in complicity with the Governments of Chile, Puerto Rico and Nicaragua, that issued passports to the counter-revolutionaries who blew up our plane and make it easy for them and others who attack our embassies and consulates to travel? The United States—the one mainly responsible for all this—should stop engaging in these actions against Cuba. Moreover, serious-minded people in the United States realize that this is a criminal, insane and discredited policy that can't go on much longer. We have given tourists, leading figures, businessmen and journalists permission to visit us, because it wouldn't be fair for us to prohibit such visits when the United States has just lifted its ban on travel to Cuba.

Two years ago, the U.S. authorities sought to get in contact with us. This was after Nixon had resigned. Such contacts were established and served to show them that we weren't ready to hold talks as long as the blockade was in effect. These contacts were limited to this. Nothing more. We still maintain this position, and I'd like to tell you why. There's a basic reason for this. We haven't imposed any blockade against the United States. We don't have any naval bases in the United States. We don't practice subversion or espionage against the United States. This is why we believe that it is necessary for the economic blockade to be lifted before any talks can be held. We believe that this is a very just position, because we wouldn't get anywhere otherwise. We admit the possibility of contacts to clear up this position—contacts, not talks.

This means that we're ready to discuss our problems

as soon as the blockade is lifted. Let me say one more thing here: I don't think that the problem of the contradictions that exist between socialism and capitalism is going to be solved through war, because we're not living in the age of the bow and arrow; this is a nuclear age, and a war could wipe out the whole world. One way or another, nations with different social regimes will have to learn to live with one another.

Let's make it perfectly clear that our solidarity with Angola will never be subject to negotiations with the United States. This is something that can't be negotiated. Wouldn't it be absurd for us to discuss, for example the withdrawal of U.S. troops from Europe, South Korea, the Philippines, Japan or Saudi Arabia? It's really absurd for the United States to set conditions of this sort. Our positions are clear, without any ambiguity.

There are those who think that certain risks are involved in letting U.S. tourists in Cuba, but we'll still let them visit us, if necessary. Perhaps there is a danger that they may succeed in corrupting an infinitesimal part of our population, but our Revolution will never be corrupted, and, if that's the price we have to pay in order to show what socialism has done in Cuba and what a communist country, such as Cuba, has accomplished in just a few years and if we can contribute in any way to laying the specter that is used to make people afraid of communism, then we think that the risk involved is really insignificant.

It is important for European and U.S. tourists to get a correct and clear understanding, by themselves, here in Cuba of what is going on in our country and of all the things that a socialist regime has accomplished in just a few years. They will realize that propaganda based on lies and slander is completely worthless. They will see how much the people of Cuba admire the members of the Communist Party, the rigorous spirit that characterizes them, the nature and extent of the sacrifices they assume, and the complete absence of privileges. They will see that all the people have respect for the Communist Party because they know that there's no room in it for opportunism, corruption, or liberalism. During the second war of liberation in Angola, the members of the Communist Party were the first to express their desire to sign up, and they left Cuba to contribute to the defense, consolidation and victory of the Angolan Revolution knowing that they would wind up thousands of kilometers away from their country and that they were taking on a very difficult task.

Part VII

Criticism
and Self-Criticism

47

CARLOS SALAZAR MONTEJO

—————— • ◆ • ——————

The "Stalinist" Parties
in Bolivia and Cuba*

✳

Trotskyism is far from being a unified movement. Its position vis-à-vis capitalism, the bourgeoisie, and "Stalinist" communism has always been weakened by the atomization of the Trotskyite groups. We present a severe Trotskyist criticism of the Communist parties in general, particularly those in Bolivia and Cuba, that is also leveled against the Trotskyite groups that united under the shadowy Fourth International, founded by Trotsky and currently centered in Montevideo. Writing in 1960, Carlos Salazar Montejo also shows remarkable insight into the future Cuban economic situation.

It would be an error to expect capitalism to succumb because of internal economic collapse, just as it would be an error to expect socialism to impose itself through the economic advances of the Soviet Union.

---

* Translated from Carlos Salazar Montejo, *Caducidad de una estrategia* (La Paz: Liga Socialista Revolucionaria de Bolivia, 1961), pp. 23–65.

Such ideas ignore the historical necessity for revolution; nevertheless, they constitute in reality the fundamental position that has been adopted by Stalinism and by the Fourth International. In fact, these gentlemen not only continue planning their strategy as if there were a situation of "capitalist encirclement"; they also replace the classical methods of class warfare and armed insurrection with disorder, anarchy, and pressures on capitalism on a world scale, without being able to set up or to organize, in any part of the world, a revolutionary movement that tends toward the winning of power. Co-existence together with "capitalist encirclement" gave satisfactory results for the survival of the internal bureaucracy of the U.S.S.R.; now it is complemented by the Cold War, a defeatist notion by means of which all types of leaders survive on a world scale, in the old and worn-out leadership of their respective parties. Stratified in their old concepts, Stalinism and the Fourth International have not realized, it would seem, that the backwardness of Russia has ended forever, that capitalism has entered into its period of disintegration, and that the encirclement has completely disappeared.

If anyone feels encircled, it is not, of course, the U.S.S.R., but rather capitalism. The situation has reversed itself. No one speaks today of communism lurking in a hiding place. It is imperialism now that is constructing atomic shelters on its own ground; this converts it into a capitalist hiding place, while all the peoples of the world rush to give final battle. But in spite of this favorable situation, the attitude that permeates the revolutionary parties continues to be defensive, merely one of continuous pressure on the enemy. They have not understood that the strategy of combat is now a strong offensive one against the capitalist regime, and that the most immediate and urgent task is to organize the proletarian uprising. It is clear that the revolutionary leaders cannot become aware of the change in strategic objectives, because this change implies as an indispensable condition the reconstruction of the old revolutionary structure, an instrument that is already inadequate for the taking over of power, but which permits them to survive as parasites, consuming the energies and the blood of the world revolutionary movement.

In fact, the slogans of the socialist revolution and of the workers' insurrection have disappeared from the leftist vocabulary; they are considered as belonging to an unforeseeable future, and have been replaced by "co-existence with capitalism" and "world peace." It is clear that in these latter terms there is no Marxism, nor anything like Marxism; but the revolutionary leaders are not worried about that, and if Marxism disturbs them with respect to their bureaucratic goals, then nothing is simpler than to throw it out . . . in the name of Marx.

The Western proletariat is thus deprived of its glorious battle flag, confused in its historical objectives and subjected to the fluctuation of innumerable negotiations. Strong Communist parties such as those in France and Italy, whose powerful influence nobody can deny, are brought to the unthinkable condition in which, instead of organizing the taking over of power and taking advantage of the favorable postwar conditions, they have preferred to cooperate with the bourgeoisie in the re-establishment of the capitalist economy . . . all this in the name of co-existence, world peace, and the other repugnant phrases that make up the present theoretical arsenal of Stalinism.

At least to the European proletariat, the socialist revolution is revealed as a probability, although a distant one. To the underdeveloped countries, not even that is conceded; the socialist revolution remains confined to the realm of utopia, and the workers' parties find themselves obliged to profess, as an objective, a bourgeois-democratic revolution, such as was justifiable in the era of capitalist expansion, but is absolutely anachronistic in the era of the liquidation of this system. And the instrument that they are to create in order to carry it out is the worker-peasant government, "an intrinsically contradictory notion" that has already been liquidated, not only by the proof of the Russian Revolution, but also by that of the Chinese Revolution.

To the extent that the relationship of forces has been inverted—that is to say, to the extent that it is favorable to the socialist camp—the leadership crisis of the proletariat is accentuated, and the most revolutionary class in history is led by a defeatist staff, shorn of fighting spirit and absolutely incapable of coming into power. The old eagles of the revolutionary world no longer fly. The truth is that the revisionists of whatever ilk, the Stalinists grown old in unconditional servitude, the canonists and pablists[1] of the other reverse-Stalinist sects, led directly or indirectly by the Moscow hierarchies, have passed onto the stage of senility and impotence, and it is certainly not through them that the revolution will be produced. The Soviet bureaucracy has reproduced itself in the external struc-

[1] Pablism was a deviationalist tendency inside the Trotskyite movement that allegedly downgraded the need for a proletarian party and a proletarian revolution [ed.].

ture of those parties and has created in their leaders a petty spirit, vain and petty bourgeois to the core. Will these gentlemen make the revolution? Certainly not. They will only postpone it, even though they know perfectly well that all delaying tactics now favor capitalism.

The fact that there exists at present a superior imperialist power—the United States—does not mean that the struggle must be confined to a struggle between the U.S.S.R. and the United States. To reduce the struggle to this level would be the same as waiting for the establishment of socialism by the military victory of the U.S.S.R. or, in the opposite case, renouncing it forever. In both cases the dynamics of the struggling forces, which resides in the structure of classes in a society and not in the greater or lesser power of one country or another, is ignored. In other words, the struggle between the bourgeoisie and the proletariat appears as a factor in the Cold War, like a battle episode between two powers. For that reason, especially in Stalinism, class struggle has been replaced by the fomenting of disorders, stone-throwing, and cat-calls, directed against the Yankees so that they will be expelled. At this rate, we will have to wait centuries for the revolution. This caricature or mockery of revolutionary struggle is similar to that of a doctor who tries to save an infected arm by cutting the patient's fingernails.

Let us examine, for example, what happened in Cuba. Here also the situation caught the Stalinist apparatus off guard, the Stalinists being experts on the subject of disorders but incapable of organizing a revolutionary movement and unable to take power at the right moment. One can easily see that the situation in the underdeveloped countries brings them to insurrectional outbursts much sooner than is being imagined by the routine bureaucratic Communists!

Nevertheless, Stalinism cannot allow a revolution, such as the Cuban one, to slip through its hands. Although Stalinism is not very skillful in the period of class struggle, it does move in its element in the field of intrigue and knows how to take strategic positions in a new administration. The doctrinal and procedural weakness of the Castro regime brings it easily to surrender to the Stalinist bureaucracy, a fact that certainly does not guarantee a revolutionary continuation, but instead disturbs its initial efforts and converts Cuba, as was Guatemala, into a factor of the Cold War.

Revolutionary support is, then, replaced by military and economic aid from the U.S.S.R., which is typical of the "economism" into which socialist strategy has fallen. But Russian aid does not solve the problems created by the breaking of the ties that once linked the Cuban economy to international markets. In fact, while the United States undermines the fundamental structure of the Cuban economy—that is, the productive aspects of the economy—Russia can take care only of consumer articles or subsistence funds—that is, the expenses. Yankee dollars are invested and grow while Russian dollars are only spent. This fact becomes a basic reality, because the relationship between constant capital and variable capital is thus destroyed. In measurable terms, we could say that the Yankee offensive reduces the active, while Russian aid increases the passive, from which can be predicted a breaking-point in the near future. The Cuban economy finds itself, in the meantime, condemned to destruction, and no revolutionary phraseology can take away the validity of that fact.

The Communist parties operate within a framework of incredible tactical opportunism. In Bolivia, the latest Communist contribution to the history of opportunism has been to proclaim as presidential candidates [1960 elections] none other than the same candidates as the Movimiento Nacionalista Revolucionario (MNR), and that after having characterized them—if only mildly—as imperialists and anti-workers. As they attempt to make their "proletarian" program coincide with the petty bourgeois program of such candidates as these, the picture is one of the most singular in modern times. The Communists have in doing so demonstrated a great amount of political imagination and even a sense of humor; the bad part of it is that they have demonstrated nothing of "Marxism-Leninism."

The Partido de Izquierda Revolucionaria (PIR), representative of the Third International, made up in its fashion what it considered to be a parliamentary republic; on the whole, however, its policy was controlled by reactionary parties. Although it had a parliamentary majority, this was so heterogeneous that its disintegration was not long in coming; but only after having slaughtered, on Jan. 28, 1947, the miners of Potosí. By 1949 the PIR had practically ceased to exist. This meant nothing more or less than the historical liquidation of the attempted parliamentary republic, drowned in an ocean of shame and ineptitude, and benefiting only the *Rosca*[2] of the mines, which persecuted the workers with more rage and passion than has ever been known in the history of America. The massacres at Catavi, Villa Victoria, Siglo XX,[3] and other places mark this hysterical period of [Bolivia], which thus owes its most bloody pages to Stalinism.

[2] The Bolivian oligarchy [ed.].
[3] These are the names of the principal Bolivian mines where the workers rose in rebellion in the 1940s [ed.].

In spite of that experience, Stalinism, which once again has appeared under the name of the Communist Party, persists in its theoretical position, maintaining as a slogan the formation of a democratic government together with "all the democratic forces of the country" (it is worth pointing out that these democratic forces would be the same parties as were in their alliance of 1946). On the altar of national unity, which they worship as the supreme remedy for all ills, the Communist Party, like its putative parent, the PIR, has committed every deceit possible, has bungled on every occasion, and has cloaked all its crimes and machinations with enemies of the proletariat and the peasants. The Communist Party has established an unqualified reputation for servility, impudence, and political irresponsibility. In truth, no other result could be expected from this historical combination of a party with such antecedents, and a theory that has been worn out for half a century.

Neither the Fourth International nor Moscow will lead the world revolution—because they are worn-out instruments, incapable of taking over power, and in their hands the revolutionary movement is immobilized, impotent, and submits to the leadership of other classes—unless they change their tactics in the struggle, renew their cadres and eliminate their corrupt hierarchies, which would seem, frankly, to be even more difficult.

48

JOSÉ REVUELTAS

———•◦•———

A Headless Proletariat
in Mexico*

✳

*Those who have been disillusioned with, or expelled
from, the Latin American Communist parties form
by now a sizable group. Many of them have endeavored to write, criticizing communism as a doctrine or merely criticizing the Party without renouncing the doctrine. The Mexican journalist José
Revueltas, who belongs to the latter group, here tries
to diagnose some of the distortions of Marxism that
have, according to him, paralyzed the Communist
Party of Mexico.*

It is not the intention of this essay to outline the historical development of the Communist Party, and for
that reason we shall not go into minute details regarding the period between 1929 and 1935, but shall
rather deal with it only in its general meaning.

The plenary session held in 1929 represented a 180-
degree change from the policy that had been carried

* Translated from José Revueltas, *Un proletariado sin cabeza*
(Mexico City: Ediciones de la Liga Leninista Espartaco, 1962),
pp. 223–245. Printed by permission of the author.

out by the Mexican Communist Party up to that time. But it also signified the beginning of changes in policy that represented an extreme effort to correct errors— a process that is in itself an eloquent expression of the collective conscience of the Party, a phenomenon that we shall discuss later.

The plenary meeting of 1929 decided to establish a new political line that, in sum, praised the break with the bourgeoisie, the frontal attack on the government, and the preparation for armed insurrection to bring the worker-peasants to power. The right wing of the Party, represented by Ursulo Galván, was expelled; within a few months, after mistimed actions by several peasant groups, which had already started to fight, the insurrection was set back and the Communist Party of Mexico went underground, where it remained until 1934.

The surprising about-face in 1929 from the political positions held during the preceding period is of extraordinary significance. It not only failed to represent the correction of errors of the right; it also created a system of functioning that, from that time on, would impede the Party from recognizing and correcting its own errors, and instead condemn it to become, strange as it may seem, a party that needed to prevent its own growth, that in the long run would end up by changing its no-growth condition into an essential one. That is, it would henceforth be a party whose leadership (regardless of who occupied the position), being prisoner of a dogma that it was not able to and did not want to examine, would try to avoid having the Party grow; later it would be faced with the need to submit the Party to periodic bloodlettings, every time a new political change had to be imposed.

The exercise of a collective conscience was thus suppressed in the Communist Party of Mexico, internal democracy was abolished, and the most authoritarian and concentrated kind of centralism was established as the Party's sole system of functioning. (We do not mean to say, of course, that under clandestine conditions centralism does not have to take precedence over democracy in regard to certain questions, but a conscientious party always makes every effort to combine centralism with democracy.)

The plenary meeting in July represented, without any doubt, the need for a fundamental change in the opportunistic policy that had been followed up to that time by the Communist Party of Mexico. But it was also evident that the Party did not understand, in a precise, scientific, and dialectical way, what that opportunistic policy of the right actually consisted of and what its historical roots were. Instead of making use of the collective conscience of the Party in order to deal with the problem, they imposed on it a simple, but no less violent change, which placed it, suddenly and mechanically, without transitions or shades of development, in a diametrically opposed posture. They did, of course, expel Ursulo Galván and the representatives who were most characteristic of the opportunistic tendency of the right. We are not discussing here the justice of such expulsions; what should have been discussed at that time and what might have helped prevent subsequent deformation of the Communist Party of Mexico were the conditions that permitted such leaders of the agrarian petty bourgeoisie as Ursulo Galván, Carolina Anaya, and others to enroll in the Communist Party of Mexico as representatives of the peasantry.

But there is even more to say about the intimate nature of the changes of direction or *virajes*. The plenary session of July 1929 was the outcome of the advice of the Communist International and of the Conference of Latin American Communist Parties which had met that year in Buenos Aires. The Conference, having made a just examination of the role of the national bourgeoisie in the bourgeois-democratic revolutions in Latin America and of the independence of the working class, adopted a series of general recommendations for the Communist parties. The Communist Party of Mexico went one better on these recommendations and then brought forth the revolutionary "putsch" and the direct attack against the government.

The essential thing to understand, nevertheless, in this phenomenon of the deformation of a Communist Party is that in Mexico it is presented as inevitable, to the point of converting itself, in time, into something that cannot be overcome, because the nature of the phenomenon itself prevents the Communist Party from understanding its historical roots. Let us try to clarify how this deformation of the Communist Party in our country was produced.

We have already seen the Communist Party of Mexico ceasing to organize itself as the conscience of the national proletariat, a process that it was obliged to carry out through the historical realization of the concrete situation in which the working class in our country found itself; on the contrary, it considered it sufficient at that time to be the Mexican section that was recognized by the Communist International in order to regard itself automatically as the conscience of the Mexican working class. The result was, in any case, that during its first period of life, until 1929, instead of playing the part of the socialist worker's conscience and thereby becoming the vanguard of the proletariat, it merely carried out the function of being the vanguard of bourgeois democracy and thus became a radical agrarian party of the petty bourgeoisie.

That is why, as we have brought out earlier, the errors of the struggle were not corrected by the plenary meeting of 1929, but instead remained intangible, in their place, ready and available to be committed again; that is why their causes—their historical essence as products of a fundamental deformation of the Party's conscience, of its not being the true conscience of the proletarian class in Mexico—were not discovered. Recognizing this, nevertheless, was not possible, because the Communist Party of Mexico, considering itself to be the vanguard of the proletariat and its authentic conscience, began by setting up the first dogma of the Sacred Scriptures of the Party at the same time as it set up its Original Sin: the correction of errors. Nor could it be recognized through the method of internal fighting over opinions, by freedom of criticism within the principles of democratic centralism. Rather, the Party established the irrational course of changes of direction which since that time has been considered by the Communist Party of Mexico as the procedure that "gets to the bottom" of problems, and which, without doubt, will take them to the bottom, just like a sinking ship, and leave floating, as survivors, those errors that they did not bother to analyze, much less to correct.

49

VENEZUELAN ARMED FORCES
OF NATIONAL LIBERATION
(FALN)

————•••————

Our Errors*

✱

The revolutionary optimism of the radical groups during the first years of the sixties came up against increasing resistance in Latin America. Evidently, as the Marxists themselves have repeated, the non-Communist forces have also tried to learn from the lesson of Cuba. Here, in a gloomy account of errors and weaknesses, the Fuerzas Armadas de Liberación Nacional (Venezuelan Armed Forces of National Liberation),[1] one of the most outstanding action groups on the continent, analyzes the difficulties of the situation.

The advances and the skill achieved by the repressive bodies in the cities must be given careful and objective study. To begin with, we must coldly recognize that many of the successes gained by the government

---

* From "Our Errors," *Studies on the Left,* IV (November 4, 1964), 129–131. Reprinted by permission of the publisher.

[1] Some interesting documents of this group can be found in the very biased book by Manuel Cabieses, *¡Venezuela Okey!* (Havana: Ediciones Venceremos, 1964).

in this field are due fundamentally to two causes, which we must energetically combat with stubborn persistence. The first is infantile subjectivism, of petty bourgeois origin—the swollen enthusiasm due to a long chain of successes which we gained for a time, which made us appear each day, in Venezuela as well as abroad, like an almost mythological force of immeasurable power, and which gave the impression that at any moment we would be able to throw Rómulo Betancourt out of the Palacio de Miraflores.

These circumstances led us to underestimate the capacity of the enemy, to consider the enemy incapable, weak, lacking in ability, etc., and to lower our vigilance, leaving us with an unfortunate balance sheet of indiscretions and mistakes which were translated into hard blows suffered by our organization.

The second cause, which on many occasions has facilitated the blows delivered by the repressive apparatus, is the open liberalism, profoundly rooted in our organization and in almost all our cadres and militants, which has led us to abandon revolutionary vigilance. This liberalism has been displayed in various ways, the most important being the following:

Exhibitionism, which constantly leads us to show off or to indicate before friends, comrades, and strangers, the tasks that we are undertaking, the secrets we know—all this with the aim of displaying before others how important one is in the organization.

The criticisms and observations voiced in familiar circles in front of people not belonging to the organizations involved. Through these circles, the enemy has become acquainted with our faults, deficiencies, and errors, taking action, consequently, on the basis of reports provided indirectly.

Covering each other's mistakes (*amiguismo*). We

will leave aside the faults and mistakes of our "friends" so they will not consider us to be tattletales or disloyal. This phenomenon has caused us damage. It is especially strong in bodies and units composed of fighters originating from the same organization, profession, or circle of friends. It is displayed in the hiding of errors, in fear of criticizing in order to avoid being criticized and in not criticizing so as not to injure the feeling of comrades.

Deviations of a military character which have been committed by the FALN on some occasions have likewise facilitated the repressive plans of the government. A deviation of this kind occurs when units are inspired to discuss or draw a balance sheet on their actions, their successes, and their errors; when they do not accept observations; when they try to resolve administrative problems; when it is thought that the faults and errors should be corrected through punishment, obviously underestimating persuasion and overlooking educational work among the fighters; when we substitute personal leadership for collective leadership; when we seek to demonstrate that we are right by raising our voice or by constantly insisting on our position as "chiefs"; and, finally, when we reject political leadership, trampling on the wise teaching that "the Party guides the rifle." Along with the political causes indicated above, and which, in our opinion, played the major role in the blows that have been received, there are others to which we must likewise call attention as important, although they are of other kinds—military, organizational, and technical—and which we will try to summarize below.

For quite a long time the FALN and the revolutionary parties have been operating in accordance with a more or less fixed schema, with procedures that have become almost clichés. This has permitted the government, once an attack has been opened, to foresee the next ones and to prepare to meet them. In this way, actions have lost their element of surprise, an indispensable condition for defeating an enemy as powerful as the one we are fighting. We can state, without fear of being wrong, that the government has learned to fight us on the basis of the political and military blows which we have delivered in the last two years.

In the magnificent battles, surrounded by popular support and enthusiasm, which the FALN fought in the *barrios* [crowded, poverty-stricken areas] and hills of Caracas, the repressive forces, as time passed, became more and more cagey and effective in fighting us, operating in the following manner: They isolated us in the area occupied by our forces without trying to take our positions. They waited patiently until we ran out of ammunition, until we became tired, or simply until the commotion died down. Then they proceeded to capture our *effectives* when they came down from the hill or tried to leave the barrio. On some occasions they waited up to three days after the end of the battles in the hills to begin the mass round-up and detention at the entrances and exits of the barrios of every youth or person who seemed the least bit suspicious to them.

Another evidence of the way the repressive bodies of the government of Rómulo Betancourt caught on to our methods of armed struggle in the city was to be noted in the tactical moves carried out by the FALN and the police apparatus in the days just before and after the elections, restricting the effectiveness of our operations. All of Caracas was divided into zones with their respective Commands, dependent on a Central Command which operated in the Simón Bolívar Center. With this distribution, they mobilized thousands of soldiers, police, traffic cops and secret agents of the Digepol, PTJ, and SIPA, who worked in a synchronized way in the capital. All the hills were taken militarily seventy-two hours before the elections, military and police effectives being placed in strategic positions with machine-guns and observation posts guarded by tanks. Likewise all the sites outside the hills were taken so that any commotion could be observed and the information flashed by radio to the posts on each hill. Where they could not do this they undertook encircling maneuvers, with extreme caution and slowness, against the focal points hostile to the government. In other cases they combed the *ranchos,* shanties, and tenements of the crowded *barrios* with light artillery.

This way of deploying Rómulo Betancourt's repressive forces revealed that they have carried out a detailed study based on reports and information, which must not be underestimated for one moment. They complement our deficiencies in this respect, the routine planning, lack of accurate information, ill-conceived militarily and even worse politically, "the popularization" of operations to be undertaken, our low striking capacity (lack of arms and explosives), our technical limitations and other deficiencies which it is not necessary to mention, all of which gravely endanger our effectives, since they (this refers to "our effectives" and "effectives" means men who are active and under FALN discipline) are trying to overcome this weakness through courage alone. All this fits in negatively with the errors that occupy us.

50

THE COMMUNIST PARTY
OF BRAZIL

———•◦•———

Self-Criticism*

✻

At the beginning of 1964, the leftist forces in Brazil seemed extremely confident of the country's immediate future. From the Peasant Leagues of Francisco Julião up to supposed socialist tendencies in the government, passing through worker, student, and political groups, Brazil seemed to be on the way toward an irreversible leftist radicalism. Then, suddenly, in 1964, a brusque, brief military coup, without major resistance, deposed the Goulart government. The leftist forces of the continent felt a certain stupor at the ease with which the overthrow took place. The leaders of the Communist Party of Brazil (Russian line) here try to find some of the reasons for their errors in evaluating the national situation.

The coup that took place in Brazil during April brought to power representatives of the most retrograde and anti-national forces, agents of American

* Translated from "La situación en Brasil," *Principios,* No. 108 (Santiago, August 1965), pp. 142–162.

imperialism, large landowners, and big capitalists in league with Yankee monopolies.

The submission of the country to the interests of American monopolies takes on unheard of proportions. The law that had placed a limit on investment earnings that could be sent out of the country was practically abolished. The volume of the wheat agreement with the United States was doubled. A mining policy was adopted in accordance with the demands of the Hanna Mining Company. The American Military Mission is making an aerial photogrammetric survey of our country. Economic and financial policy is dictated by the International Monetary Fund.

The dictatorship is putting into practice a foreign policy that is based on total dependence on the United States government. It severs relations with Cuba. It is an instrument and spokesman for the Department of State in the O.A.S. It makes common cause with Yankee aggression against the Democratic Republic of Viet Nam and with the brutal assault on the sovereignty of the Dominican people. It permits the construction of bases for rockets and nuclear arms on Brazilian soil, under the pretext of scientific experiments.

In examining the present situation of Brazil and the situation of the Party, in the framework of the new set of problems that we must now face, the Central Committee places prime importance on the need to carry on and vastly expand the process of self-criticism in which we find ourselves and which should culminate in the Sixth Congress.

The Central Committee hails the concern for criticism and self-criticism that is manifest in the entire Party, as we search for our errors and for the causes that have led to our setbacks. It sees in this concern a healthy revolutionary spirit of love for the Party and an ardent aspiration to raise the ideological level of its ranks.

In order to stimulate this process of self-criticism, we are informing the Party of the main conclusions that the Central Committee has been able to arrive at so far in its analysis of the events that have to do with the successful coup of April 1, with respect to errors and failures in Communist activities.

The success of the military coup brought to light many of our most serious weaknesses. The events took us by surprise; we were unprepared, not only to face them but also to continue our activities safely and efficiently, in the light of the new conditions in the country. The confidence we had placed in Goulart's military machine proved to be false. The outlook for an easy and immediate victory, which we presented to the Party and to the masses at that time, was also false. Our class illusions, our *Seguidismo* [tailism] with respect to the sector of the national bourgeoisie that was in power, became evident. We should therefore analyze the process that led us to such a situation.

The result of an arduous political and ideological battle, the line approved by the Fifth Congress was a powerful revolutionary instrument in that it enabled the Party to strengthen its relations with the masses and to participate actively in public life, thus contributing to the advancement of the revolutionary process. Mad with rage, enemies of the revolution rose up against our Party. But with the rise of Goulart, which was the result of an understanding between the national bourgeoisie and reactionary forces, we had begun to withdraw from the political line, because of our concern with the fight against conciliation. This process reached its peak during the last months of the Goulart government, when we actually abandoned the fight for the just application of the line.

It was undoubtedly indispensable to combat steadily the policy of conciliation. It was due to the struggle against the policy of conciliation that the reactionary attempts of April and October 1963 failed (when Goulart tried to take measures, under the pretext of attacking the right, to contain the spread of the popular movement). We were meanwhile carrying on the struggle against conciliation inadequately.

In practice, our activity with regard to the Goulart government was oriented as if his policies were almost entirely negative. We scorned its very important positive aspects, such as (under his foreign policy) the defense of the peace, of the self-determination of peoples, of the principle of non-intervention, and of the development of diplomatic and trade relations with the socialist countries. In the field of domestic policy, we did the same thing with his relative respect for democratic liberties, and his meeting the claim of the workers. Our opposition to the Goulart government became a struggle against an appeaser government, our main objective being to unmask it before the masses.

We acted on the understanding that the struggle against conciliation was the concrete way in which the greatest enemy of our people, American imperialism, should be combatted under existing conditions. Such a political position could lead only to a shift of the onslaught, which then fell on our national bourgeoisie. Instead of concentrating our fire on American imperialism and its domestic agents, we directed our attacks mainly against the policy of conciliation, with the result that imperialism received only the secondary or side effects of those attacks. This explains the lack of concern with combatting such unabashed agents of American imperialism as Lacerda and Ademar. This explains the lack of concern over the maneuvers and machinations of imperialism itself, over the intensification of its aggressiveness toward the peoples that it dominates. This explains the underestimation of the danger of a rightist coup, which was considered to be a mere scarecrow, intended to frighten the masses. Concentrating our fire on the government, we demanded more and more drastic measures while overlooking our own weaknesses and the shortcomings of the national-democratic movement, as well as the effective correlation of social forces that existed at that time. This attitude lays bare the persistent influence of subjectivism in our activities.

We ignored the fact that the very advance of the democratic process threatened the privileges of foreign monopolies, of large landowners, and of the upper bourgeoisie, which still occupied strong positions. A false evaluation of reality prevented us from seeing that the correlation of social forces, during the last months of the Goulart government, was daily becoming less and less favorable to the national-democratic forces. Reactionaries and lackeys (*entreguistas*) joined hands and succeeded in attracting into their camp wide sectors of Brazil's bourgeoisie of the urban petty bourgeoisie, who were unhappy over the situation and who were not in agreement with the growing threats against the system of government that was in force at that time. Rightist forces took up their arms and swiftly prepared the coup.

At the beginning of 1964, when Goulart, prompted by his own political objectives, tried to draw closer to the popular forces, the separation from the line of the Fifth Congress became sharper in our activities. We underestimated the importance that the holding of elections had for the Brazilian people, and we did not ensure the implementation of the electoral resolution that had been approved by the Central Committee of the Party. At the same time, we were encouraging Goulart's tendency to extend illegally his term in power. Instead of alerting the masses and calling them to arms against the threat of a rightist coup, which was clearly revealed by the actions of Lacerda, Ademar, and their military backers, we issued the March 27, 1964, Note of the Executive Committee in which, together with demands for the immediate formation of a new government that "would put an end to the policy of conciliation," we transferred the center of attack to Congress, by demanding constitutional reform and making threats against it. "The plebiscite," said the Note, "should be called by Congress, or, in case of default, postponement, or refusal by the latter, by the executive branch itself." In this way, we allowed the forces of reaction to use the defense of legality as a way of deceiving wide sectors of the population and sweep them along in the reactionary coup. For all practical purposes, we had completely abandoned the tactical orientation contained in our party line.

The root of our errors lies in a petty bourgeois misconception of the Brazilian revolution, which has manifested itself predominantly at decisive moments in our revolutionary activity, independently of the political line (whether right or wrong) that we had adopted. It is a conception that sees revolution not as a mass phenomenon but rather as the result of group action and, at best, of action by the Party. It gives our activities a sense of immediacy, a petty bourgeois haste, which turns us away from a persistent and continuous struggle for our basic and strategic objectives through the process of a gathering of forces and the conquest of proletarian hegemony.

The self-critical examination of our errors and the analysis of their deepest causes constitute the decisive factors in the struggle for the just application of our political line.

51

**CENTRAL COMMITTEE
OF THE VENEZUELAN
COMMUNIST PARTY**

———•••———

The Venezuelan Communist
Party Replies
to Fidel Castro[*]

✳

On several occasions, following a line of increasing radicalism, Castro has criticized the Soviet Union for dealing with non-socialist governments in Latin America and has made contemptuous remarks about the lack of revolutionary spirit of the Latin American Communist parties. Venezuela is a particular zone of friction, for since 1966 the Cuban government has been expressing increasing support for guerrilla fighters, like Douglas Bravo, who are in open and bitter polemic with the Venezuelan Communist Party. In March 1967, the friction reached a breaking point with the murder of Julio Iribarren Borges, brother of the Venezuelan Foreign Minister. While in Havana a spokesman of the FALN (Armed Forces of

[*] Translated from "Respuesta del Partido Comunista a Fidel Castro," *El Nacional* (Caracas, March 17, 1967), p. D-9.

National Liberation) credited the organization with that terrorist action, the Venezuelan Communist Party (PCV) condemned the murder and disassociated itself from those terrorist methods. On March 13, in a speech full of the usual criticism for the "pseudo-revolutionaries," Castro aimed the full power of his diatribe at the Venezuelan Communist Party. And then, for the first time since Castro took power, a Latin American Communist party shot back at the until then untouchable Fidel Castro. Following are some excerpts from this significant document.

1) Fidel Castro, Secretary General of the Cuban Communist Party, in power, and Prime Minister of the Cuban socialist government, profiting from the comfortable vantage point of his position, has attacked the Venezuelan Communist Party, a clandestine party with hundreds of its militant members in prison, with dozens of them slain in the mountains and on the streets of the country, and subject to an implacable persecution which every day—even at the same time when Fidel Castro was speaking—claims new victims. The same man whose verbal excesses are tolerated because Cuba is in the front line of the anti-imperialist struggle should have the simple generosity of restraining his language when referring to the Communist party that struggles in the country which of all Latin America is most penetrated by *Yanqui* imperialism and fights under the worst conditions. With a world audience and being who he is, Fidel Castro has not hesitated to insult a Communist party that, because of suppression, is hardly able to respond to him. . . .

2) Fidel Castro has not only expressed a negative

judgment about the murder of Iribarren Borges but even asserts his right to give his opinion on the subject. Nevertheless, with amazing impudence, he presumes to deny that same right to the PCV. Apparently Castro wants the Venezuelan Communist Party, which operates in Venezuela, which is in Venezuela, to express no opinion, to form no judgment on a Venezuelan political event occurring on Venezuelan soil and therefore directly affecting the life of the PCV. . . . According to his peculiar point of view, when *we* speak we play into the hands of the government; when *he* speaks he presumes to be the voice of an intangible revolutionary oracle. . . .

3) The PCV asserts its right to form its own policy without interference from anyone. Because Cuba has traveled a hard revolutionary road honorably, she is for us an example and an inspiration; but what we have never been, are not now, and shall never be are Cuba's agents in Venezuela, just as we are not agents of any other Communist party of the world. We are Venezuelan Communists, and we do not accept tutelage from anyone, no matter how abundant his revolutionary merits. If there is a revolutionary group in Venezuela that gladly submits to the tutelage and paternalism of Fidel Castro, it is that group's own affair. The PCV will never do it. If that displeases Fidel Castro, too bad for him. But why does Fidel Castro intervene against the PCV precisely at this moment? Because the PCV has already begun to defeat not only ideologically but also practically the anti-party outbreak of Douglas Bravo. . . . Precisely for that reason Fidel Castro has thrown all the weight of his prestige against the PCV in a desperate attempt to "help" the anarcho-adventurist group which he

sponsored and encouraged to split from the PCV. . . .

4) In a new demonstration of his irritating tendency to consider himself the sole possessor of bravery and courage, Fidel Castro has labeled as "cowards" the leadership of the PCV. We Venezuelan Communists are not puerile exhibitionists who go about proclaiming our good qualities. . . . The history of the PCV, which is a political history, is also the history of men who faced the terror of Gómez and Pérez Jiménez;[1] who guided the insurrection of January 23, 1958; and through whose efforts Fidel Castro was able to receive a plane loaded with weapons when he was still in the Sierra Maestra. . . .

5) In his speech Fidel Castro wants to assume once again the role of arbiter of the revolutionary destinies of Latin America and of super-revolutionary who, had he been in the place of all the Latin American Communists, would have already made the revolution. On another occasion we shall refer to the characteristics of the Cuban struggle and to the place where Fidel Castro would still be had he had the idea of raising the red flag in the Sierra Maestra. But for the moment we only want to reject the role of revolutionary "Pope" which Fidel Castro arrogates to himself. We categorically reject his pretension of being the only one who can decide what is and was is not revolutionary in Latin America. . . . To this Fidel Castro, supreme dispenser of revolutionary titles, who asks himself what North Viet Nam would say if Cuba should trade with South Viet Nam, we only want to ask if he thinks about what the Spanish people say

[1] Juan Vicente Gómez (1857–1935), Venezuelan dictator from 1908 to 1935. Marcos Pérez Jiménez, dictator from 1950 to 1958 [ed.].

of his commerce with Franco and the Spanish oligarchy or what the black people of Zimbabwe (Rhodesia) and the patriots of Aden can say of his trade with imperialist England. Or is it that Fidel Castro considers opportunism in others that which, in himself, is cleansed by the lustral waters of his self-sufficiency?

6) This is an unpleasant controversy which makes the enemy jump for joy. But evidently it could no longer be avoided. Fidel Castro's speech forced us to go over the edge. So be it. We shall have discussions. . . . We say to Fidel Castro that the descendants of Simón Bolívar and Ezequiel Zamora do not tolerate from anyone the provocative and insolent language that he used in his speech of March 13. . . .

7) We are not unaware that acts like the one by Fidel Castro will cause us difficulties. But we do not despair. We have the tranquil conviction of he who knows that he is right. And we possess the revolutionary fervor to defend it.

52

TEODORO PETKOFF

The Left on Trial*

*

Teodoro Petkoff has had a remarkable and rather agitated political career. A student leader, a member of the Miranda State Legislative Assembly and of the National Congress, he has also known the underground life of a leftist, has been in jail and has escaped from it. A leader of the Venezuelan Communist Party, he became increasingly critical of the strategy of the party until 1970, when the publication of his book "Socialismo para Venezuela?" provoked the final break. After the break, Petkoff and a group of Communist leaders moved out and founded MAS (Movimiento al Socialismo). They were officially expelled from the party in January 1971¹ Though it focuses on

---

*From Teododo Petkoff, *Proceso a la Izquierda, o de la Falsa Conducta Revolucionaria* (Caracas: Editorial Planeta, 1976.)

¹For the Party's accusation of Petkoff, see "Venezuelan Renegade," *World Marxist Review*, XIV, No. 6 (June 1971), 173–175, and for an attack on his ideas, Pedro Ortega Diaz, Antonio Garcia Ponce, *Las Ideas Antisocialistas de Teodoro Petkoff* (Caracas: Ediciones Cantaclaro, 1970). An interesting history of the crisis can be found in Eleazar Diaz Rangel, *Como se Dividió el Partido Comunista Venezolano* (Caracas: Editorial Domingo Fuentes, 1971). For Petkoff's own version, "La Division del Partido Comunista de Venezuela," *Libre* (Paris), No. 1, (September-November 1972?).

the Venezuelan situation, his deep and honest criticism of the dogmatism and narrowness of many leftist groups has, nevertheless, penetrated well beyond the borders of his country. Petkoff's ideas are totally a subject of debate in all of Latin America. MAS has rapidly become a political factor to count with in Venezuela.

In our polemic with the Communist Party, we pointed out some of the factors which limited—not to say made impossible—the capacity of an "orthodox" Communist Party, modeled by the III International, to guide successfully a revolutionary process. We concentrated on two factors: "vanguardism" and "Stalinism." Vanguardism imagined the struggle as a simple act of will, promoted by a heroic vanguard, to which was given the miraculous capacity to bring about a revolution out of nothing. The violent criticism—not totally unjustified—of the passivity of the Communist parties created a slogan which was worse than a tautology: "the duty of a revolutionary is to make the revolution." The revolution was supposed to come out, as a rabbit from the hat of a magician, from the will of those who wished it and had the courage to go to the mountains.

Unfortunately, reality showed that a revolutionary will, deprived of favorable circumstances and supported by generalities like "Latin America is ready for revolution," could do nothing when faced with those "stony eyes" of the Bolivian peasants who looked at Guevara without understanding his efforts to communicate with them.

On the other hand, the Stalinist only looked and

trusted the Party. For Stalinism the Party is sacred. The organization of the Party, its rules, its structures, have lost all character, all historical perspective, to become external forms of a new mysticism. For Stalinism the Party is an end in itself. The Revolution (with a capital *R*) is reduced to the condition of a distant mirage whose basic purpose is to keep alive the spirit of the Party, to sustain its glorious life.

From the perspective of years, it could be said that since 1967 the whole effort of the left has been a desperate struggle to save herself from what could have been a historical collapse. In April 1967, the central committee of the Venezuelan Communist Party "officially" took the decision to suspend its armed actions. This was called a "tactical retreat." It should have been admitted that the movement actually had been defeated. In any event, in this case the CP demonstrated a not too common capacity to understand the political reality of a country where, as the democratic channels were still open, it was possible to save the movement by returning to a legal political struggle.

To the fanatics of the armed struggle, this looked like a surrender, but looking back, we can see that there was no other alternative. Those who rejected this decision—and remained loyal to the tactics of violence—have been reduced to a sterile and hopeless fight carried out on the periphery of the national life. Not even with a great deal of generosity can we call the sporadic actions of those groups "an armed struggle."

But we don't gain anything by analyzing this or that revolutionary "deviation." The Communist orthodoxy had filled innumerable volumes denouncing real or supposed deviations inside or outside the Party. It is much more creative and important to explore what a "revolutionary condition" is. A "false revolutionary condition" is easy to detect in the aberrant positions of the "ultra-left." But it happens that the ultra-left is only carrying to the absurd certain concepts considered "normal" by the orthodox left. The problem is not to make a dissection, so easy to make, of the ultra-left, but to analyze how many of the concepts we criticize in the "ultra" exist among us, albeit in more sophisticated and mature forms. In what other way could we find an explanation of the fact that each generation of revolutionaries repeats almost exactly the mistakes of its predecessors?

We could begin by examining two of the idological arguments used by the right against the left, and how the left itself helps to reinforce them.

One of the most common arguments—but still very effective—is the supposedly "foreign" character of the revolution. The right continually uses the accusation "foreign agents." In that way it kills two birds with one stone: it uses for its own benefit the worst expression of chauvinism and the "defense" of nationalism while, at the same time, depriving the revolution of its national and social roots. As foreign agents, leftists find themselves, not discussing the possibilities of socialism in their nations, but arguing about Cuba, Russia, or China.

But the left usually acts as if the argument were true. Educated in the old and beautiful tradition of "international revolutionarism," willing to identify itself with the struggles of all "socialist brothers," the left tends to confuse solidarity with the exploited with solidarity with the parties who rule socialist countries. There is almost no leftist party or group in Latin

America which does not feel the need to find an international pole or model to define its own position. This
colonial mentality forces those groups to defend te-
naciously—and at times exaggeratedly—the virtues of
their respective Vaticans. That distorted loyalty gives
water to the mills of the right. To defend a nation's
need for a socialist transformation while refusing even
a limited measure of critical discussion of the socialist
models which now exist contributes enormously to the
image of a left too submissive to a foreign country.
The argument that such open debates will "give weapons to the enemy" has petrified anti-democratic structures in the socialist parties, has helped one small
group to monopolize political activities and expressions, and has helped to create that ridiculous para-
noia which regards any dissident poet as a menace to
the system or as an agent of the CIA.

A typical example of what we are saying is the reaction of most leftists to Solzhenitsyn. Many of them
not only justified the expulsion of the writer but would
even have defended his execution. But the essence of
the problem is not, as they have tried to present it,
the ideas and the writings of Solzhenitsyn. Hard-
headed Stalinists place all dissidences in the Soviet
Union on the same level. They anathematized Solzhenitsyn in 1975 with the same sacred passion with
which they condemned Denikin[2] in 1920.

It is true that the religious mysticism of the great
Russian writer could be translated into a very reactionary political position. But that is not the point. The
real problem is to know if the new society which we
are offering to our people is one where any general
dissent—and Solzhenitsyn represents a very general
form of dissent, without any concrete appearance of

subversion, as the mere human right to disagree—is going to be punished with utmost severity. Judging by the attitudes of the average leftist, that could be the conclusion of the ordinary citizen. The right knows too well how to use that kind of impression.

This dogmatic, narrow approach manifests itself in many of the left's other conceptions, producing the same type of ideological confusion. Take, for example, the extreme simplification of the nature of political power in general and of the state in particular. In this case, the left reasons through a syllogism: the state is the machinery by which one class oppresses another; Venezuela is dominated by Yankee imperialism, and the Venezuelan bourgeoisie only executes its orders; thus, the Venezuelan state is there just to follow Washington's orders.

The consequence of this reasoning is that each time the Venezuelan state acts in a way which evidently contradicts or opposes imperialist policies, the left is disconcerted and forced to appeal to magical explanations: the whole process is "a maneuver to deceive the people." Instead of examining the changing social and political conditions, national and international, which affects every particular moment, the left, anchored in its deterministic simplifications, explains everything with abstract, theoretical dogmas almost totally deprived of contact with political reality. The perplexity and the theoretical equilibriums that the left has made to explain a process like the Peruvian are proof enough of how it lacks valid interpretations once reality breaks its dogmatic framework.

One of our conclusions is that the "classic" forces

[2]A general and leader of the White Russians who fought against the Red Army.

of the left have blockaded themselves. They have created a manner of being revolutionary, a conduct, a theorization, that far from helping the historical birth of a new society tends to reinforce the status quo. The task facing us is to find a "new way to be socialist," an authentic revolutionary conduct capable of triumphantly surmounting the present difficult situation. It is a hard work of re-education. Again and again we will fall into the old and comfortable formulas, into the accepted dogmas which spare us the necessity of thinking. But to avoid that temptation we can always ask where we are, what we are trying to do, from what depths we are trying to climb, because none of this would be necessary if we were speaking from the top of a mountain of victories. But the recognition of the left's long history of failures is precisely what must galvanize us to find a true revolutionary conduct. To break out of the ghetto where the left dwells and open the possibility of a revolutionary road is the fuel which feeds our struggle.

53

PARTIDO MARXISTA-LENINISTA (MAOISTA) DEL URUGUAY

Maoist Criticism of the Tupamaros[*]

✻

This document offers a typical example of Maoist literature in Latin America. It attacks with the same virulence the Tupamaros and all the sectors of what they call the "traditional left" (from anarchists to Trotskyites), and especially the "revisionist" pro-Soviet Communists. The arguments, nevertheless, show a realistic appraisal of the Uruguayan situation and predict, quite accurately, the defeat of the Tupamaros. The document also serves to demonstrate the confusing ideological situation of Marxism in Latin America. In spite of their mutual antagonism, the Maoist's criticism of the Tupamaros is remarkably similar to that of the pro-Soviet Communists when they also dismissed the "revolutionary" capacity of the Tuparamos.

In this work we will give our opinion on certain aspects of the Tupamaros' activities. The destiny of

---

[*]From Partido Marxista-Leninista (Maoista) del Uruguay, *Tupa-

Uruguayan revolution depends on how correctly we face the issues of the present national situation. . . . And we begin by ratifying Lenin's words "without revolutionary theory there is no revolutionary movement."

In our country the proletarian party has just begun to form and to "separate" itself from the non-proletarian revolutionary movement. Ideological questions are, thus, vital to the growth and development of the proletarian vanguard. That is why we maintain a constant ideological battle against the Tupamaros, who are the principal representative of the petty-bourgeois anti-imperialist ideology. Using Mao's thought as our guide, we disagree with the Tupamaros on all practical and theoretical questions. To begin with, the Tupamaros have tried to copy a foreign experience. The Cuban Revolution is their model. They have followed to the letter Castro's line, principally in its "guerrilla form" theory. This is a basic mistake.

The Cuban Revolution was at its beginning (even as a petty-bourgeois anti-imperialist revolution) a mass struggle. Its revisionism came later, precisely because in Cuba there was no proletarian party. Guerrilla foquism is, thus, a deformation of the Cuban experience, and it is a revisionist deformation that leads to failure. The Cuban model became important only because of the deep crisis of the parties which formed the so-called "traditional left" (Socialist, Communist-revisionist, Trotskyite, and Anarchist), which had stagnated during the peaceful period of our bourgeois-democratic regime. The frustration of many elements of our youth, dazzled by Fidel Castro, gave

maros; *Conspiración o Revolución?* (Montevideo: Ediciones Voz Obrera, 1970).

birth to the Tupamaros, an amorphous organization without ideology or any defined policy. Becoming a national version of the "foquista theory," they proclaimed Fidel and Ché as their guides, and repeat that to make a revolution only guts and weapons are necessary.

True Marxist-Leninists know that war is the continuation of politics by other means. Every armed struggle is essentially a political struggle. There is no struggle which can ignore class struggle. In practice, either one consciously applies a proletarian policy, or one applies consciously or unconsciously a bourgeois policy. By rejecting all theory, the Tupamaros are actually rejecting proletarian ideology and accepting bourgeois policies.

The Tupamaros have been able to achieve notoriety in and out of our country. But to be well known does not imply having influence on the masses, and precisely the capacity to mobilize the masses is the measure of a revolutionary force. Furthermore, the Tupamaros have always displayed a conciliatory attitude toward the "revisionist" traitors of the Uruguayan Communist Party. They say that to criticize Arismendi and his gang is "to divide the left." But the recent history of Latin America is full of tragic examples of revolutionaries who believed they could initiate an armed struggle without first combating "revisionist" influence on certain sectors of the population. They believed that their discrepancies with the "revisionists" were only related to tactics and methods of struggle. They all paid dearly for that mistake. Abandoned and betrayed, Luis de la Puente Uceda in Peru, Fabricio Ojeda in Venezuela, Ché in Bolivia, and

many others, are clear examples of how the "revisionists" deal with these "revolutionary forces."

Never have the Tupamaros tried to gain or convince
the masses. Quite the contrary, they pretend to carry
on a war without the masses. They reduced the
masses to mere spectators of their armed actions, carried out by petty-bourgeois groups coming from the
more unstable segments of the "intelligentsia." The
idea is to gain the admiration of the people with daring and sensational attacks. This is the favorite type of
struggle of the petty-bourgeoisie: it expresses its in-
dividualism and its fear of joining the proletariat. Any
of them is willing to place a bomb or participate in a
direct action, but none is willing to get immersed in
the masses to carry on hard, patient, long, and anony-
mous work. They reject all political theories because
"they divide the left"; they are proud of "not knowing
where they are going." If they will study Lenin and
Mao, they will certainly know where they are going
and how they are going to end.

APPENDIX

Diplomatic Relations of the Independent Latin American States with the U.S.S.R. *

✳

Argentina, Federal Republic of *relations established June 6, 1946*

Barbados *no relations*

Bolivia, Republic of *relations established April 18, 1945; representatives not exchanged*

Brazil, Federation of the United States of *relations established April 2, 1945; broken off October 20, 1947; restored November 23, 1961*

Chile, Republic of *relations established December 11, 1944; broken off October 21, 1947; restored November 24, 1964*

---

* From *International Affairs* (Moscow, March 1967), pp. 110, 112.

Colombia, Republic of *relations established in 1935; broken off in 1948; restored in January 1968*

Costa Rica *relations established May 8, 1944; representatives not exchanged*

Cuba *relations established October 14, 1942; broken off April 3, 1952; restored May 8, 1960*

Dominican Republic *relations established in 1945; representatives not exchanged*

Ecuador *relations established June 16, 1945; representatives not exchanged*

El Salvador *no relations*

Guatemala *relations established April 19, 1945*

Guyana *no relations*

Haiti, Republic of *no relations*

Honduras, Republic of *no relations*

Jamaica *no relations*

Mexico, Federal Republic of the United States of *relations established August 6, 1924; broken off January 26, 1930; restored February 12, 1942*

Nicaragua, Republic of *relations established December 12, 1944; representatives not exchanged*

APPENDIX (*409*)

Panama, Republic of   *no relations*

Paraguay, Republic of   *no relations*

Trinidad and Tobago   *no relations*

Uruguay, Republic of   *relations established August 22, 1926; broken off December 27, 1935; restored January 27, 1943*

Venezuela, Federal Republic of   *relations established in 1945; broken off in 1952*

A BIBLIOGRAPHICAL NOTE

The present picture of Marxist studies on Latin America is far from bright. Many of the important independent periodicals mentioned in the first edition, such as Uruguay's *Marcha* and *Revista Civilização Brasilera,* have been suppressed by military regimes. The majority of Communist and Socialist publications have suffered the same fate. *Unidad* and *Documentos Políticos,* organs of the Peruvian and Colombian Communist parties, are two of the few still published with some regularity. Of the new, somehow ephemeral, left-oriented publications, *Alternativa,* edited by novelist Gabriel Garcia Marquez in Colombia, is perhaps the most interesting.

Books with Marxist interpretations abound in Spanish, although invariably devoted to problems or periods of a particular Latin American nation. Apart from anti-imperialist subjects, no general study of Marxism on the continent nor any wide Marxist analysis of historical and economic conditions is visible. The reader can find sources for the former type of publication in the title lists of Siglo Veintiuno and El Caballito, two Mexican editorial houses devoted primarily to Marxist authors.

The situation is not much better in the United States. The collapse of the Chilean socialist experiment, the evanescing leftism of the Peruvian government, and the sovietization of Cuba have apparently dampened interest in socialism in Latin America. Besides the most recent and important books on the subject already footnoted in my new Introduction, I will limit myself to a brief list of suggested readings.

Alexander, Robert J., *The Communist Party of Venezuela* (Stanford: Hoover Institute Press, 1973).

Castro, Fidel, *Balance de la Revolución* (México: Ediciones Cultura Popular, 1976).

Chaliand, Gerad, *Revolutions in the Third World* (New York: The Viking Press, 1977).

Clissold, Stephen, ed., *Soviet Relations with Latin America, 1918–68* (London: Oxford University Press, 1970).

Debray, Regis, *La Guerrilla del Ché* (México: Editorial Siglo Veintiuno, 1975).

Herman, Donald L., ed., *The Communist Tide in Latin America* (Austin: University of Texas, 1973).

Hodges, Donald C., *The Latin American Revolution* (New York: William Morrow & Co., 1974).

Horowitz, Irving L., ed., *Cuban Communism* (Transaction Books, 1970).

Loscher, Ivan, *Escrito con la Izquierda* (Caracas: Libros Tequy, 1977).

Santos, Theotonio Dos, *Socialismo o Fascismo* (Buenos Aires: Ediciones Periferia, 1973).

Walter, Richard J., *The Socialist Party of Argentina, 1890–1930* (Austin: University of Texas, 1977).